Effective

Leadership

in Action:

Health Care's

Focus on

Accountability

A CCOUNTABILITY

John K. Wong
Iowa State University

**Academy for
Health Services
Marketing**

AMERICAN
MARKETING
ASSOCIATION

Conference Digest

Effective Leadership in Action:
Health Care's Focus on Accountability

tm

(Effective Leadership in Action):
Health Care's Focus on Accountability

Academy for Health Services Marketing
American Marketing Association
250 S. Wacker Drive
Chicago, Illinois 60606   (312) 648-0536

Proceedings Series

Library of Congress Cataloging-in-Publication Data

Effective leadership in action.

   (Proceedings series / American Marketing Association)
   Proceedings of the 7th Annual Symposium on Health Services
Marketing, held Mar. 1-4, 1987, San Diego, Calif.
   1. Medical care—Marketing—Congresses. 2. Health services
administration—Congresses. 3. Leadership—Congresses.
I. Wong, John K. II. American Marketing Association.
III. Symposium on Health Services Marketing (7th : 1987 : San
Diego, Calif.) IV. Series: Proceedings series (American Marketing
Association)
RA410.56.E34 1987   362.1'O68'8   87-976
ISBN O-87757-186-4

TABLE OF CONTENTS

INTRODUCTION TO

EFFECTIVE LEADERSHIP IN ACTION

HEALTH CARE'S FOCUS ON ACCOUNTABILITY

As a student of marketing, I have been impressed by the
rapid diffusion of marketing in the health care delivery
system over the past decade. Even to the casual observer,
there is ample evidence that supports the conclusion.
While new converts are won daily, many health care
marketing practitioners have acquired a new sophistication in their management outlook and practice.

This is very much in evidence in the wide range of topics
and the level of treatment these topics have received in
The Seventh Annual Symposium on Health Services Marketing.
Not only are the backgrounds and experience of the
contributors impressive, their contribution to these
proceedings also reflects a sophistication that is
equally striking. Working with these men and women on
the forefront of our discipline has been an enjoyable
experience. It is an honor for me to be able assist the
Academy in this effort and to serve as the Editor of
these proceedings.

Organizationally, the papers in this collection are
grouped within each of the tracks as indicated in the
Symposium program. Introductory remarks to each track
are provided to help readers focus on the key ideas
presented by the contributors in that track. As is true
in most conferences, some tracks attract more attention
than others. This, together with a high attrition rate
in the review process has resulted in the variation in
the number of articles in each of the tracks.

I am indebted to Carla Windhorst and Idelma Baro and the
staff of the Academy for their help in this project. The
contribution and cooperation of the authors are gratefully
acknowledged, for without their effort neither this
Symposium nor this compilation of the proceedings would
be a reality. This truly has been an enjoyable venture
in which many have participated.

FINANCIAL EFFECTIVENESS

With increasing competitiveness in the health care industry, the financial aspects of marketing management have gained in importance. Even in the more traditional area of price-setting, the need for creativity is paramount. Goldman and Gershon's paper provides a basic yet comprehensive overview of pricing strategies and the rationale behind each.

Shorr's paper presents a scenario where mergers and acquisitions in the health care industry will become more frequent and commonplace. The question then becomes not whether merger, acquisition or joint venture will take place, but how these can be managed with greater effectiveness. He proposes a process in which more effectiveness can be injected into the conduct of these activities. In the third paper, Kelsey suggests an approach to integrating marketing and financial information for hospital management.

INTEGRATION OF MARKETING AND FINANCIAL INFORMATION
FOR HOSPITAL MANAGEMENT

RONN R. KELSEY
VICE PRESIDENT, CORPORATE MARKETING
SAINT AGNES MEDICAL CENTER

JOHN M. THOENS
EXECUTIVE VICE PRESIDENT & CHIEF FINANCIAL OFFICER
SAINT AGNES MEDICAL CENTER

ABSTRACT

The ability to do timely business planning, is both a
necessity and almost an impossibility in today's changing
healthcare environment. This is the result of cumbersome,
scattered information; and fragmented healthcare
organizational structures.

The financial and management/marketing information
systems of the past hinder the timely analysis of new
and existing departments/programs. The inefficiency of
these systems is exacerbated by what is quickly becoming
archaic structures.

We discuss two innovative approaches which solve these
problems through:

1. Standardized approach to business planning

2. Reporting system which integrates clinical,
   financial and market dynamics

These two reports allow management to review new programs
and over sixty hospital departments in a timely fashion.

> "MOST HOSPITALS HAVE THE INFORMATION THEY NEED FOR
> MORE EFFECTIVE MANAGEMENT...IT'S JUST NOT IN THE RIGHT
> CONTEXT FOR TIMELY MANAGEMENT REVIEW AND USE."

INTRODUCTION:

STANDARDIZED BUSINESS PLANNING....A WAY TO INTEGRATE
MARKETING AND FINANCIAL INFORMATION AND REDUCE BUSINESS
RISKS.

The Standardized Business Planning process provides a
blueprint for reducing business risks and overcoming
organizational obstacles.

Today's competitive healthcare environment requires
increasingly sophisticated market analysis and business
planning techniques to identify and tap hospital's
most promising profit center potential. Since the
allocation of resources is such a critical decision,
business marketing risks must be minimized in the
planning process.

As a result business planning efforts require a systematic
approach for demographics, case mix, hospitalization
rates, physicians, revenues and utilization information.
Also essential is an understanding of market perceptions
regarding the hospital and services desired. To be most
effective, this planning must integrate marketing/
financial considerations with the clinical/operational
expertise of departmental manager who best know the
market. The integration of a variety of information
resources, plus total management involvement, establishes
a context for asking the right questions - a key component
of the planning process.

KEY INDICATORS PERFORMANCE REPORT....A WAY TO MONITOR
MARKETING AND FINANCIAL PERFORMANCE.

The appropriate planning process is only part of the
answer to the integration of marketing and financial
information for more effective healthcare management.
The "right" marketing and financial information in today's
environment is vital in monitoring new programs as well
as everyday department performance.

In order to capture the "right" information a computerized
monthly report was developed which reflects the marketing,
financial and management performance of key hospital
departments in a format which can be easily reviewed and
understood by upper management, as well as operational
level managers.

Ultimately, the two approaches for planning and monitoring
will reduce business risks and optimize profit potential.

STANDARDIZED MARKET/FINANCIAL PLANNING....A WAY TO
DECENTRALIZING THE MARKETING PROCESS

One of the difficulties in developing a standardized
approach to market planning is the traditional
fragmentation of hospital organizational structure and
management. Departmental managers have little
familiarity with the marketing approach, and often find
it threatening. Marketers and Executive Management, on
the other hand, need more than numbers and readouts to
develop strategies; they need the input of those who are
actually serving the market as well as from the marketplace itself.

To compound these problems management must overcome other
obstacles inherent in a typical hospital organization,
including:

* A wide variety of people doing different types of
  planning at all levels.

* The traditional fragmentation of hospital departments
  and management.

* Managers' inexperience with business and market plan
  development.

* Lack of planning guidelines.

* Inaccessibility of marketing information resources.

* The perceived "threat" of marketing.

* Inability to make meaningful program comparisons.

* Undefined performance guidelines.

To overcome this counterproductive situation, St. Agnes Medical Center adopted a systematic planning approach (developed by one of the authors for International Business Management) which involves the total management team in the marketing/business planning concept. One of the primary goals of the St. Agnes marketing department is to facilitate and support the business planning process at the operational level. To achieve this, department managers had to realize that marketing had no intention of running their programs. Instead, by working with marketing's support and combining their expertise, they could develop more profitable programs and a more cohesive management team.

The Business Planner is the primary vehicle for building a trusting, cooperative working relationship between marketing/finance and departmental managers. It brings the marketing approach to various department managers and helps them structure and evaluate potential market opportunities. It forms the basis for re-packaging current services or creating new or expanded services. On a corporate level, it is a tool for analyzing joint venture opportunities. In all cases, the approach creates a standardized context for organized market/ financial analysis, planning, implementation and tracking. Ultimately, it is the means for formulating meaningful assumptions used in generating "realistic" profit-and-loss analyses.

WHAT IS THE STANDARDIZED BUSINESS PLANNER?

The guide provides a prepackaged format that facilitates departmental participation in the marketing and financial planning process. It also provides an overall context and consistent format for business planning assumptions and profit-and-loss projections.

The planner format gives management a means to expedite program evaluation and implementation, and more importantly prompts managers to ask the right questions and provides the context for capturing the answers.

ASKING THE RIGHT QUESTIONS....HOW DOES THE GUIDE DO THAT?

The first phase of the business planning process is developing a thorough understanding of critical market factors, i.e., demand, competition, hospital capabilities, physician manpower, relative costs, available capital and revenue potential. By confronting the key business issues from the outset, managers often can quickly grasp the true potential of various program ideas, and pursue only those offering the greatest return on investment and provide the best base for future growth.

The standardized business planning process expedites this initial analysis by prompting managers to ask the "right" questions. Following are examples of some of the questions addressed by the standardized business planning process guide.

* What consumer need does the program address?

* Who else will be competing to meet the same customer need?

* What is the hospital's advantage over alternative solution, and how sustainable is this advantage?

* How big is the market?

* How fast will it grow?

* What financial return can be expected immediately? In 1-2 years? In 5 years?

* What are the key success factors in the program? Where should management focus its efforts?

* What would happen if the hospital did not provide this service? Strategically? Financially? Reputation?

ADVANTAGES EXPERIENCED BY USING THE STANDARDIZED BUSINESS PLANNING CONCEPT.

1. Integrates the planning process throughout the hospital.

    a. Sets expectations for doing planning.
    b. Merges marketing/clinical/financial/administrative expertise of hospital staff.
    c. Helps managers ask the right questions.
    d. Links operational managers activities with strategic planning objectives.
    e. Facilitates delegation of planning tasks.

2. Encourages hospital entrepreneurs.

    a. Expedites their evaluation of programs.
    b. Gives them tools to evaluate new business ideas.
    c. Eliminates time wasted pursuing dead-end programs.

3. Helps managers exploit market opportunities by capitalizing on hospital's strengths.

4. Expedites planning process - managers can evaluate program potential in weeks instead of months.

5. Facilitates full management team involvement - decentralizes planning process down to "where the action is" at the operational level.

6. Establishes a context and end point for sound business planning.

7. Permits management to make program evaluations earlier in the planning process.

8. Provides a consistent format that allows management to make "apples to apples" program comparisons based on "realistic" profit-and-loss financial projections.

9. Reduces business risk and optimizes profit potential.

10. Perpetuates sound business planning through consistency and increased management participation.

KEY INDICATIONS PERFORMANCE REPORT....FINANCIAL INFORMATION IN A MARKETING AND MANAGEMENT CONTEXT

By utilizing available hospital financial information the Key Indicator Report format facilitates monitoring and review of the key performance indicators for departments or businesses against current budget and last years performance by placing the information in an easy to use marketing/management context.

> "PEOPLE TEND NOT TO USE INFORMATION UNLESS THEY PERCEIVE IT OF SOMETHING OF VALUE TO THEM....
> SO THE TRICK IS....GIVE THEM SOMETHING OF VALUE."

The report details the following key indicators in spreadsheet and graphic formats:

1. Volume Performance

2. Full Time Equivalents (FTE's)

3. Revenue

4. Expense

5. Margin

SEE EXAMPLES OF KEY INDICATOR REPORT FORMAT

EXAMPLE OF KEY INDICATOR GRAPHIC FORMAT

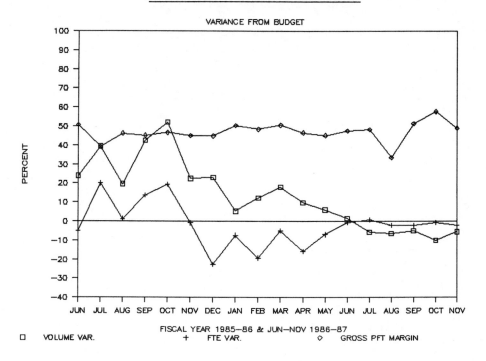

VARIANCE FROM BUDGET

FISCAL YEAR 1985—86 & JUN—NOV 1986—87

□ VOLUME VAR.   + FTE VAR.   ◇ GROSS PFT MARGIN

The most powerful and effective parts of the key indicator report is the graphic overhead format which depicts and visualizes the spreadsheet information in a way that allows the key members of the management team to review variations from budgeted performance for volume, FTE's and gross profit margins. Because the information is presented in a simple graphic format, deviations from budgeted performance and more importantly, trends as well as marketing, operational or physician issues can be easily spotted and explained by one or several of the management team or assigned to a member for investigation and explanation.

EXAMPLE OF KEY INDICATOR SPREADSHEET FORMAT

PROGRAM OR SERVICE INDICATORS		FISCAL YR	JUN	JUL	AUG	SEP	OCT	NOV	DEC	JAN	FEB	MAR	APR	MAY	Y.T.D
Vol.	Actual	1986-87	264	245	215	190	180	189							1283
	Budget	1986-87	260	260	230	200	200	200							1350
	% Var.	1986-87	1.54	-5.77	-6.52	-5.00	-10.00	-5.50	0.00	0.00	0.00	0.00	0.00	0.00	-4.96
	Actual	1985-86	455	453	482	506	525	506	517	493	504	526	555	503	2927
	% Chg	FY86-87	-41.98	-45.92	-55.39	-62.45	-65.71	-62.65	0.00	0.00	0.00	0.00	0.00	0.00	-56.17
FTEs	Actual	1986-87	13.9	14.1	13.7	13.2	13.4	14.7							13.8
	Budget	1986-87	14.0	14.0	14.0	13.5	13.5	15.0							14.0
	% Var.	1986-87	-0.71	0.71	-2.14	-2.22	-0.74	-2.00	0.00	0.00	0.00	0.00	0.00	0.00	-1.19
	Actual	1985-86	20.9	22.7	23.7	24.2	23.9	24.6	18.9	25.2	24.3	24.6	25.6	27.2	23.3
	% Chg	FY86-87	-33.49	-37.89	-42.19	-45.45	-43.93	-40.24	0.00	0.00	0.00	0.00	0.00	0.00	-40.71
Rev.	Actual	1986-87	110049	116337	91410	118670	136836	122963							696264
	Budget	1986-87	112124	112124	112124	112124	112124	112124							672744
	% Var.	1986-87	-1.85	3.76	-18.47	5.84	22.04	9.67	0.00	0.00	0.00	0.00	0.00	0.00	3.50
	Actual	1985-86	187772	172316	185822	182871	196285	196496	190000	188324	196557	216237	210902	216106	1121562
	% Chg	FY86-87	-41.39	-32.49	-50.81	-35.11	-30.29	-37.42	0.00	0.00	0.00	0.00	0.00	0.00	-37.92
Exp.	Actual	1986-87	57711	60262	60828	57629	57844	62623							356896
	Budget	1986-87	61555	61555	61555	61555	61555	61555							369327
	% Var.	1986-87	-6.24	-2.10	-1.18	-6.38	-6.03	1.74	0.00	0.00	0.00	0.00	0.00	0.00	-3.37
	Actual	1985-86	92408	104806	99932	100391	104646	108088	104692	93393	101289	106755	112581	118684	610271
	% Chg	FY86-87	-37.55	-42.50	-39.13	-42.60	-44.72	-42.06	0.00	0.00	0.00	0.00	0.00	0.00	-41.52
	Margin	1986-87	52339	56075	30583	61041	78993	60340	0	0	0	0	0	0	339369
	Margin	1985-86	95364	67510	85890	82480	91639	88408	85308	94931	95268	109482	98321	97422	511291
	% Chg	FY86-87	-45.12	-16.94	-64.39	-25.99	-13.80	-31.75	-100.00	-100.00	-100.00	-100.00	-100.00	-100.00	-33.63
Gross Pft Margin		1986-87	47.56	48.20	33.46	51.44	57.73	49.07	0.00	0.00	0.00	0.00	0.00	0.00	48.74
Gross Pft Margin		1985-86	50.79	39.18	46.22	45.10	46.69	44.99	44.90	50.41	48.47	50.63	46.62	45.08	45.59

Report format allows quick review of current months performance against budget, year-to-date performance, as well as monthly and yearly-to-date performance against previous years performance. Each key indicator volume, FTE's, revenue and expenses is easy to track since (%) percentage variation from budget is included as well as (%) percentage change from last years performance. Gross profit margins are also reported to allow managers to see the "bottomline" impact of their management activities. In the near future we will add contractual allowances to the report to allow us to better report and track the "true" bottom lines of each department or program. Trend can also be seen easily as the reports rolls forward a fourteen (14) month reporting basis.

In addition, the method can be used to analyze pricing/ discount strategies, new business growth, clinical markets and communication program performance. The report has an added benefit of being utilized in future bonus or pay for performance programs where performance against budget is used as a management reward.

SUMMARY:

Using the Key Indicator Report and the standardized approach to business planning to tap its most valuable resource...the expertise of it's marketing, business planning, financial and clinical management...the hospital can perpetuate innovative and sound business planning at all levels of its organizaiton.

FUTURE EVOLUTION:

It is clear that the integration of marketing and financial data will lead to major improvements in the quality of decision making relative to new markets and the management of current markets and businesses.

From a global viewpoint, the key to future performance will be sound strategic planning, out of which is developed a marketing plan which supports the strategic direction for the hospital or medical center. Once these two are in place, the financial plan can be developed which synergistically supports the entire strategic marketing and financial plans in such a way that "the engine of competition" becomes self-fueling. The key to the synergistic approach outlined above, is clearly high-quality data from marketing and finance integrated into a sound strategic vision supported again by marketing, finance and performance based compensation.

ACKNOWLEDGMENT

Special thanks to Sister Ruth Marie Nickerson, CSC, President & Chief Executive Officer, Saint Agnes Medical Center, for her support and for providing the environment and "space" to develop and implement these two powerful management programs.

WHY TO CHARGE WHAT TO WHOM WHEN

Ellen F. Goldman, Lammers+Gershon Associates, Inc.
Howard J. Gershon, Lammers+Gershon Associates, Inc.

ABSTRACT

The importance of pricing of health services is increasing as the industry becomes more adept at responding to market forces. The strategies for service pricing fall along a wide spectrum from a cost floor to a ceiling dictated by the marketplace. The conditions under which a strategy is effective vary, as do associated tactics of implementation. Inputs to price decision-making are many - including information of an internal, competitive, market, legal, and strategic nature. While price-setting follows a logical step-by-step process, the complexity of pricing activities may require dedicated resources. This paper highlights strategies which may be employed in pricing, identifies input requirements, and outlines the price decision-making process.

BACKGROUND

Historically, the pricing of health services has been executed on a "cost plus" (a mark-up) basis. As payment moved away from cost formulas and competition for volume increased, many healthcare providers initially reacted (to each other) by cutting prices. While this may have provided quick action, price cuts may not have increased either profits and/or volume. As providers continue to enter non-institutional markets, negotiate contracting proposals and become further de-regulated, the opportunties for using price as a strategic tool will increase.

STRATEGIES

Pricing strategies applicable to healthcare services fall into a spectrum where the market-place dictates the ceiling and cost coverage dictates the floor, as shown in Figure 1.

FIGURE 1

```
                    MARKETPLACE
                        |
Skim.......... ---|  ---
                        |
Slide-Down..... ---|  ---
                        |
Phase-Out...... ---|  ---
                        |
                        |
Follow......... ---|  ---
                        |
                        |
Penetration.... ---|  ---
                        |
Pre-Emptive.... ---|  ---
                        |
Loss Leader.... ---|  ---
                        |
                        |
                      COST
```

Adapted from the American Management Assoc.

Midpoint Strategy

The midpoint of the spectrum is follow pricing, or pricing relative to (usually below) the market leader. This is used when you have a service which can not be differentiated, low market share and acceptable profits. As was typical of the auto and steel industries for years, any price agressiveness by a "follower" would be met with an acute reaction by the leader. The medical/surgical services of a community hospital in a multi-facility and specialty area might consider "follow pricing".

High Spectrum Strategies

Higher-priced strategies are defined and used as follows:

Skim - pricing at the "cream" with a unique service with high value, such as a high-tech piece of equipment or a highly intensive procedure.

Slide Down - moving prices from the top down for a highly price sensitive service with a long life-cycle and economies of delivery, such as mammography screening.

Phase-Out - pricing high to discourage demand or to reduce inventory of a service or product which you can not flatly withdraw or for which you have an improved version, such as indemnity insurance.

Low Spectrum Strategies

Lower-priced strategies are defined and used as follows:

Pre-emptive - pricing low to discourage competitive entry when you have a strong position, such as initiating tiered emergency room pricing to discourage urgi-center development.

<u>Penetration</u> - pricing below the prevailing
level in order to steal share for a
sensitive, but undifferentiated service
to which you do not expect competitors to
react. Hospitals have tried this for both
obstetric services and HMO products.

<u>Loss Leader</u> - pricing part of a complementary
service low to attract buyers to the other,
higher priced service, such as low cost
dental exams for which profits are made up
on orthodontic work.

Segment Strategies

Services which are useful to several different
markets can be priced differently, particularly
if elasticity varies, attributes can be

high. Hospitals have used segmentation for VIP
suites, weekend admissions and self-care units.

Growth vs. Share Mapping

One way to help determine price strategy is to
estimate market growth and market share. On a
simple high vs. low basis, four different
strategies are indicated, as shown in Figure 2.

FIGURE 2

		LOW MARKET SHARE	HIGH MARKET SHARE
MARKET GROWTH	HIGH	PENETRATE	PRE-EMPT
MARKET GROWTH	LOW	PHASE-OUT	SKIM

MARKET SHARE

Where share is low and growth not expected,
prices can be raised to "phase-out",
particularly if substitutes are available.
Where share is low but growth high, a lower or
"penetration" strategy may increase share if
there is no competitive reaction and the service
will not be labelled as low quality. If both
growth and share are high, lower "pre-emptive"
pricing may discourage competitors as long as
customers are highly satisfied. Lastly, if
share is high but growth low, then high "skim"
prices will increase profitability if the
service is unique.

Tactics

Regardless of which strategy is employed,
numerous tactics can be used as part of the
price perception. These include:

<u>Discounting</u> for quantity purchases, payment
terms or functions (i.e. frequent user);

<u>Bundling or unbundling</u> features in lieu of price
increases or decreases;

<u>Psychological pricing</u> at 95 or 99 for prices of
100 etc., so they appear less expensive;

<u>Visibility</u> of competitive prices which are
likely to be compared (i.e. room rates);

<u>Timing</u> of announcements to appear more or less
competitive; and

<u>Optics</u> of presentation which focus on benefits
(vs. restrictions) and clearly show savings.

INPUTS

The complexity of price strategy determination
requires much information and analyses.
Generally, inputs fall into five categories of
internal, competitor and market information;
legal considerations; and strategic decisions.

Internal inputs include service costs, cost-
volume relationships, life-cycle position,
profitability and financial objectives. The
ability to manipulate this information to
proposed volume changes is critical. One of
pricing's common fallacies is "cut the price, we
will make it up in volume". In fact a 10% price
cut on a service with a 30% gross margin will
require a 50% volume increase to maintain the
same profitability (assuming equal fixed costs).

Competitor inputs include current pricing
levels, policies, tactics and strategies, as
well as reactions they may make to your proposed
changes. This may necessitate the need for
other market information (which you should have
anyway) regarding share, positioning and
customer characteristics.

Market information of importance includes buyer
characteristics, factors relating to their
demand, sensitivity to price changes,
perceptions regarding the price-value of
services, and reactions to non-price
alternatives. The hardest area to determine is
sensitivity. The conditions under which a
service is highly price sensitive include:
frequent purchase, low personal involvement in
care delivery, little or no insurance coverage,
many available alternatives, low intensity of
care, and high personal knowledge of treatment.

Legal concerns of pricing relate to federal and
state laws prohibiting such things as trade
restraints and price discrimination. Activities
which have been deemed anti-competitive in and
of themselves include price-fixing agreements
and tie-in arrangements.

Finally, pricing decisions must be based on
strategic inputs regarding target markets,
objectives, timetables, positioning and
marketing mix.

PROCESS

The complexity and amount of input in pricing
decisions may leave many organizations
vulnerable to common pricing fallacies, such as
"just follow the competition" or "raise the
price to meet our ROI target". The steps in
price-setting, however, are quite straight-
forward, as follows:

1. Identify your objectives.
2. Gather cost, demand, and competitor
   information, and perform necessary
   analyses.
3. Determine what strategies and tactics fit
   your situation.
4. Evaluate the fit of your chosen strategy
   within the marketing mix.
5. Develop monitoring and contingency plans.

As marketing practices become more sophisticated
in healthcare, separate pricing functions may be
developed. This area would deal with the timing
and players involved in price setting and
changing; credits and collections policies;
research regarding pricing decision inputs and
outcomes; and the communication of prices and
price changes.

CONCLUSIONS

Numerous pricing strategies and tactics can be
employed by healthcare providers. The success
of each strategy depends on the appropriateness
of the conditions for its use, which in turn
requires the input of much information and sound
evaluation. Pricing can be a pressure point,
but it is also a strategic marketing tool; one
which will continue to grow in importance in
healthcare services delivery.

REFERENCES

The Conference Board, Inc. (1982), Pricing
Practices and Strategies, New York, NY.

Goldman, Ellen F. and Gershon, Howard J. (1986),
"Pricing: Pressure Point or Strategic
Tool?," Health Care Competition Week
(Special Report) (July 21).

Modern Healthcare (1986), "Providers not picked
by price," (November 7).

Nimer, Daniel A. (1986), "Nimer on Pricing,"
Healthcare Forum, (all issues).

Pointer, Dennis, PhD, and Zwanziger, Jack, PhD
(1986), "Pricing Strategy and Tactics in
the New Hospital Marketplace," Hospital and
Health Services Administration, 31 (6),
5-18.

"Pricing for Profit: Strategies and Tactics,"
(1986), A Business Week Executive Program,
(December 16 and 17) (Philadelphia).

MANAGING MERGERS & ACQUISITIONS PROFITABLY

Arthur S. Shorr,
Arthur S. Shorr & Associates,
Tarzana, California

ABSTRACT

As a growth strategy for the 1990s, medical practice mergers and acquisitions must be well managed in order to capture market-share and to achieve profitability goals. The development of acquisition strategies must be based upon creative interpretation of operating data with sensitivity to the internal strengths and needs of the organization. Once done, senior level executive and board support becomes the key to successful implementation. To evaluate a potential candidate, all legal financial, and community factors must be considered. The responsibility to assure continuing profitability and growth of the new business relationship rests with all parties to achieve common goals. Whether these skills are in-house or contracted through third party facilitator, the outcome must be a win/win situation for all participants.

INTRODUCTION

Although institution merger and acquisition activity has slowed among the major hospital corporations recently, healthcare providers on the local level are under increasing economic and competitive pressures to find ways to protect current market-share.

In light of today's circumstances, the question is no longer one of the possibility of merger, acquisition or joint venture but with whom, when and how many can we manage successfully.

Adopting a market-share sensitivity and orientation is the first step. The objective is to see the logic of extending an organization's reach around the largest possible population within its catchment. For some organizations, this market reach may be within a city; for others, a larger regional view is appropriate. Capturing market-share can be accomplished by going beyond the promotion of traditional episodic treatment into wellness, preventative medicine, multi-phasic screening and other community sensitive programs.

New program development should be viewed as the means of acquiring those practitioners who can attract the patients and implement the programs. To succeed in these new business ventures, healthcare administrators are well advised to be attentive to the process and the projected outcomes of such business relationships.

THE INTERNAL ISSUES

Before embarking on a merger/acquisition course of action, executive management must address the internal issues and policies of the organization. Organizational and specific acquisition strategic plans must be developed based upon:

- Making an internal assessment of needs. Knowing the organization's clinical strengths and weaknesses helps defines the type, number and kind of partners and business relations desired. For instance, if a hospital's center of excellence is in cardiac care, medical practices or geographic areas with a heavy concentration of mature and elderly people are logical targets.

- Identifying solid product lines and their markets. Know what kind of in-patients or out-patients are wanted, where they are and, most importantly, if they desire this service. It is no longer enough to assess that a service is needed; it must also be determined if the market actually wants and will use this service. Obviously, finely tuned market research is essential.

- Targeting underserved geographical areas and populations. The "outpost" theory of market-share business development comes into play here. An organization establishes, through merger/acquisition/joint venture, a new outpost or base of operation at the furthermost reachs of its feasible geographic market area with the intention of capturing as much of the patient population between the outpost and the home base. Once accomplished, the next step is to back fill this area with other patient care delivery sites for greater market penetration.

- Arriving at strong, valid rules of thumb for profit margins. Selected decisions can and should be made "at the margin." However, one must pre-determine the criteria to make the decision easier. There may be some unusual factors in an acquisition/merger/joint venture situation - such as a practice situated in the path of explosive population growth - that weighs heavily in its favor. At times, "at the margin" decision-making should overrule the classic accounting criteria.

- Involving the Chief Financial Officer. With the CFO's direct participation in acquisition strategy, hard financial data, resource allocation, and evaluation techniques can be focused to target and prioritize potential new business partners.

- Inventorying every healthcare provider in the primary and secondary catchment areas. This may include non-physician run healthcare businesses or providers and, most importantly, those physician practices NOT already known to you. Know the:

     -nature and number of practitioners,
     -type of practice,
     -number and type of patients/clients,
     -number and types of admissions,
     -practice variables and
     -a host of other data.

- Using the good offices of a consultant as a neutral third party negotiator. This is especially valuable when dealing with medical practices or physician controlled business. For many physicians, being approached by a hospital with financial motives can be reason enough to discourage a relationship that could otherwise be developed by a neutral third party. As a confidential facilitator between the parties, his primary objective is to serve the best interests of all concerned throughout the deal.

- Know the organizational/financial benefits for the candidate and promote them. The variety of "value added" business services an organization can bring to the deal include:

     -access to capital,
     -strategic planning,
     -product line business planning,
     -business management skills and
     -new career paths for the principals.

- Gaining concensus among executive management. Otherwise known as spinning your wheels, concensus must be obtained beforehand to smooth the course of the business negotiations with a promising candidate.

- Establishing a concerted program to attract candidates while monitoring the universe for changes, discontent and new players. Let interest be Known by tapping into the "profes ional grapevine" of physicians, consultants and others who are involved in the medical services community. Become an attractive resource by providing information and skills the candidates may not have. Set up seminars or host informal meetings which emphasize business management skills of the organization or its consultant-resources -- people who can make a candidate more profitable through association with your organization. Be mindful of the "shop talk" among medical community members and ever alert to spot and create new opportunities as conditions develop and change.

THE EXTERNAL ISSUES

Legal/Financial Issues

Where corporate practice of medicine laws exist, a hospital or corporate entity can not legally buy a medical practice. In this case, the organization's role is to act as a facilitator, positioned as a third party between the buying and selling principals who affiliate with the organization. For example, a hospital, given its greater access to capital and business management expertise, can assist a young physician in acquiring a practice or aid an established medical group expand, market its services or gain a foothold in an underserved geographic area. All are ways to extend the hospital's market-shared reach.

The specific structure of the merger/acquisition/joint venture can take various legal and organizational formats, depending on the needs and desires of the parties. In strucuring the financial and legal arrangements, the contract must provide, to the extent possible, a lock-in of patients while allowing for equitable treatment of the principals. Achieving this delicate balance can result in an economic gain for all parties.

Methods of Evaluation

Somewhere in the process, establishing a mutual value of the candidate's business/practice must be addressed. Valuation is a complex, delicate process, best left to specialists in the field of healthcare appraisal and brokerage.

One key issue in determining a valuation basis is identification of the buyer. A physician acquiring another medical practice presents a remarkably different set of valuation criteria and guidelines than does an organization seeking market share and inpatient referrals.

These basic considerations generally hold true:

1. A thorough analysis of the candidate's worth must include, but is not limited to analysis of such items as:

    -profit and loss statements,
    -capital assets (land, building, equipment),
    -patient lists,
    -goodwill.

2. Cost of providing "value add" services. The question here is how much of the organization's resources and business management expertise will be required to maximize current and potential revenue.

3. Projection of revenue based on market demographics against current and planned operating assumptions. For instance, how much will be

gained with a computerized billing and patient recall system? Will it be worth the commitment of resources to achieve these gains?

4. Clinical compatibility of the candidate. Does the candidate's practice/business complement the current and future financial and operational goals of the organization?

5. Comfort level of the candidate. Beyond the financial attraction, one has to look at the candidate's comfort level in associating with the organization. Factors of personality, short and long terms goals and issues of control must be evaluated separately for each candidate.

Perhaps the most sensitive issues arise when the subjects of money and control are placed on the agenda. Although larger organizations have deeper pockets and other appeals, these very attractions tend to generate extra anxiety among a potential partner. Issues of control, clinical latitudes and prerogatives, management and financial understandings must be aired before a contract can be signed.

It may be wise to consider the appointment of a mutually acceptable neutral third party to facilitate and bring to closure the proposed business deal. The facilitator serves as an impartial, confidential sounding board to address the emotional issues for both sides. The best approach is to minimize as much emotional baggage as possible by emphasizing for the candidate what will be gained by the new association.

The organization needs to identify, understand and find a way to reconcile the candidate's hidden agendas. These will vary depending on the party, but tend to include:

    -immediate vs. retirement income,
    -degree of practice control,
    -concerns and perceptions of the sellers changed status,
    -perceptions of the new relationship and
    -responsibilities to the organization's executive and management team.

One should be continually sensitive to these and other human elements as the negotiations progress. Then as the contract takes shape it can be structured to maximize the potential for success.

The facilitator, because of his impartial status, can build the foundation of trust and establish a common meeting ground so that all parties are satisfied when the contract is signed.

...AND AFTERWARDS

Now the success of the venture will rest heavily on the development of the on-going working relationships between the new partners as the venture unfolds. The organization has the ongoing responsibility to encourage, motivate and maintain the productivity of its new business partners as it does for its own activities. Viewed not as a take-over or employment situation, the new relationship will have a greater chance for success and profitability if it is seen by all concerned as a partnership structured to accomplish mutually beneficial goals.

HOW TO FAIL AT MANAGING MERGERS & ACQUISITIONS

1. Ignore the market share view. Pay attention only to your organization's inner world and not what is happening to the other players within your arena. However,

by being aware of the dynamics of the entire playing field, you are much better positioned to plan and act on new opportunities as conditions develop and change. Better yet, a proactive stance allows your organization to become a market leader rather than a follower.

2. Skip the homework. Successful mergers and acquisitions first depend on accurate information and intelligent interpretation of data to target and assess profitable candidates. The process of gathering, sorting and evaluating the data has to be done well. Know what you're doing, learn how to do it or find the right people who can accomplish the task for you.

3. Don't set objectives and corporate policy or obtain executive and board consensus. You must have a pre-established, measurable set of objectives to know with whom, where and what to deal. Then, you can properly evaluate if the proposed business is appropriate for your organization. You must also involve the key people in the organization so you are able to fulfill the ultimate aim of increasing market share efficiently... and with no surprises at the end of the road.

4. Be insensitive to the parties' hidden agendas. Depending on the age, status, peer pressures and a host of personality factors, each party brings to the negotiating table individual concerns. Know what these are and be able to deal with them up front. You also need to know what is happening in the community that influences the agenda.

5. Be indifferent or neglect the principals after the contract is signed. Besides the traditional financial and marketing monitoring devices, build in ways to empower the principals so that they have continual pride of ownership and thus productivity. Gently educate them in the responsibilities of the new partnership. All parties should feel they have a stake in the development of it.

SUMMARY

Creating and implementing a profitable merger or acquisition is not without its hazards, but, then, it also has its rewards. Given the realistic consequences of not doing it well, there are relatively few creative alternatives to growth and profit in the years ahead. Well conceived and managed from start to finish, your organization's reputation for fair dealing for all parties will quickly spread among the community. The fourth deal will be much easier than the first.

RESEARCH AND INFORMATION

This collection of papers provides evidence that there is a growing sophistication among health care managers in the use of marketing research as a management and decisional tool. The discussion in this section covers a wide range of issues pertaining to the proper use and role of marketing research in a variety of settings in the health care industry.

As Yeargain and Cantor suggest in their paper, there is more to field research than the basic cross tabulation of data that market research vendors generally provide. They list a number of multivariate tolls that collectively can throw more light and a better understanding of the market that is being studied. They further propose a checklist to assist health care managers in the evaluation, selection and collaboration with market research suppliers. Tobin and Kaufher's paper provides arguments for and against the use of focus groups as a research methodology. They advocate its use mainly as a precursor to the more expensive and complicated quantitative phase of marketing research. The authors also provide a "how to" approach to conducting focus research.

The goal of marketing research is to provide timely and useful information for decision makers to formulate effective marketing strategies based on a sound understanding of the target audience and market forces. The two articles by Navarro/Rubinger and Rexroad highlight the importance of bridging the process of marketing research and the formulation and implementation of appropriate marketing strategies. Scheuerman illustrates how this can be accomplished via a case study of the distribution channel for orthopedic services.

BEYOND CROSS TABS:
HEALTHCARE MARKETING RESEARCH COMES OF AGE

Eve W. Yeargain, The Marketing Works, Austin, Texas
Murray Cantor Ph.D, MRC Research, Austin, Texas

ABSTRACT

This paper will introduce healthcare marketing managers to advanced statistical techniques which create more reliable, insightful, and valuable market research data. The underlying concepts and benefits of cluster analysis and discriminant analysis are explored through case studies. The paper concludes with practical approaches to reaping maximum value from commissioned market research studies.

OVERVIEW

When marketing isn't working, it's often because it isn't really Marketing.

Marketing that works can only emanate from a thorough knowledge base. Good instincts and risk aversion are not enough. Good marketing requires an intimate understanding of customer needs, characteristics, purchase behavior, preferences, and loyalties.

So when marketing isn't working, it is often due to inadequate - or faulty - market research.

In our opinion, healthcare marketing research must come of age if marketing executives are to allocate resources where they will reap the most desirable returns. The industry must become more knowledgeable about various market research options, know how to conduct and analyze primary research studies, and raise both its expectations and standards for market research products.

The use of advanced statistical techniques can bring richer, more reliable and more useful data to bear on strategy development for healthcare marketers. Custom research can meet the unique objectives of a healthcare provider more aptly and reliably than generic surveys or secondary data. Even the highly standardized products widely commissioned across the country can be measureably improved with better questionnaire design, sample construction, creative cross tabulation, and more comprehensive analysis.

Our objective is twofold. First, we wish to acquaint healthcare marketers with advanced statistical techniques (such as cluster and discriminant analysis) which yield marketing research data that are more accurate, more understandable, and more easily translated into effective actions. Secondly, we wish to show marketing managers how to reap the maximum benefits from existing and future marketing research studies which have been analyzed by cross tabulation.

PART I: HOW MULTIVARIATE ANALYSIS CAN MAKE YOUR LIFE EASIER

Consider an all too familiar scenario. The marketing director of a health care center becomes concerned about his hospital's position in the market in anticipation of some planned changes. Perhaps an expansion or reduction of services is under consideration. Perhaps market share is eroding and no one is sure why. Perhaps there is a general sense that the physician base is eroding.

It is decided that a market survey is an appropriate tool. A study is commissioned. The research is conducted competently and a report provided with lots of graphs and tables tabulating the responses. The volume of information is overwhelming. The results are interesting, real information is conveyed, but a nagging feeling remains that the research fell short. The answers are still not there.

The market research may fail to provide management the answers it needs not because the data collected is insufficient, but because there has not been sufficient analysis to bring out the answers.

It is our experience that two of the standard multivariate techniques of survey research, cluster analysis and discriminant analysis, have proven useful in healthcare marketing. This paper is a non-technical introduction to the use of those techniques.

Multivariate Analysis

Multivariate analysis is simply using more than one of the variables (questions in the survey) at a time, which allows one to establish and understand relationships among the responses. The answers follow from these relationships.

A frequency table and the usual descriptive statistics (mean, median) involve only one variable, and so are not multivariate. A cross tabulation is one way to look at the relationship of two (or occasionally three) variables and so may be considered multivariate. More general multivariate techniques can study tens of variables at a time.

Two techniques that are especially applicable to the sorts of questions that arise in healthcare market research are cluster analysis and discriminant analysis.

Cluster Analysis

Often many of the questions on a survey are related. There may be several attitude questions about a service or several questions about usage patterns. In most communities the demographic variables (age, income, education, profession, stage of life, marital status, ...) are related. The patterns of these relationships can vary from neighborhood to neighborhood. For example, the relationship of age to income can be very different in the inner city than in the suburbs.

Studying related questions individually ignores the very fact that they are related. Also, because the questions are related the responses tend to come in constellations or clusters. A fundamental step in understanding the responses to sets of associated questions is finding these patterns of responses. Often there are five or fewer groups of responses that characterize virtually the entire population. The mathematical technique for identifying these groups is cluster analysis.

For example, a hospital's marketing director could study market share by age, income, education, ... individually and suspect that some important patterns are being missed. The preferences of those with high income must be to some extent related to those with high educations.

What this marketing director needs is a clear picture of the demographic make-up of his market area. Further more, he needs to know to what extent the different segments use his hospital. This can be done by developing demographic segments and tabulating hospital usage against these segments.

Demographic Cluster Case Study. The following case study involves hospital in a predominantly hispanic neighborhood in a southwestern city (population approximately 1,00,000). Although the hospital had been in the neighborhood over 70 years, it had only 20% market share for households living within one mile of the hospital.

A bilingual survey of recent healthcare consumers (400 screened surveys) in the immediate neighborhood of the hospital was conducted. A cluster analysis determined that the local healthcare consumers were made up of four demographic clusters:

1. Old Folks. The members of this group had a median age of 65 and lived in households without children. This group were less educated and had lower household incomes. This group made up approximately 20% of the market.

2. Older Children. These households had children in their twenties (in some cases [about 20%] with the children's children) still living at home. The household income for this group was higher than average for the neighborhood. The median age of the head of household was 54. This group also made up about 20% of the market.

3. Nuclear Family. This group made up 40% of the sample. It consisted of households with a mean of three children. The average age of the head of household was 34.

4. Young Folks. This group (about 20% of the sample) consisted of single adults (with or without children) or married adults without children. The median age of this group was 28. This group was somewhat better educated than the average.

When membership in these groups was cross tabulated against hospital usage and opinion, Chi-square significance of .003 were observed. However, cross tabulations against the individual demographic variables yielded no significance. Only by combining the variables did a usage pattern emerge.

It was found that the hospital was only getting its share of the market with Young Folks. At first this was surprising given the time the hospital had been in existence. It turns out, however, that for much of its existence the hospital was an extended care tuberculosis center and was actively avoided by the residents. What we found is that only with the Young Folks were these habits breaking down.

The actions required were clear. First, the hospital needed to reacquaint the neighbors with the hospital with community relations outreach programs. A promotional campaign with testimonials from older members of the community about the "new" hospital would also be in order.

For the longer term, the marketing department along with other hospital planners were able to determine the needs of the various population segments and which of those segments could be served best. Thus a basis of a strategic marketing plan was established.

Physician Opinion Case Study. A different sort of case study involves a hospital that was very concerned about dissatisfaction among the staff physicians. In particular it was felt that physician dissatisfaction was affecting referrals.

A survey was administered to the admitting physicians. The questionnaire included twelve questions that measured the physicians' attitudes about the hospital, its management, and their relationship to the hospital.

Tabulation of the individual responses showed that on the average the physicians were neither highly dissatisfied nor satisfied with the hospital. Cross tabulation of the responses to these questions against the usual staff demographics (age, specialty, length of service) yielded no significant patterns. In other words, standard cross tabulation techniques would not reveal whether a problem existed or not.

A clustering analysis was applied to these questions. It was found that there were two distinct groups:

1. Generally Satisfied. This group expressed strong agreement with such statements as:

   - "(The Hospital) is a better place to practice than 5 years ago."

   - "(The Hospital) is responsive to my needs."

   - "The management solicits my input into long-range goals."

   - "(The management) considers my opinion on issues that affect my practice."

   and others. This group constituted about 60% of the staff.

2. Less Than Satisfied. The members of this group disagreed with all of the above statements as well as the other questions about attitudes. This group made up about 40% of the staff.

Clustering analysis brought out the fact that there was a group of 40% of the physicians that were unhappy with the hospital and felt alienated from the management. The discontented physicians were not distinguishable by specific demographic criteria other than their collective dissatisfaction with management. Further, these "Less Than Satisfied Physicians" were in fact decreasing their referrals to the client hospital.

So although the management was doing well with 60% of the physicians and well overall, they still had a serious problem with their staff.

Conventional data interpretation methods would not have affirmed this very serious problem.

Discriminant Analysis

Often a population can be divided into a few categories which are of primary interest to the management of a healthcare facility. An example of this could be users and non-users of the facility. The management might want to know what are the characteristics that differentiate the two groups. The tool for doing this is discriminant analysis.

The first step in discriminant analysis is to attempt to develop a method for scoring the respondents using responses to various other (predictive) questions. The idea is to predict which group a respondent belongs to on the basis of this score. The score (or discriminant function) has a cut-off value with respondents having a score below this value most likely to be in one group and those with a score above the cut-off most likely to belong in the other group.

By computing to what extent a variable is related (correlated) to the discriminant function, one has a direct measure of the importance of that variable in sorting out the groups. Those variables that are highly correlated (either positively or negatively) with the discriminant function contribute to the choice, and the functions that are not correlated do not.

Of course, one could cross tabulate the predictive variables against the predicted variable to accomplish much the same analysis. However, discriminant analysis (when it can be used) provides several advantages:

- Discriminant analysis does not require the loss of information inherent in breaking continuous variables (such as age) into a few classifications required for statistically valid analysis of cross tabulations.

- Each variable is assigned a number that is directly comparable to the numbers assigned to the other variables in measuring its relevance to the group assignment. No such measure of association exists for cross tabulations.

- One can determine by the sign of the correlation coefficient whether a variable contributes positively or negatively to the likelihood of being in one group or the other.

- Many variables can be considered at once and the technique will automatically determine the important ones.

Hospital Market Share Case Study. A hospital in a predominantly white working class neighborhood has for several years strived to upgrade its services. The improvements have not yielded a commensurate improvement in market share, and the hospital management commissioned a marketing study as a first step to developing a marketing plan.

Over 400 users of healthcare in the primary market area were interviewed. A discriminant analysis was performed in which twenty-five variables were analyzed as possible predictors. These variables included demographics and household location, reported importance of hospital features, reported role in hospital choice, previous hospital use, and hospital preference.

A discriminant function was derived that predicted actual usage correctly in about 90% of the cases. Using this function it was found that the only variables that currently contribute to use of the client's hospital are:

- distance to hospital (negatively correlated)

- previous use (positively correlated)

- hospital preference (positively correlated)

- physician's recommendation (positively correlated)

- importance of others' opinions (negatively correlated)

- quality of emergency care (negatively correlated)

In other words, users of this hospital primarily lived in the neighborhood, were swayed by their physician, and were less concerned with other people's opinions and quality of emergency care as criteria for hospital selection. Those who cared about other people's opinions and emergency care were more likely to use other hospitals.

Based on this research the hospital could work with its physician base to expand its patient market into neighborhoods adjoining its current core market area. Emergency services improvement sprang to the top of its product line marketing objectives. Public image and word of mouth referral strengthened in importance. The marketing manager can proceed with confidence knowing that many of the other issues that may have affected market share (such as heavy advertising by competing facilities) could be safely ignored.

Benefits to the Manager. Multivariate analysis requires a significant amount of time from a competent statistician. This understandably adds to the cost of the research. These costs are offset by several benefits and (as we have seen) may make the difference in the success of the study.

The 17th century mathematician and philosopher, Blaise Pascal, once wrote in a letter to a friend, "I have made this letter longer than usual only because I have not had time to make it shorter." The point is that proper analysis clarifies the research results so that the report can be focused, to the point, and actionable.

While anyone commissioning a study is entitled to frequencies and cross tabulations, it should not be necessary to wade through these in order to discern some meaning in the data. Furthermore, by using cluster analysis to combine the variables in meaningful ways, fewer but more useful cross tabulations need be interpreted.

More importantly, the marketing manager is given a clear picture of the structure of his market and his services' positions in it by using these techniques. In addition, he can be confident that the important relationships in the data have been considered and rejected. He or she is then able to efficiently plan the appropriate strategy.

Another benefit of higher order multivariate techniques is that they permit the study of more subtle and difficult concepts. It may take more than one question to measure such concepts as physician satisfaction, role in decision making, and perceived benefits of various services. As we saw in the physician case study, by combining responses to several questions one can establish clear answers to these problems.

If the study is initially founded, the additional expense of sufficient analysis should be compensated by the efficient use of the manager's time and the forthrightness with which he or she can proceed with actions based on the data.

FURTHER ISSUES

The two advanced multivariate techniques discussed here, while very useful, are not simple. Many statistical packages such as SPSS offer clustering and discriminant packages. But having a good set of tools does not make one a craftsman. The right tool in the wrong hands can do more harm than good.

Both techniques require:

- careful questionnaire design so that the data is in appropriate form for the analysis

- proper data preparation after collection (such as creating dummy variables for discriminant analysis or rescaling for cluster analysis)

- sufficient number of completed surveys (especially for discriminant analysis)

- proper concern of the subtlety of the techniques so that they are not misused.

It is important that multivariate analysis should be planned from the beginning when the goals of the research are set and just not be an added afterthought.

Making sure your analysis is in experienced, competent hands and that the analyst is included in the early stages of the research planning will give you a greater likelihood of a successful research project.

CONCLUSION

There are other higher order multivariate techniques such as factor analysis, conjoint analysis, and multiple regression. It is likely that conjoint methods will be used more often in healthcare research the next few years.

In conclusion, although multivariate analysis may be somewhat more costly and require more careful research, the proper use of these techniques

- increases the likelihood of obtaining actionable results

- provides a sounder basis for planning and implementation of strategic marketing plans

- generally makes better use of the money expended to collect the data.

PART II: SO WHAT ABOUT CROSS TABS?

Cross tabulation of the variables remains the fundamental tool of survey research. It can be used to refine one's understanding of the data and to test causal relationships. There are many good sources of information and discussion on the subject of cross tabulations (see especially [1]). However, we would like to make some points not normally presented.

- The overall sampling error often reported by the survey firm does not apply to the row and column percentages. The sampling error must be computed using the number of cases in each row or column separately. Often the number of cases in a given row or column is less than 10 and so the sampling error is very large. We have seen examples of researchers misinterpreting row percentages with as few as three cases. Because of this phenomenon, many researchers prefer drawing samples as large as 600 to 1200 (when the budget permits) so that there can be confidence in the individual row and column percentages.

- The standard statistical test of significant (Chi-square) requires that fewer than 20% of the cells have expected cell size (the number of cases one would expect to be in each cell if the variables were independent) less than five and none with expected cell size less than zero.

- It follows from the above two points that proper use of cross tabulations requires that there be as small a number of categories as possible in the coding of the individual variables. If this is done, then the row and column frequencies as well as the expected values will be larger.

- Running three-way (or higher) cross tabulations exacerbates the cell size problem.

- Combining variables using clustering analysis as presented above often makes the cross tabulations more meaningful. The establishment of a small number of meaningful market segments permits easily interpreted, reliable cross tabulations.

- An advantage of cross tabulation is that it requires no data preparation other than proper coding. Many other statistical techniques make assumptions about the underlying population (such as fitting a bell-shaped curve). This is not the case for cross tabulations.

- On the other had, there is a loss of information when taking such continuous variables (such as age) and assigning categories (such as 18 to 24) for use in cross tabulations. We have seen examples where significant relationships were missed when this was done. Generally, one should collect continuous values (not categories) whenever possible and apply methods (such as discriminant analysis or some modern non-parametric test) which use the data more efficiently.

Generally, cross tabulation is a rough-and-ready research technique that is generally easier to use than the other tests. It requires little concern about data quality. However, sometimes cross tabulations will miss significant relationships that could be found with other techniques.

PART III: HOW TO COMMISSION BETTER RESEARCH STUDIES

Routine consumer and physician studies customarily contain far more exciting, meaningful, and usable data than are ever mentioned in the consultant's written report. The data tables can provide a treasuretrove of market facts and insights, but the study must be constructed so that these important tidbits are available and accessible.

Set Objectives. If you do not have clear objectives in mind for what you wish to accomplish, you run considerable risk of wasting time and money on a frivolous study. You will also be sending signals to your potential research vendor that you have fuzzy expectations, a set of circumstances that can lead to your getting a standardized study that does little more than add to the research vendor's data base.

Before you even shop for a vendor, you should know:

- What do we need to know about the market?
- What hypotheses should be explored?
- How will we use the information?

Select the Right Vendor. Vendors should be selected on credentials, quality standards, service range, flexibility, and value.

Treating market research as a commodity has become a popular but dangerous habit in healthcare. Firms differ substantially in their approaches to survey research, their ranges of experience and capabilities, their flexibility, and their fees. To reap the utmost from your research study, it is important to have the full support and cooperation of your vendor. Ethical research firms welcome knowledgeable - and discerning - clients. Points to cover in your discussion with potential vendors include:

- Who owns the data? You will want to have perpetual access to your data. If you have computer capability, you should have the option of taking actual possession of the survey responses on tape or diskette.

- How many cross tabs will be allowed? Some firms limit cross tab selection to 12 or 24, depending on the restrictions of the their internal software. Pulling additional cross tabs can be costly. Negotiate in advance the terms of cross tab runs. You should strive for optimum flexibility in running tabs in several sequences, if desired.

- What are the limitations of the standard cross tab tables? You will want your tabs to include actual frequencies, row percentages, and column percentages. Not all vendors have this capability.

- What statistical validity tests will be performed, and how will results be reported? You cannot interpret cross tabs without testing the relationships between the variables. Comparing simple percentages can lead to false assumptions. Your cross tab tables should indicate where relationships between variables exist, and the degree of significance by Chi square testing.

- What formats can be used to show relationships among multiple variables? When variables to be used as cross tabs are suspected to be related (such as age and income), the cross tab variables should ideally be run simultaneously against the primary question. Tables can be generated which show these interrelationships. Interrelated variables should not be considered separately against the primary question.

- What will the report contain? Some vendors are excellent at interpreting numbers, but do not excel at the marketing implications of the numbers. Some promise to deliver everything, including advertising theme recommendations! Determine what skills you need from your vendor, how much interpretation you can handle internally, and what each vendor's strengths and weaknesses are. Then, you can negotiate to purchase the scope of analysis you really need.

- How involved can you be in questionnaire development? Generally, the more you know about survey research and the objectives of your study, the more involvement you should have in designing the questionnaire and the study itself. If you delegate too much responsibility to your vendor, you are making a leap of faith that the research firm knows more about your hospital, market, and CEO's expectations than you do - a risky business! It is wise to let your potential vendors know up front that the standard questions asked on most surveys may not meet your needs and objectives.

Make or Buy? Before you negotiate budget parameters for a survey, you should determine what extent of services you need from the outside vendor. Data analysis and interpretation is a time consuming and costly business. Much can be done to extract extra value from a fairly standard report, provided you have good cross tabs to begin with, and you have easy access to additional data. Most research vendors are happy to bid on increments of analysis. If you have more staff time available than hard dollars, however, you may wish to commission only a standard report product, which you and your staff then flesh out in additional detail.

Custom or Canned? Because market research is often viewed as a commodity, many vendors strive to be the low cost producer/low bidder. They exchange wide margins for volume, attempting to streamline projects as much as possible. The result is usually a highly standardized product which varies little between one client and another, given comparable objectives and survey targets.

Again, there are trade-offs which the marketing manager must consider. If price is the primary consideration, the standardized study may meet your needs. Custom research, although often more costly, has the advantage of being designed specifically around your individual market circumstances, competitive environment, and objectives. Custom research can be expected to deliver a richer, more insightful product which may also be a more efficient use of research dollars.

Most firms purport to deliver customized research. In actuality, survey instruments for community attitude studies or medical staff satisfaction studies often tend to have large blocks of identical questions - which are used to develop "national norms." National norms may be interesting, but for most single-market or regional providers, other questions may be more relevant.

Marketing managers should discuss with prospective research vendors the level of customization offered in their respective proposals. As a rule of thumb, if you are being quoted a per response price, and if the vendor has not quizzed you at length on the specific study objectives, you probably are not receiving a bid for highly customized research.

Sample Size and Construction. Cross tabs are not meaningful if the data is sliced too thin. Insufficient sample sizes are one of the primary reasons that cross tabs are not used more extensively in market survey analysis.

Sample size for consumer opinion studies in healthcare generally hovers around 400 responses, which (at 384) provides a confidence level of 95% certainty with sampling error of $\pm$ five percentage points. Consumers are customarily selected at random, with nominal screens introduced for adult head of household, non-employment in healthcare, etc. Rather than arbitrarily set a goal of a 400 random sample, however, you may wish to consider if other configurations might yield more value.

For example, a sample of 650 responses will create a much stronger data base for statistical analysis, and will afford more confidence in the cross tabs (both in row and column calculations).

If you wish to analyze certain geographic segments individually, you must sample each segment in sufficient quantity to support independent analysis.

Many hospitals have geographically constricted service areas which penetrate only fractions of their respective metropolitan areas. This type of hospital often confines a community attitude study to its service area, and loses the value of a citywide perspective of demographic market segments, competitors' strengths and weaknesses, variations in media preferences, etc.

Hospitals in locations where zip code-specific utilization data is unavailable can use market studies to build strategic data bases on market share by zip code or neighborhood. The difference in cost between a sample size of 400 and one of 1000 can often be minimized through efficient questionnaire design. The additional data can yield much richer, sounder, and reliable interpretation.

Cell sizes can be increased without increasing total sample size by oversampling the relevant population. If your study is intended to reveal the behaviors and preferences of actual hospital users, for example, you should sample a disproportionate percentage of people who have had recent inpatient experiences. Depending on the complete objectives of the study, you may even wish to sample only recent hospital users. Otherwise, when you attempt to unravel the issues surrounding market share and actual usage patterns, your cell sizes may be too small to explore fully.

Questionnaire Design. It's all too easy to fill a 15 minute telephone survey with interesting questions. Confining your survey to the questions that will ultimately yield the desired results, on the other hand, can be quite challenging. Again, a clear sense of purpose is your best tool for efficient survey design. Your task is to know what you want to get out of your study and how you expect to use the results.

When designing the survey, you should try to make the questionnaire as concise as possible. Don't pad it with questions that are merely interesting. Instead, try to make it as short as possible and use the money you've saved on survey length to increase the number of responses.

Why commission a 15 minute survey of 400 responses if you can get better information by conducting a tightly written eight minute survey among 800 respondents?

Coding. Cross tabs deal with categorical data. If the original responses have not been coded properly, the resulting cross tabs can be spurious. Similarly, the categories of responses must make sense, and should be used in the largest aggregate possible.

We heartily recommend that healthcare marketing managers occasionally crosscheck the accuracy of their research vendor's coding. An excellent way to do this is to request raw data on a question such as top of mind awareness. Not only will such an exercise show you how well responses are being categorized, but these particular responses can be incredibly rich with insight and nuance. Consider the difference between a raw response of "I wouldn't send my dog to Hospital X" versus its collapse into a category of "general negative responses."

Response categories are often so small that they lose meaning. For example, one research vendor listed 20 categories of response to the question, "Why did you select that hospital?" These categories can usually be collapsed into more meaningful, larger categories with much larger cell sizes, which can then be isolated (such as physician-directed choice) and used as a predictive cross tab.

Similarly, when you have one response category of "honesty" explaining the most important physician characteristic, and another of "trustworthyness," you must wonder why the coder did not simply collapse these responses into the same category.

Collapsing categories where you can without losing important distinctions will allow more options for exploratory analysis.

Creative Cross Tabbing. Don't confine your analysis to simple demographic cross tabs and other obvious choices. Cross tabs can be used to build simple models and explain choices and behaviors. A little right brained conceptualizing and a cooperative research consultant can help you mine the data to produce a rich knowledge basis.

Examples of cross tab analysis that we have employed successfully include the following:

- Developing a patient-driven hospital selection group and a physician-driven hospital selection group, then tabbing against actual hospitals used.

- Isolating an advertising-sensitive segment and determining what, if any, differences exist in their hospital choices.

- Identifying physician referral patterns by consumers' physicians' locations, specialties, and hospitals used.

- Discerning loyalty entrenchments to various facilities by tracking preference, last hospital used, and previous hospital used.

- Clustering homogeneous zip codes to develop neighborhood-specific competitive rankings and utilization.

Cross tabs can test hypotheses that flow from the initial analysis. They can be used to cross validate other responses. They can also stimulate and refine behavioral analysis that leads to better targeted marketing strategies. With proper interpretation, cross tabs can be used as components of market models and feasibility studies for a variety of issues.

As an exploratory device, cross tabulation is time-consuming, costly, and not without interpretive risks. We encourage competent research counsel to guide you in determining what is meaningful and valid.

Interpret the Market, Not Just the Data. Most research vendors will not be on intimate terms with your local market and competitive environment. You must not accept conclusions drawn from statistics without determining if they make sense within the context of your unique circumstances. A few cautions are in order.

- Be wary of overinterpreting the value of national norms. The fact that your facility's rating is akin to national norms is irrelevant if that rating is significantly lower than your rival hospitals'.

- Look for the bad news. Many consultants fear bringing bad tidings. Once in a while, the messenger does get shot! Read your consultant's report very carefully. Often the news is sugar coated. No one likes to know that the situation is dire - but if that is reality, you must face it before you can change it. Be very certain you understand the implications of the data from your own, more knowledgeable, perspective.

By following these practical tips, we believe that you will glean added value from every research study you commission. Your investment in a sound and thorough knowledge base is an investment that will pay off dearly. Let the numbers tell you where truth is, and your marketing plans will have a much higher probability of success.

CONCLUSION

Healthcare marketing's new Age of Accountability requires marketers to employ the most reliable and cost-effective means to develop marketing strategies that meet performance objectives. Healthcare marketers must raise their standards and expectations for the marketing research studies that guide their marketing planning. Advanced statistical techniques and a thorough understanding of how to construct, commission, and interpret marketing research will create a better foundation for developing successful marketing strategies.

REFERENCES

Zeisel, Hans (1968), Say It With Figures, 5th edition, Revised, New York: Harper & Row Publishers, Inc.

Myers, James H. and Tauber, Edward (1977), Market Structure Analysis, Chicago: American Marketing Association

FOCUS GROUP RESEARCH: DO-IT-YOURSELF

Ellen Tobin, Health Surveys and Marketing, Inc.
Columbia, Maryland

M. Keith Kaufher, Geisinger Health Care System
Danville, Pennsylvania

ABSTRACT

Health care facilities are seeking better ways to gain insights into their various markets. In a more competitive environment, market managers are looking for cost effective ways to enhance decision making; to help them economically discover characteristics of the market response to products or services; and to generate ideas. Focus group research, a form of qualitative research, provides an in-depth, subjective understanding of the problem being investigated. The major impediments to consistent use of focus group research are the cost of hiring external consultants, the lack of appropriately trained people within the organization, and organizational barriers. This paper examines the uses of focus group research, highlights the potential obstacles to conducting the research with internal resources, and presents an approach to the development of in-house capabilities.

INTRODUCTION

A number of techniques have been developed to elicit subjective information on people's feelings and impressions: in-depth interviews, projective techniques, and focus group interviews.

The focus group interview technique evolved from group therapy methods. Its use aids in the discovery of factors that motivate a particular behavior. A focus group is a meeting of eight to twelve persons, with a moderator who elicits in-depth responses during a discussion of a particular issue. Although focus group research is widely used in industrial marketing research, its applications in the health care field have only recently emerged.

Focus group research is often the precursor to more costly quantitative research. The focus group can determine important issues for the customers of a health care organization: former patients, community members, referral sources, physicians, community leaders, and employees. Focus group interviews follow an open discussion format, resulting in a high level of spontaneity and candor.

The objective of this paper is to demonstrate the issues involved in developing an in-house focus group research program. Supporting these discussions will be the experience of Health Surveys and Marketing in conducting focus group research for health care facilities and in assisting in the development of in-house capabilities. Also presented as a case study are the efforts of the Geisinger health care system to incorporate focus group research as part of internally managed marketing research.

Examples of focus group uses include providing opinions and testing on:

o   strengths and weaknesses of health care services or a delivery system

o   proposed changes in service delivery

o   facility design

o   product concepts

o   design of survey questionnaires

o   clarification of quantitative research results

o   communication/advertising strategy

Although focus group research has proven widely successful, the technique has its limitations. The research is a non-scientific form of data collection and is not projectable to the universe. There can be bias because participants tend to be risk takers and there are a small number of respondents. Results cannot be quantified and analysis is left to the moderator's interpretation.

There are also reasons not to conduct some focus group research totally with in-house staff. In some cases, there is the need for outside objectivity, e.g., research on a new facility, program, or product line. In other cases, the lack of expertise in some aspects of the research would be a limiting factor. A research program should be managed to accomplish some activities in-house and seek necessary outside assistance from objective, professionals who can assume either a consultative or more direct role.

OBSTACLES TO HEALTHCARE FOCUS GROUP RESEARCH

What stands in the way of focus research within health care facilities?

1)   Cost

     In focus group research, the cost per respondent as compared to surveys, can be high, e.g., renting a focus group facility, recruiting participants, gratuities or honoraria, a professional moderator, video taping, written transcriptions of tapes and preparing reports.

2)   Unavailability of experienced people

     For the research to be successfully executed, there must be individuals with training, experience, and a combination of skills. While it is possible for management within your organization to attend off-site training programs in focus group moderation, most of the training programs are expensive and frequently not practical or useful for the unique needs of a health care facility.

3)   Bias introduced by internally conducting focus research

     Providers and administrative staff have a vested interest in the quality of services and frequently have "ownership" of an idea or product being tested. At other times, management responds defensively when consumers perceive that the hospital has weaknesses.

4)   Difficulty in convincing management to approve focus group research

     There are two difficulties to be overcome. The first is the recognition of the necessity for any marketing research. The second (assuming that the first difficulty is overcome) is the difficulty in convincing management of the need for an internally managed and executed focus group program.

5) Organizational problems

Many organizations have fragmentation of marketing responsibilities and varying points of view of various disciplines. For example, patient opinion research is frequently valued by patient representatives or by patient relations, quality assurance, and risk management staff. However, the marketing department is charged with marketing research and there may or may not be cooperation between the departments.

6) Time constraints

Focus group research demands time to establish the issues, train the moderators, recruit, make logistical arrangements, develop the analysis, prepare the report and present results.

THE SITUATION AT GEISINGER

Geisinger is a growing, diversified, multi-institutional health care system in central and northeastern Pennsylvania. The system includes medical group practices, a regional specialty referral center, medical and allied health teaching programs, medical research, a community hospital, outreach specialty clinics, alcohol and chemical abuse centers, an HMO and a biomedical engineering company. Geisinger has been considered the standard setter in its region from its beginning in 1915.

The marketing functions within Geisinger are diverse and decentralized. The chief executive officer is, in a very real sense, the chief marketing officer as well. The organization has well developed marketing management resources.

Marketing management style is high-touch and largely intuitive. Marketing research has been mostly secondary or anecdotal. Some quantitative baseline research has been done. Preliminary and follow-up surveys have accompanied advertising campaigns. Communication tools are regularly evaluated by readership testing. Standard patient response "safety value" opinion gathering techniques have been in use for years.

Use of primary marketing research is limited among top management and demand for it comes largely from those directly responsible for staffing the marketing functions.

In response to several requests from consumers, we developed focus group research. Due to the number of different needs and the desire for year-round sampling, the cost of a program completely dependent on outside consulting was judged to be prohibitive. The alternative was to initiate a program of internally managed research.

The system was developed, a pilot series on needs of the geriatric community was run. Geisinger, assisted by HSM, developed the approach, recruited participants, handled logistics and focused the issues.

Three members of Geisinger's marketing staff and two carefully screened local residents received training from the consultant in conducting focus groups. Senior staff assisted in the pilot focus group moderation. The people who had received training observed the focus groups and were part of de-briefing afterward. The consultant prepared a final report.

Two very basic conclusions came out of the focus groups. First, while the geriatric segment of our market is burgeoning, it views itself as well taken care of. Second, there is little we would currently change in managing services for our 65 or older segments that would markedly enhance their care and improve the system's revenue and profit picture. Subsequent secondary research has supported these conclusions.

The program for internal management of focus group management presents important advantages. First, the job of answering critical questions about market characteristics gets done. Second, management maintains control of the process without having to do the job as well. Third, able consulting expertise provides necessary support, quality control and credibility. And, finally the approach is much less expensive and avoids dependence on outside consulting.

The single, most outstanding problem is the same in hundreds of organizations. Focus group research and, more broadly, marketing research have not established themselves as essential elements in management of health care. Until marketing research does gain acceptance, well conceived and executed marketing research or good management of the process simply won't be enough.

TRAINING STAFF

The following aspects must be considered within a training program:

1) The moderator

The choice and the training of the moderator is second only to the commitment for developing the program.

The moderator must be able to direct the discussion and encourage participation. He or she must be skilled at eliciting responses without encouraging bias. The skill and experience of the moderator are essential when discussing sensitive issues or when handling difficult situations.

When selecting a staff person to be trained, the following qualities are sought: intuitive skills as a facilitator; a warm, sensitive, self-effacing person; and very important and frequently overlooked, one who understands the issues and the purpose of the research.

The training of the individual moderators includes techniques in rapport building, group dynamics, handling of difficult situations, and ensuring that the information elicited is as bias-free as possible.

2) The moderator guides

The development of the moderator guides depends on the issues to be studied. However, certain rules apply. The most important axiom is that the guide must be structured in a way which allows for flexibility and for encouraging group interaction. One must remember that the process, while important, is not the end product. For patient/consumer research the guide takes the following form:

   a) Introduction

   b) Ground rules

   c) Introduction of participants to the group

   d) General health care selection criteria and usage/low anxiety questions/rapport building

   e) Specific questions, patient satisfaction, in-depth investigation, needs not being met

f)   Testing of concepts

g)   Written response form

h)   Closure

3)   Recruiting

The composition of the group is extremely important. It
has been our experience that homogenous groups are
preferable, e.g., former maternity patients, geriatric
consumers in a certain geographical location, breast
cancer patients, referral sources, etc. Recruiting is
quite easy. Using a script or screener, the recruiter
calls the participants. Recruiting consumers from the
general community is another matter. This demands time,
patience, and good salesmanship. Honoraria or gratuities
are provided and confirmation letters and thank you
letters are appropriate.

4)   Logistical arrangements.

We have had much success conducting focus groups within
healthcare facilities (in a board room or a group therapy
room). Not only is the cost sharply reduced but there are
few barriers to arriving at the facility. Refreshments
are provided. Video taping and viewing through a two-way
mirror are optional. Audio taping is provided.

5)   Analysis/interpretation/reporting

Reports can be either of the "reporting" or "analytical"
style and are frequently a combination of the two. The
type of report and the length of the report depend on
several factors: 1) the expertise of the analyst; 2) the
use of the research; 3) the time available for report
preparation. Any type of report should rely heavily on a
large number of verbatim responses. Interpretation and
recommendations must be based on serious consideration of
the results.

CONCLUSIONS

Implementing an in-house focus group research program is not
without difficulties. Why bother? Because as health care
marketing professionals, our job is to stay close to our
customers and to be up- to-date about their points-of-view.
Health care is in the early stages of evaluating and
implementing techniques for marketing research. Methods we
choose must be useful, actionable and cost effective. The
various techniques for enhancing management's sense of the
markets must fit into the context of the organization's
business picture as well as into accepted standards of good
marketing research.

Focus group research can meet these standards. The technique
becomes even more attractive when managed internally with
modest support from a marketing research consultant.

References

Hisrich, Robert D. and Michael P. Peters (1982) "Focus Groups:
An Innovative Marketing Research Technique, Hospital and Health
Services Administration, (July/August) 8-22.

C112/a

PROFILES OF ATTITUDES TOWARD HEALTHCARE:
A POWERFUL SYSTEM FOR HEALTHCARE MARKETING SEGMENTATION

Fred Navarro
Marc Rubinger
The Peabody Group
San Francisco and Cleveland

ABSTRACT

Using a multivariate approach to define segmentation within the healthcare market, The Peabody Group has developed a computer-assisted procedure to predict healthcare needs in any specific market. Documentation for the methodology and testing involved in this procedure is provided in this paper.

Attendees of the Seventh Annual Health Care Marketing Symposium will be the first to hear the results of a nation-wide study based upon this procedure.

OVERVIEW

Recognizing that well-documented market segmentation is essential to the success of healthcare marketing, The Peabody Group is currently involved in the development of a landmark market segmentation study. This effort began with a primary research pilot study for a North Carolina hospital, supported by secondary research. The pilot research has been followed with an extensive literature review and a comprehensive prototype primary research study involving five major hospitals. Numerous researchers have found that traditional customer attitude and life-style profiles may be misleading indicators of market segments. Classic analysis of product- or service-specific customer benefit characteristics may also be misleading, especially if product purchase is situation dependent (Harrel and Fors 1985, Young, Ott, and Feigin 1978). Peabody analysts have developed a system for assessing qualitative and quantitative characteristics of any healthcare market, developing focused information about a reliable set of consumer market segments.

Initially, The Peabody Group contracted with a North Carolina hospital to conduct a study of market segmentation among five hundred women throughout a five-county area. Utilizing a cluster-based segmentation approach (Wind 1978) involving twenty-two original psychographic, healthcare-specific, attitude, interest and opinion measures, Peabody identified seven distinct segments of the women's healthcare market, based on dimensions suggested by Harrel and Fors (1985). As with all psychographically-based segmentation typologies, solutions are not meant to be evaluated independently of geographic, demographic, and socio-economic information. "Psychographics can put flesh on demographic bones (Wells 1975)," and it is within this context that Peabody analysts identified and employed these psychographic dimensions.

The pilot study identified specific market segments, based upon previously suggested segmentation bases, consisting of identified actionable product/service specific attitudinal and behavioral dimensions affecting healthcare consuming behavior. Using these dimensions as the basis for segment-ation, Peabody identified preliminary segments and assisted with development of a successful marketing strategy for that hospital.

The Peabody Group has successfully identified a set of attitudinal and behavioral characteristics relevant to the healthcare concerns of men and women. Peabody's proprie-tary healthcare market research and the literature indicate that knowledge of the following characteristics is essential to the development of actionable marketing strategies:
- Health emphasis (physical fitness vs. nutritional fitness)
- Propensity to experiment ("shop")
- Self-confidence in decision making
- Involvement in decision making (individually and for the family)
- Healthcare information seeking
- Propensity to avoid healthcare
- Degree of family orientation
- Price/quality consciousness
- Tendency to plan for the future
- Attitudes toward medical professionals
- Receptivity to healthcare advertising
- Health apathy (level of health involvement)
- Health optimism

These dimensions provide information that accurately evaluates general and situation-specific healthcare consumer strategies, activities, and benefit requirements.

This technical paper explains and documents the methodology used to develop a healthcare market segmentation typology. The presentation in March will focus totally on the actual findings of this research, rather than on the methodology outlined in this document.

METHODOLOGY

To identify consistently similar segments across geographic markets, five hospitals across the country were invited to participate in the prototype study. To broaden the geographic base of the study, and increase the likelihood that identified healthcare market segments would be applicable to the majority of U.S. markets, Peabody selected an additional five localities to survey.

Peabody's questionnaire was designed to assess healthcare attitudinal and behavioral dimensions, as well as to provide insight into health insurance and medication shopping behavior; satisfaction with available healthcare options; use of hospitals; the mechanism for hospital choice (e.g., does respondent, doctor, or health plan drive the decision?); the presence of a personal doctor; interest in switching doctors; use of preventive health check-ups, common personal healthcare referent sources (e.g., spouse, parents, friends); and common media sources of healthcare information.

Traditional demographic (age and sex) and socio-economic (education, income, and occupation) measures were also addressed. Statements were scored as five-point, Likert-type, strongly agree-disagree items.

Two thousand completed telephone interviews, each averaging seventeen minutes, were conducted from Peabody's in-house central telephone bank in San Francisco. Two hundred interviews were conducted in each of the participant hospital service areas (Manchester, NH; Pittsburgh, PA; Columbus, OH; Indianapolis, IN; Louisville, KY) and in each of the markets represented by Jacksonville, FL, Dallas, TX, Denver, CO, Seattle, WA, and the combined populations of Glendale, Pasadena, and Arcadia, CA. Random digit dialing insured that both listed and unlisted telephone households would be represented; random telephone numbers were generated by prefix according to the proportion of telephone households within each prefix. Only heads of households were interviewed, and up to three call-backs were made to each household, if necessary, before alternate numbers were used. Approximately 15% of completed interviews were with people who initially refused to be interviewed; comparison between these refusal "conversions" and initial non-refusals was used to assess non-response bias.

DATA ANALYSIS

Psychographic Inventory Reduction

Prior to segment development, two R-type factor analyses were used to identify the number of statements necessary to precisely determine defined psychographic dimensions. Fifteen factors were identified in each R-type factor analysis using the Kaiser eigenvalue criterion and Varimax rotation. The number of factors identified (15), relative to the proportion of variance explained (about 65% in each analysis), demonstrates that the original items Peabody selected were successfully measuring distinct, independent dimensions, and that factor structures were similar.

Classification Procedures

Recent research has demonstrated the superiority of Q-factor analysis over alternative clustering routines (Funkhouser 1983, Hagerty 1985, and Peabody's own comparisons of both techniques) and Q-factor analysis was employed in the identification of homogeneous clusters within each of the ten geographic locations. Split-half samples of 100 respondents each were used to produce two Q-correlation matrices for each market, and each matrix was factor analyzed using orthogonal Varimax rotation. Two initial subject clusters were potentially identifiable for each factor and the positive and negative loadings of all subjects on all factors were examined. Subjects were then assigned to the factor clusters on which they had the largest positive or negative loading, and subjects not attaining a minimum loading value of at least ± 0.33 were not assigned (Stephenson 1953).

Q-factor analyses of data from both the pilot North Carolina study and the present prototype study indicated that rotated factor solutions accounting for 70% of the variance across subjects were sufficient to insure that all subjects in each split-half sample met the minimum criteria for classification in a cluster. Screen tests of eigenvalues indicated that this cut-off level was appropriate. Nine to ten rotated factors were produced in each market using this criterion.

Clusters were entered into a multiple discriminant analysis. This procedure produced mean and standard deviation profile vectors for each cluster, provided an evaluation of the classification matrix and assessed the clustering of subjects.

Validating Segments Within Markets

Reliability of cluster solutions within markets was determined by calculating distance indices between each cluster solution within the split-half samples. Each distance index was constructed using an unweighted average of the Euclidian distances between cluster profile mean vectors (Lehman 1979, p. 559). This produced a C1 by C2 matrix of distances in which C1 referred to the number of clusters produced in the split-half samples with odd cases and C2

referred to the number of clusters produced in the split-half samples with even cases. The minimum distance between each cluster profile in one split-half solution and the set of profile mean vectors in the other solution was then identified. An average of minimum distances was used as the index of optimum similarity (Lesser and Hughes 1986, p. 21).

Cluster solutions within a market were further evaluated by comparing the mean of split-half minimum distances with the mean of minimum distances developed by replacing each cluster profile vector in the odd split-half sample with Monte Carlo synthetic-random mean profile vectors. A statistically significant smaller mean for the actual split-half sample minimum distances provides evidence supporting reliability of the solutions. Given that clusters identified using Q-factor techniques are not orthogonal in a statistical sense, the original factor loadings were examined to determine if the mix of respondents who load negatively on one factor was similar to the mix of respondents who load positively on another factor. Pairs of clusters exhibiting high similarity in composition of respondents and low distances between them were combined within each market and identification and validation of the market segments within a market was completed.

Validating Segments Across Markets

A set of across-market distance matrices was calculated to evaluate the similarity of cluster solutions. A statistically insignificant difference between the mean distances across markets and the mean distances within markets indicates that differences across markets are no larger than differences within markets; a statistically significant, lower across-market minimum distance index, as compared to a minimum distance index derived from synthetic random profile distances, provides evidence that profile vectors across markets are more similar than expected by chance. This procedure provides strong evidence regarding the occurrence of similar healthcare consumer segments across markets and assesses whether psychographically based healthcare segments, as defined by Peabody's selected dimensions, are generalizable across markets.

Cross-tabulation of segment membership with additional healthcare behavioral and attitudinal data (e.g., frequency of health service use, health insurance shopping behavior, use of hospitals) insures consistency between perceived healthcare behavior profiles and psychographic characteristics. The nature of the relationship between segment demographic and socio-economic profiles and segment psychographic traits is particularly important. Information about age groups, the distribution of males and females, the size and structure of the family, and the relative buying power (as indicated by per-capita income levels), is clarified through understanding this relationship.

Similar market segments across the ten geographic healthcare markets were then combined according to the distances between pairs of profiles, and a set of distinctly different healthcare consumer types was identified. Preliminary analysis of these data suggests that there are 6 to 8 major healthcare consumer market segments occurring in most markets and that 70% and 80% of all healthcare consumers will belong to these segments.

STRATEGIC MARKETING IMPLICATIONS

The questions raised by this research are numerous, interdependent, and important.

- How involved in the decision-making process are potential consumers of the healthcare product or service?

- Do they tend to make all healthcare decisions themselves, or do they rely on others?

- How receptive to healthcare advertising is the targeted consumer?

- Is the consumer attentive, suspicious, or ambivalent?

- What kind of health information or product will appeal
  to the consumer?

- Is the consumer highly involved in maintaining personal health, or is the consumer apathetic?

- Where should services be based?

Information derived from this type of analysis is essential
to the successful targeting of educational and promotional
efforts.

Peabody's newly-developed process answers all of these
questions and provides reliable healthcare marketing advice
to those organizations who require such assistance. Cross-
tabulated segment membership information provided the North
Carolina hospital with clear direction regarding services
required, potential users for those services, and market
opportunity. Having advanced knowledge regarding healthcare consumer segments presented a definitive strategic
advantage.

REFERENCES

Funkhouser, G. Ray (1983), "A Note on the Reliability of
Certain Clustering Algorithms," Journal of Marketing
Research, 20 (February), 99-102.

Hagerty, Michael R. (1985), "Improving the Predictive Power
of Conjoint Analysis: The Use of Factor Analysis and
Cluster Analysis," Journal of Marketing Research, 22
(May), 168-84.

Harrel, Gilbert D., and Matthew F. Fors (1985), "Marketing
Ambulatory Healthcare to Women: A Segmentation Approach," Journal of Health Care Marketing, 2 (Spring),
29-36.

Lehman, Donald R. (1979), Market Research and Analysis,
Homewood, IL: Richard D. Irwin, Inc.

Lesser, Jack A., and Marie Adele Hughes (1986), "The Gene-
ralizability of Psychographic Market Segments Across
Geographic Locations," Journal of Marketing, 50 (January)
18-27.

Stephensen, William (1953), The Study of Behavior, Chicago:
University of Chicago Press.

Wells, William D. (1975), "Psychographics: A Critical
Review," Journal of Marketing Research, 12 (May), 196-
211.

Wind, Yoram (1978), "Issues and Advances in Segmentation
Research," Journal of Marketing Research, 15 (August),
327-37.

Young, Shirley, Leland Ott, and Barbara Feigin (1978),
"Some Practical Considerations in Market Segmentation,"
Journal of Marketing Research, 15 (August), 405-12.

BUILDING BRAND LOYALTY AMONG OLDER HEALTH CARE CONSUMERS:
THE ROLES OF RESEARCH IN PRODUCT LINE DEVELOPMENT

Sharon K. Rexroad, The Methodist Medical Center of Illinois, Peoria

ABSTRACT

Research was undertaken to measure interest in the
general concept of a membership club for older adults and
specific "benefits", to develop a pricing strategy that
would lead to the optimal balance between members and
revenues, and to design a promotional strategy that would
effectively reach the target audience. This project
included primary and secondary quantitative research and
two-stage concept testing. The program model also
included mechanisms by which consumer response is evaluated and research effectiveness measured.

BRAND LOYALTY -- THE CONCEPT

The concept of building "brand loyalty" to a health care
facility is relatively new. Techniques used by marketers
in consumer goods and service industries to build such
loyalty are only now being tested in the health care
arena. In addition, older adults (defined, for this
article, as those persons age 65 and over) have only
recently gained attention as an economically desirable
target market for both goods and services. Consequently,
little formal research has been performed in the area of
building brand loyalty among older health care consumers.

One loyalty building tool used in other arenas, most
noticeably the financial and airline industries, is the
membership club. By belonging to a club, the member
receives special benefits. It is hoped that these
benefits will serve as an incentive to use the sponsoring
organization's primary services.

Previous research, to be discussed later in this article,
indicated both a high level of satisfaction among current
users of the medical center and a latent preference for
the hospital among older adults that was not being
realized in terms of market share. In an effort to
to reinforce loyalty among current older adult patients
and to tap into the latent demand for the facility, the
medical center researched the feasibility of "borrowing"
the membership club concept from other industries.

Results obtained from the research enabled the medical
center to:

- measure the level of interest in a membership club
  for older adults

- select appropriate services to offer as "benefits" to
  club members

- develop a pricing strategy that would lead to the
  optimal balance between members and revenues

- create a promotional strategy that would effectively
  reach the target audience

The resultant proposal for a membership organization for
older adults was then reviewed and modified based on
anticipated moves by the competition. The program was
implemented in September of 1986. Its effectiveness in
building brand loyalty to the medical center is being
measured on an ongoing basis.

SITUATION ANALYSIS

The "brand loyalty" project did not occur in a vacuum.
Rather, it is one component in the medical center's
overall marketing strategy to attract older adults. In
order to place the program in its proper context, a brief
description of the medical center's efforts in the area
of older adult services follows.

The "Graying" of the Marketplace

The medical center is located in a metropolitan area of
366,000 that is surrounded by a predominantly rural
population. Although persons age 65 and over represent
only 12% of the population in this medical center's
primary service area, they accounted for 32% of all
discharges and 44% of hospital revenues at the time that
the research was initiated. Competition among area
health care providers for the older adult market is
intense with each of the major hospitals in the area
offering services geared toward this segment.

The population in the medical center's region, like that
of the rest of the nation, is aging. Between 1970 and
2020, it is projected that persons age 55 and over will
have increased by nearly two-thirds in the medical
center's immediate service area. Given unfavorable
economic conditions in the area, resulting in a recent
exodus from the region of persons in their 20's, 30's and
40's, the older adult population may currently represent
a greater proportion of the local population than is
typical nationally.

In terms of medical center utilization, the impact of the
aging of the population is already being felt. Using
1983 as the base, the following increases in older adult
patient days have been projected for the medical center:

- 7% increase by 1990

- 13% increase by 2000

- 19% increase by 2010

- 52% increase by 2020

The dramatic increase between 2010 and 2020 reflects the
maturation of the baby-boom generation.

Market Share

Exact market share data, broken out by age, is not
readily available in the medical center's geographical
area. Age-specific utilization rates for the medical
center itself were, however, approximated by combining
internal patient origin data with population information
available from state and local agencies. By comparing
these utilization rates with national rates of admission
per 1000 population age 65 and over, the medical center
was able to estimate its share of the 65+ market at the
end of 1984 at just under 30%.

Preference among this age bracket for the medical center
appears, however, to be significantly higher than this.
In May of 1985, the medical center commissioned a

telephone survey of older adults living in the six-county area surrounding the facility. Research findings from this survey indicated that among those who had been treated at the Medical Center in the preceding three years, more than three-fourths would make the same choice in the future for non-emergency care. In contrast, of those who had used another facility in the past, more than one-third would now choose to come to the medical center. Overall, more than 45% of the older adult population preferred the medical center over its competitors for treatment other than an emergency. In comparing this with an estimated 30% market share, it is clear that an opportunity exists for the medical center to make significant gains among older consumers.

Matching Waiver Programs

All area hospitals began waiving Medicare deductibles and coinsurance payments for persons with Medicare parts A and B in the summer of 1984. Despite some differences between the specific programs, the core benefit of each was the absorption of all out-of-pocket hospital expenses incurred while an inpatient or outpatient for anyone with Medicare A (hospital) and B (medical) coverage.

Although the medical center's program had the highest overall awareness level in mid-1985, as measured by the six-county survey, consumers had difficulty in differentiating among the various hospitals' programs. In early 1986, all area hospitals significantly modified their waiver programs due to Justice Department interpretation of the Medicare regulations. These modifications resulted in lessened benefits for older adults at all area hospitals.

Diversification Strategies

In the area of services to older adult, the medical center's diversification strategies have focused on five basic arenas: health care (further broken down into institutional care, ambulatory/outpatient/community care, and home care); education; communication; consumer products and services; and entertainment and leisure. In early 1986, the medical center formalized its commitment to older adults by creating a corporate Senior Services Division and hiring a Director of Senior Services.

PROGRAM SPECIFIC RESEARCH

With this as background, the medical center's Marketing Department explored the basic concept of a membership organization for older adults. The basic goals set for the organization included:

- reinforcing the medical center's image as a provider of special services for older adults

- differentiating its senior services from those of its competitors

- "cushioning" the back-lash against the modifications in the waiver program

- increasing older adults' utilization of the medical center

In developing a preliminary program "model", the older adults programs offered by other hospitals throughout the country were reviewed and analyzed for applicability. The internal marketing groups that focused on older adult services and preventive medicine reviewed potential program options.

The six-county survey of older adults, conducted in May of 1985, had already indicated that the availability of special services or benefits for adults was a "very

important" factor affecting hospital choice for 37% of the survey respondents and an "important" factor for an additional 49%. The availability of such services was particularly important to those respondents who already preferred the medical center over its competitors, with 41% rating this attribute as being "very important" in their choice of a health care facility. However, in terms of actual services that older adults wanted the medical center to provide, the survey respondents were vague.

Consequently, it was determined that further formal research with older adults was necessary. The methodology selected was two-stage concept testing, based on:

- modified focus group sessions using an already established Older Adults Advisory Board

- one-on-one interviews with 14 older adults in the community

It was felt that this methodology was the most appropriate means of testing and fine-tuning the concept.

Stage One: Modified Focus Group

Although generally qualitative in nature, an element of quantitative research was built in during the focus group sessions. The Older Adults Advisory Board (a 10 person cross-section of senior leaders and lay persons, urban and rural members, and persons from various economic, racial and religious groups) was presented with the basic idea of a membership organization or club for seniors, preliminarily named "Senior Connection". As part of the discussion, members were verbally "walked through" 16 potential components or benefits. Each person was given a form and asked to rank each potential benefit as to whether it should "definitely", "probably", "probably not", or "definitely not" be part of Senior Connection. After each participant had done his/her own ranking, a group discussion on the rankings ensued. Additional discussion centered on health screenings for older adults, pricing strategies for belonging to Senior Connection (beginning with a high dollar figure and then working down until an acceptable price was reached), and a review of potential logos for the organization.

Stage Two: One-on-One Interviews

Based on the responses of the Older Adults Advisory Board, a concept board was developed for use during the one-on-one interview process. The goals of these interviews were to substantiate (or not substantiate) the opinions of the Older Adults Advisory Board regarding:

- the "top five" benefits for Senior Connection members

- interest in specific health screens

- annual membership fee

In addition, interviewees were asked to respond to alternative names for the organization and to discuss the most effective means of getting information about membership to older adults.

RESEARCH RESULTS

Analysis of the responses of the Older Adults Advisory Board resulted in the following "top five" benefits to Senior Connection membership:

- CLAIMS MANAGEMENT -- free help in filing Medicare and supplemental insurance claims, by phone or in person.

- HEALTH SCREENS -- every month, free or discounted screens that address the health concerns of older adults.

- EVENT-OF-THE-MONTH -- Discounted or free social outings to community activities such as the theatre or sports events.

- QUARTERLY NEWSLETTER -- information about ways to stay healthy, new services for seniors, and upcoming events for members.

- PHYSICIAN LISTINGS -- physicians who accept Medicare assignment.

The "core benefits" were substantiated during the one-on-one interviews. Three other program options received enough interest to be considered as "second tier" benefits: an insurance counseling program, a discounted transportation service, and discounts in the hospital's retail pharmacy.

The interviews did not, however, support the pricing strategy developed on the basis of the focus group session. Whereas the Advisory Board felt that an annual fee of $50 or $75 was appropriate (with the group split evenly between the two) the interviews indicated that this was too expensive. Generally, those interviewees who would be interested in joining Senior Connection were willing to pay annual fees in the $15 - $40 price range. It should be noted that three of the interviewees would not join Senior Connection at any price, mainly because they felt that their health was so good that they would not use the benefits.

In terms of specific health screenings for inclusion in Senior Connection, the Advisory Board placed the most emphasis on blood pressure, blood sugar, skin cancer, cholesterol levels and pulmonary function tests. Generally, however, the individual interviewees were not able to prioritize among twelve possible health screens.

Based on the questions presented in both phases of the research, the promotional strategy for the proposed membership organization should include:

- the name "Senior Connection"

- the use of the hospital's logo as opposed to a logo developed just for the organization

- direct mail, supplemented by newspaper advertising, as the media of choice

- public presentations to senior organizations

The general guideline of using a larger-than-normal point (type) size in materials geared towards older adults was reinforced during the interview stage of research.

MODIFICATIONS BASED ON A COMPETITIVE ANALYSIS

Prior to implementing Senior Connection, an analysis of anticipated countermoves by the competition was undertaken. This process resulted in two major modifications to the proposed membership club: a service package expansion and the elimination of the membership fee.

Although concept-testing had narrowed the core benefits down to five, it was concluded that a pro-active approach would be to include more benefits in the membership. Consequently, the final Senior Connection package consisted of thirteen distinct benefits to members.

The decision to offer Senior Connection memberships at no charge reflected the desire to promote "good will" among

older adults in one of the earliest offerings of the new Senior Services Division. In addition, it was determined that the additional memberships would lead to increased overall revenue to the medical center through increased utilization of hospital services.

IMPLEMENTATION AND EVALUATION

The Senior Connection program was implemented in September of 1986. A full-page newspaper ad introduced the program in a special "older adults" insert in the area's major newspaper. This was supplemented by direct mail, advertising in local papers geared toward the older adult population, and presentations by the Director of Senior Services to local organizations. Additional publicity came via word-of-mouth advertising.

Initial response to the program was positive. In the first four months, more than 1000 older adults joined Senior Connection. Subsequently, applications continued to come in on a reduced, but steady, basis.

In order to measure the true effectiveness of the program and, in turn, the effectiveness of concept testing as a research methodology, on-going evaluation of the success of Senior Connection was planned. In addition to focusing on actual membership numbers, this research was designed to monitor the utilization of specific services within the medical center by Senior Connection members. Future additions and modifications to the program will be based on these evaluations.

CONCLUSION

The results of this study indicate that the concept of a hospital-sponsored club for older adults that gives members access to free or discounted services is a valid idea. The use of the two-stage concept testing methodology permitted refinement of the product offering so as to maximize success. Further refinement occured following an analysis of the competition.

As a final note, it is necessary that the medical center evaluate over time as to whether the membership club has 1) reinforced brand loyalty among those currently favoring the hospital sponsor and 2) resulted in shifts in loyalty among those currently favoring other health care facilities. This type of measurement is required to accurately test the validity of the "brand loyalty" tool in the health care arena.

COLLECTING STRATEGIC MARKET DATA ON INDUSTRIAL MARKETS AND USING IT EFFECTIVELY

Joseph A. Boscarino, Ph.D.
Jersey Shore Medical Center
Neptune, NJ

ABSTRACT

Accurate data are required in order to evaluate key healthcare market decisions. Often, healthcare marketers lack information of this type in "industrial" markets. The following presentation offers insight on how this data can be collected and used effectively. Collecting accurate data on area industry is not easy. The following is based on years of experience in survey research collecting data on thousand of companies nationwide.

FIRST DEFINE YOUR TARGET MARKET

It is important to identify the geographic limits of the market when conducting any market research. With companies, the market could be nationally based, or it could include only a region of the United States or a local area — it depends on the product. However, for hospitals, the market normally encompasses a local service area. The question which needs to be asked is what service or product is to be marketed to companies and, realistically, how large is this market?

Often, it is clear that the product being marketed has limited geographic reach. As a rule of thumb in industrial markets, the "principal of 75%" is often helpful. That is, answering the question of from where do (or could) 75% or more of my customers normally come? Once this is answered, the geographic marketplace is usually clear. (An HMO, for example, could be marketed on a regional or county level.) Once the geographic market is defined, then the "sample frame" can be constructed at that level. Of course, when working in smaller markets, no sample is required, because every eligible company is attempted contact. However, when your're working with a smaller target population of less than several thousand (random sampling error is based on larger populations), then your "sampling error" will be smaller than normally found in large population surveys. This is important to remember (see Sudman, 1976). There are several sources of data normally available to develop an accurate sample of companies. These include the following:

° Local business directories.
° Local yellow pages.
° Dun and Bradstreet.
° American Business Mailer list.

If yellow pages directories cover your geographic market, then this can be an excellent source. If you have a broad geographic market, then the yellow pages may be difficult to use. It is also not a good source if you need to contact certain types of firms (e.g., larger companies). One of the best sources for developing a sample of area companies is typically the local Chamber of Commerce. (They usually have the best lists.)

THE FOCUS GROUP METHOD

The focus group method is a qualitative consumer research technique. This method permits a detailed "qualitative" level of analysis. Although, it does not permit statistical generalization, it does allow the researcher to probe the depth and breadth of commitment with respect to a number of variables. To successfully conduct a focus group among firms, the following rules must be closely adhered to:

°The groups must be conducted anonymously, meaning that neither the firms nor the client should be identified.

°Incentives must be used to recruit. (Typically, $50 to $150 per person is necessary.) The higher up you recruit, the larger the incentive. In health care you need to reach "benefit managers."

°You must begin recruitment at least two weeks ahead of time and use followup and reminder calls (as well as letters) to confirm "appointments" for the focus group.

°A week night "buffet" is usually effective (6:30 p.m.). Typically, you need to recruit from 8 to 12 benefit managers for the focus group to be successful.

°The focus group must be held in a neutral facility. Usually, a hotel conference room or a formal focus group room can be rented for this.

°Quotas must be established (representative of the target market) and reasonably adhered to, otherwise, the group may be too biased. The biggest problem here is getting too many small firms or "secretaries."

Any deviation from these rules can result in very poor focus group performance. Typically, it will require an experienced moderator to lead this type of a group, and the group should run about 90 minutes. Tape recording is advised. It should be pointed out, however, that focus groups in this market are not easy. One of the greatest failures here is the failure to callback and remind participants the morning of (or the day before) the group. This last-minute callback greatly improves the "show up" rate. Also, the researcher needs to be careful of the quotas while recruiting, so as to not end up with a biased group. The size and types of firms represented should mirror your actual market (see Cox and Higginbotham, 1979).

Focus group data can be analyzed in a number of ways. Generally, the analyst is looking for the intensity of response as well as frequency of response to specific issues. The exciting thing about the focus group is that, unlike the structured questionnaire method, you can uncover factors not suspect before. In the telephone or mail survey, you are limited with regard to uncovering new, serendipitous factors. A focus group allows you to probe as deep as necessary to uncover the reasons why. In addition, focus groups are often the only way to get through to managers in many metro markets. They are simply "over-surveyed."

THE MAIL SURVEY METHOD

The mail survey can also be utilized to survey area firms, if properly conducted. If done improperly, the mail survey produces very inaccurate and misleading results. Generally, you need at least a 25% response rate (i.e., 25 out of 100 questionnaires returned) to consider the data representative of a given market. The following are the rules to consider when designing a mail survey:

°The questionnaire must be simple, "open end" questions should be minimized.

°The questionnarie should be short and anonymous for both participant and client, to avoid bias.

°A postage-free, mail-return envelope must be used.

°Multiple mailings will be required.

°Monetary incentives could be used to boost response rates. Typically, only a small incentive (from $1 to $2) can increase the response rates significantly.

°Monitor quotas based on the corporate profile in the market. If a serious bias is uncovered, the data must be statistically weighted to adjust for this (e.g., too many small firms).

In a survey, the response rate is critical, because unless you get a good response, you never know whether the responders are truly different than those who did not respond. This holds even if no bias is found in the profile obtained, because the bias may be attitudinal (see Babbie, 1973). The only way to minimize potential bias is to maximize (25% or greater) the response rate.

Once the sample lists of companies have been prepared, mailing labels should be typed three or four across (same label). This will allow you to do multiple mailings and track responses. This way, all sets of labels could be numbered (same number across), and the last set of labels could be used as a control set to track responses to the survey.

The critical factor to consider with this method is the response rate. Corporate personnel are so over solicited today that reasonable rates are impossible in many markets. Also, mail surveys, unlike phone surveys, can't screen effectively for the proper respondent (potential buyer), which is an additional negative factor. For these reasons, the mail survey method is becoming a less common research tool in industrial markets.

THE TELEPHONE SURVEY METHOD

The telephone survey method has been proven to be one of the most accurate and effective ways of collecting statistical data on a target population (see Groves and Kahn, 1979). The greatest advantages of the telephone survey are the speed of data collection, the ability to screen and probe, and accuracy. Two major disadvantages of the telephone survey with firms are the cost of the survey (usually $50 to $100 per complete interview) and the completion rate. Often completion rates are low here, because of the difficulty in reaching managers during business hours. Important rules about the telephone surveys are:

°Multiple callbacks must be used (up to 4 or more).

°Only experienced telephone interviewers can be used.

°Decision-makers higher up are difficult to reach, thus, require more persistence.

°Anonymity is recommended for both client and respondents.

°Monetary incentives are sometimes recommended (used as a "fee" in the range of $20-$30) to complete an interview.

°As with the other methods, quotas must be watched and biases adjusted statistically as required.

In order to achieve a good phone completion rate with mangers, a minimum of 4 callbacks are required. Typically, the best way to do this is to schedule the interview and set up callbacks on 3 X 5 index cards, doing callbacks in the morning, early afternoon and late afternoon hours. The 3 X 5 cards can be passed on to the different interviewers. They simply pick up the cards and begin the callback procedure again. Remember, just as with the mail survey, the lower the response rate, the less generalizable and the more biased the survey can be, so use quotas and adjust the sample by weighting if necessary.

SELECTING A MARKET RESEARCH FIRM

Typically, it is important for a market research firm to have experience in surveying this population. They should also have expertise in healthcare, although this should not be the only prerequisite. It is critical, however, that they have interviewers that are familiar with medical terminology.

The price ranges should run within the following, and should include data collection, data processing, analysis, and a report:

SERVICE RATINGS BY AREA EMPLOYERS

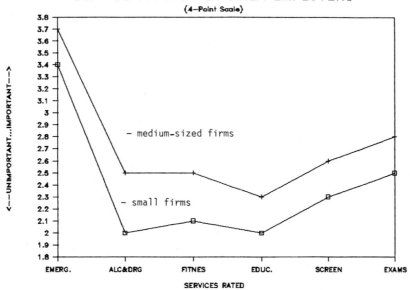

(4-Point Scale)

°Industrial focus groups should cost about $1,500-$3,500 each, for about 10 managers per group.

°Mail surveys should range from $5,000-$13,000 for 300 completed questionnaires, based on a completion rate of 25% or better.

°Telephone interviews completed with 100 managers should range from $6,000-12,000, with a minimum 25% completion rate.

The importance of maintaining anonymity cannot be over-emphasized when conducting this type of survey. If the client's position is known, this could jeopardize the accuracy of the market research. Often, research firms will discourage anonymity because it can negatively impact on the completion rate, and it also costs more. Typically, clients don't understand this. What works in phone surveys and focus groups is to simply pay the managers a "fee" for their opinions. For a focus group, the incentive is anywhere from $50-$150. For a telephone interview, anywhere from $20-$30 is normally effective.

HOW TO USE THE DATA

Industrial market research data collected with focus groups, mail and telephone surveys have potential for use in a number of areas. These include the following:

° Feasibility studies.
° Product testing.
° Quality of care issues.
° Loyalty and attitudes.
° Needs assessment.

Industrial market research data when properly collected provides a wealth of information. There are some serious ethical issues which are related to the use of this information, however. In order to collect accurate and

objective information, very often, strict respondent anonymity must be maintained. Market research data and/or focus group information should be kept anonymous and should not be used to make sales calls on individuals, unless they request this. It should only be used to analyze and report data in terms of the group. The American Marketing Association's Code of Conduct should be strictly adhered to here. If not, problems can result.

CASE EXAMPLES

The following presents case examples from two industrial healthcare market surveys. The first was based on a survey of 100 small and medium-sized firms in a Mid-western city. Here the client (a local hospital) wished to test the feasibility of specially-tailored services for smaller area firms (less than 35 employees). Benefit managers (many times "owners") in these firms were contacted anonymously by telephone in a 10 minute interview. A graph is presented which shows that these firms rated specific services differently, based on the importance of them for their operations. As a matter of fact, the study confirmed that it would only be profitable to pursue medium-sized companies, and only in-so-far as emergency medical care and physical exam services were concerned (see graph).

The next study presented was conducted in a Southeastern city. It was conducted by telephone (15 minutes) and with 200 benefit managers from medium-sized and larger firms. In this study, the client (a large medical center) was not only interested in specific products but in actual demand estimates, pricing, and brand loyalty. These were all successfully measured in the survey.   Product demand was measured through the following method:

Likely Use Response	Reported Potential Fitness Center Use % (A)		Proportion Would Actually Use (B)		Firms In Market (C)		Market Potential (D)
Very Likely	3%	x	.60	x	1212	=	22
Somewhat Likely	13%	x	.40	x	1212	=	63
Somewhat Unlikely	31%	x	.20	x	1212	=	75
Very Unlikely	51%	x	.00	x	1212	=	0
Don't Know	3%	x	.05	x	1212	=	2

TOTAL FIRMS = 162

The above example shows how to use a survey to measure demand.   The percentage of firms that report they would send employees to a "hospital-sponsored" fitness center is recorded in column "A". This is multiplied times ("B"), the estimated actual proportion that would use this service when it becomes available in the market. Column "B" represents the best estimate of "slippage" between the reported intent to use a service (or product) and the actual use in the marketplace.   All things being equal, reported use should always be higher than actual.   Critical factors in determining what your proportions should be here are the size of your advertising budget and market, and the time from the survey to product introduction.   The figures presented above are the averages for a broad range of healthcare services nationwide.   They should be adjusted for specific "intervening" variables in your market.

The figure above of 162 firms represents the total potential market.   The client's market share would not normally be 162 firms, but a proportion of this figure.   This is a factor which can be determined, along with other qualifying factors, in the text of the survey.   The global demand estimates (162 firms) provide the base figure for the analysis.   For example, you can measure the percent increase or decrease in "likely users" of a service by asking them if they would be more likely or less likely to use the defined service if:

    °The price is changed,
    °The sponsorship is different,
    °The location more convenient,
    °The service expanded, etc.

These factors were measured in the study, and as a result, the client was able to develop much more "demanded" products for local firms.

CONCLUSION

To conclude, three different methods of data collection have been presented.   All methods have their merits.   When properly conducted, industrial research data can be extremely important in product or service development. Which technique to use is determined by a number of factors: budget, time, the number of companies that need to be contacted, etc.   This presentation has, hopefully, provided insights as to which method would be useful in specific situations.

REFERENCES

Babbie, Earl R., Survey Research Methods, Wadsworth Pubs., Belmont, CA 1973.

Cox and Higginbotham, Focus Group Interviews: A Reader, American Marketing Association, Chicago, 1979.

Groves, Robert M. and Kahn, Robert L., Surveys By Telephone, Academic Press, New York, 1979.

Sudman, Seymour, Applied Sampling, Academic Press, New York, 1976.

Vichas, Robert P., Complete Handbook of Profitable Marketing Research Techniques, Prentice-Hall, Englewood Cliffs, NJ 1982.

TRACKING AND INTERCEDING IN DISTRIBUTION CHANNELS FOR HEALTH CARE PRODUCT LINES

Janet L. Scheuerman, Herman Smith Associates, Hinsdale, Illinois

ABSTRACT

While health care marketers have zealously adapted and
applied business/services marketing techniques and language to health care marketing endeavors in recent years,
channels of distribution concepts have gained little
attention or application. However, those providers who
are applying the concept to determine exactly how their
patients get to them are gaining valuable information on
where they can most effective deploy their marketing
efforts and spend their marketing dollars. Two case
studies are reviewed here. Others will be included in
the full presentation, including results from a referral
study completed for a major urban ambulatory care center.

INTRODUCTION

Lost patients. Patients forgotten in exam rooms or in a
procedure room, or even in a soiled linen holding area.
How often they're the subject of a newscast! How often
they're the topic of a joke!

But lost patients aren't a joke anymore. As the health
care marketplace moves rapidly from a sellers' market
into a buyers' market, hospitals, clinics (group practices) and solo practitioners alike are seeking ways to
find patients and to keep patients, particularly through
awareness of distribution channels.

In the early 1980's the proverbial "handwriting was on
the wall." Per capita inpatient rates began what has
become a precipitous decline. Inpatient health care, the
primary source of revenue for hospitals, had become a
mature industry. Concurrently, the first glimmerings of
the physician glut became evident in selected communities. The emerging outpatient market, a promising new
source of revenue for hospitals, was met head-on by competition from physicians who needed alternative revenue
sources to supplement declining patient revenue, and by
other nontraditional providers who saw revenue opportunities in the nonregulated portion of the health care
marketplace.

Almost overnight, taking care of sick people became the
health care industry and a new mindset and operating
environment took over. It was not surprising that the
new health care industry began to look to other industries to borrow techniques that could insure at least
survival, if not success in the new environment.

It did not take the health care industry long to discover
marketing. Shrinking profits were invested in marketing activities, but as hospitals adopted one marketing
strategy after another from the capital goods and other
service industries, one concept never seemed to join the
others. That marketing strategy was distribution.
Whether it was a strategy that didn't have as much pizzaz
as the others, whether industrial techniques seemed to
defy reformatting by the health care providers, or whether they just had low priority, until very recently, distribution concepts have not been pursued in an indepth,
organized manner by many hospitals.

However, a few of the more farsighted providers did
struggle with the concept of distribution and have

reaped handsome rewards. They are not losing patients --
indeed they are finding patients that they never had
before. In the process they have learned that the lost-
and-found game is not played the same way for all patients and that there are a variety of techniques that
really succeed.

The goal of this paper is to show how hospitals and other
health care providers can answer three essential questions:

1. How do we get patients?

2. What do we do to continue getting patients and to
    get more patients? (Included in this question is
    a side issue of, what have we done to get pa-
    tients in the past?)

3. How is the market likely to change and how should
    we position ourselves relative to the organiza-
    tion and to capital?

Case studies best demonstrate the application of distribution strategy in health care.

DEVELOPING THE CHANNEL OF DISTRIBUTION
ROAD MAPS -- A CASE STUDY IN ORTHOPEDICS

Orthopedics represents about 6% of this client hospital's
total inpatient market and substantial revenue in the
outpatient business. How did this client identify and
reinforce its channels of distribution?

First, some homework to understand the basics about the
orthopedic market. Here's what the assignment was:

o   Establish market share.

o   Establish revenue and net income for the orthope-
    dic market (and for unspecific DRG groups within
    orthopedics).

o   Hypothesize market channels (Exhibit 1).

Exhibit 1
ORTHOPEDICS MARKET CHANNELS

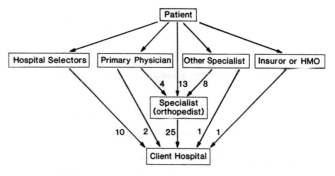

o   Estimate market share, growth trend, and pro-
    fitability by market channel (Exhibit 2).

Exhibit 2

ESTIMATED ORTHOPEDIC MARKET SIZE, GROWTH TREND AND PROFITABILITY BY MARKET CHANNEL

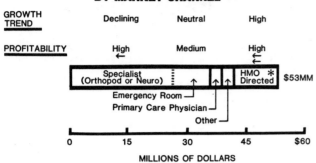

GROWTH TREND

| Declining | Neutral | High |

PROFITABILITY

| High | Medium | High |

Specialist (Orthopod or Neuro) — HMO * Directed — $53MM

Emergency Room
Primary Care Physician
Other

0   15   30   45 $60

MILLIONS OF DOLLARS

✳ Based on HMO Penetration

Exhibit 5

PHYSICIAN SURVEY RESPONSES

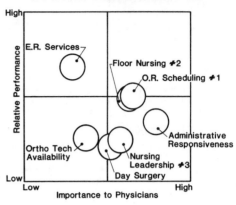

E.R. Services
Floor Nursing #2
O.R. Scheduling #1
Administrative Responsiveness
Ortho Tech Availability
Nursing Leadership #3
Day Surgery

Relative Performance — High / Low
Importance to Physicians — Low / High

Armed with these facts, the hospital analyzed the various channels by:

o Surveying orthopedists in the market area to determine:
-- Primary loyalties (Exhibit 3).
-- How their orthopedists distributed their business (Exhibit 4) and why (Exhibit 5).

o Conducting patient surveys to complete the profile of market attitudes.

The information collected and assessed indicated key areas for strategy development. Emphasis was on the physicians who quite clearly were the primary channel of distribution. Based on an assessment of survey findings, the hospital developed:

o Overall strategy (Exhibit 6).

o Physician-specific strategies (Exhibit 7).

o Consumer/emergency room strategies (Exhibit 8).

Exhibit 3

ORTHOPEDISTS PRIMARY HOSPITAL LOYALTY

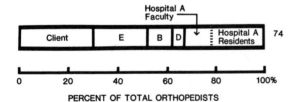

Hospital A Faculty

| Client | E | B | D | ↓ Hospital A Residents | 74 |

0   20   40   60   80   100%

PERCENT OF TOTAL ORTHOPEDISTS

Exhibit 6

STRATEGY FOR PATIENT ACQUISITION

| Bond Current Hospital Physicians to Hospital | Increase Hospital's Share of "Practice Splitters" | "Win Back" Selected Physicians | New Practice Development |

EXHIBIT 7

Specific Strategies/Physician Channel

o Concentrate on loyalists (who currently represent 70 to 75% of orthopedic revenues).

o Develop orthopedic business in DRG's where market share is low and profit potential exists.

o Adopt organizational changes to eliminate perceived lack of a "can do" attitude and to counter more positive perceptions of competitor hospital in the area of elective surgery.

o Implement a customer approach to physician relations.
-- Build on appreciation of key physicians regarding the hospital's concern for the physicians.
-- Target needs of two loyalists who are "waivering."
-- Investigate and respond to needs of "splitters."

o Assist loyalist physicians in practice development.

o Investigate recruitment opportunities.

o Evaluate and encourage joint venture opportunities.

o Test importance of geographical location to patients.

Exhibit 4

ORTHOPEDIST REVENUES BY HOSPITAL RELATIONSHIP CATEGORY

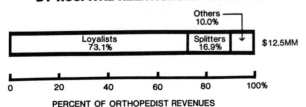

Others 10.0%

| Loyalists 73.1% | Splitters 16.9% | ↓ | $12.5MM |

0   20   40   60   80   100%

PERCENT OF ORTHOPEDIST REVENUES

EXHIBIT 8

SPECIFIC STRATEGIES

Emergency Room Channel

Key Decision Factors	Prior Hospital Experience (65%)	Location (20%)
Primary Data Used	Nursing and other staff interactions	Proximity to home and/or accident
Influencing Mechanisms	o Reinforce positive experience o Create center of excellence message	o Take Advantage of multi-locations -- Local newspaper advertising -- Direct mailings -- Phone stickers

In summary, analysis of the orthopedic channel of distribution identified existing channels, how to reinforce them and amplify on their effectiveness, and what kind of changes needed to be built into the distribution system to anticipate the continuing evaluation of the local orthopedic market place (Exhibit 9).

EXHIBIT 9

SUMMARY

o Physician channel critical.
   -- Competitive pressure for physicians will increase.
   -- Opportunity exists to stabilize and strengthen physician relationships.

o HMO channel to become increasingly important.

o Self-selector channel virtually non-existent, except for emergency room.
   -- Prior hospital experience crucial to patients' decision.
   -- General surgery market accounts for over 40 percent of emergency/orthopedic admissions.

o Is self-selector channel profitable?

Next Steps

o Practice building with interested loyalists/physicians.

o Assessment of geographical importance through consumer interviews.

o Primary care physician survey.
   -- Help specialists.
   -- Identify potential for referrals directly to the hospital.

SUMMARY

Follow up was also of key importance in this channel investigation. Results were shared with the medical staff in an effort to build commitment. Definitive action plans were developed to match strategies with recommendations. And, with staff and administration, means were developed to evaluate change and success.

THE OBSTETRICAL MARKET --
A DIFFERENT CHALLENGE

The health care marketing literature abounds with studies that identify women as the primary decision makers in numerous health care situations. Concurrently, the literature reinforces the importance of a positive obstetrical experience in aligning a woman with a particular institution. Taking these as given, how can an institution secure the obstetrical distribution channel and ultimately the allegiance of the women decision makers?

The basic process outlined in the orthopedic case study was followed -- the findings funneled hospital energies in different avenues.

Step 1 -- Do the homework relative to the obstetrical market. Three channels surfaced -- physicians, consumers, and HMO's (Exhibit 10).

Exhibit 10

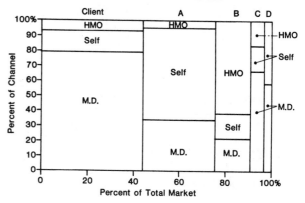

SELECTORS/OB MARKET

o Assess the influence of the selectors on the area providers (Exhibit 11).

o Assess the reimbursement implications by market channel (Exhibit 12).

o And, estimate market share and growth trends (Exhibit 13).

On to Step 2 -- Complete market research.

o Of special importance was the consumer. Selected questions from the consumer survey and findings appear in Exhibit 14.

And finally on to the strategy and change aspects.

o Reinforce the self selector females, especially in the younger age groups (Exhibit 14).

o Develop the physician channels (Exhibit 15)

Exhibit 11

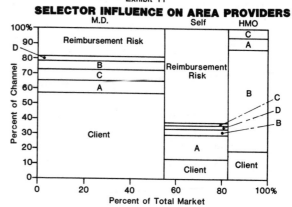

SELECTOR INFLUENCE ON AREA PROVIDERS

Exhibit 12

REIMBURSEMENT IMPLICATIONS

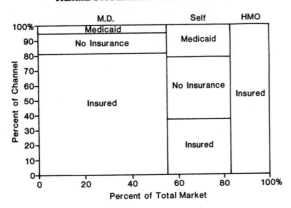

MD's compared before making selection:

	Total Sample	Age 18-24
Got one name, saw, was satisfied	67	56%
Got several names, saw one, and was satisfied	11	23%
Got names and saw several	22	21%

Exhibit 13

ESTIMATED AVAILABLE MARKET SHARE AND GROWTH TRENDS

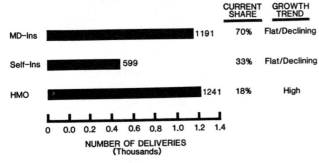

The area obstetrical market summary incorporates a dual approach to building on existing strengths and opening new channels to compensate for market changes in the future (Exhibit 16).

EXHIBIT 14

Community and Patient Market Research

Patients were asked who selected the hospital for their most recent delivery. Self? Family/friends' recommendations? Obstetrician/gynecologist? Family doctor? HMO/insurance plan?

Responses were cross tabulated with respondents' ages, yielding these results:

			Age	
	Total Sample	18-24	25-34	35-44
Self	24	41%	20%	29%
MD	59	41%	63%	49%
HMO	17	18%	17%	22%

When patient first saw obstetrician/gynecologist on a regular basis:

Age	Total Sample	Self Selector	MD Selector
15-18	40	60%	40%
19-24	40	30%	50%
25-34	20	10%	10%

Exhibit 15

M.D. SELECTOR CHANNEL

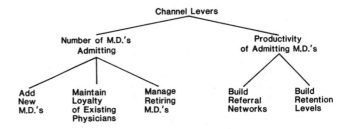

EXHIBIT 16

Summary/Obstetrical Market

o Decline in the client hospital's market share is due mainly to penetration of HMOs in the marketplace.
   -- HMO penetration expected to reach 50% by 1990.

o Increasing hospital market share in the HMO market is crucial to regaining overall market share.
   -- Limited opportunity to market more aggressively to the HMO's.
   -- Key will be growing Health Plus.
      - Current market position poor.
      - Need to exploit the hospital's provider reputation and evaluate potential for growth.

o The hospital's "monopoly" in the physician channel has eroded slightly but remains strong.
   -- Must continuously reinforce message that MD's are our key customer.
      - Respond to their needs.
      - Formal "customer executive" program.
      - Nursing education on importance of channel.
   -- Neonatology/perinatology may offer significant profit potential as well as demonstrating responsiveness to MD's.

o Opportunity to increase market share in the physician channel will be difficult since the hospital already has dominant position.
   -- Opportunity exists to work with physicians to add physician presence in specific geographic areas.
   -- Increasing the hospital physicians' retention of patients is largely a defensive strategy but also offers opportunity for share gain.

CONCLUSION

Hospital resources will increasingly flow toward investments, both operational and capital, that build the channels of patient distribution. For hospitals with astute marketing departments there will no longer be lost patients.

ORGANIZATIONAL EFFECTIVENESS

There is little debate among health care managers that
the health care industry is beset by rapid change in its
technological, economic, legal and social environments.
There is also general concensus that the best approach to
survival in such a turbulent environment is to build
flexibility within the organization that will allow it to
effectively respond to any disequilibrium in its universe.
However, there is little agreement as to how this can be
accomplished.

In this section, the authors of the three papers help to
shed some light on this issue. Franklin and Welker
present a case for developing organizational innovativeness by combining a new concept of organization structure
with some basic management principles. The remaining
papers by Gee/Folger and Henderson/Leibman advocate the
adoption by health care managers of the product line
management concept that has generally been widely and
effectively utilized in the consumer goods industries.

BUILDING AN INNOVATIVE ORGANIZATION

Daniel P. Franklin, Illinois Health Plans, Inc., Springfield
Susan J. Welker, Illinois Health Plans, Inc., Springfield

ABSTRACT

To compete in today's rapidly changing health care environment, an organization must be innovative. An effective
organization builds innovativeness into its core operations
enabling it both to effectively discharge its internal responsibilities and to respond positively to the challenges
and opportunities of its dynamic external environment. The
authors present a case for developing organizational innovativeness by combining a new concept of organizational
structure with pragmatic management principles.

INTRODUCTION

The health care sector of the American economy continues
to experience the stresses of rapid change. Changes in government involvement and reimbursement programs, new competitive forces, and increasing consumer awareness and demands are all causing health care institutions to reexamine
their delivery mechanisms and operations.

One of the results of this reexamination has been intensi-
fying efforts to build market share, reduce costs, and establish a broader range of integrated services and alternative delivery systems. New products and services such as
HMO's/PPO's have evolved along with a corresponding rush
to form or affiliate with networks or systems (regional/
national linkages) which might provide a competitive edge
in the escalating battle for patients.

With the need for alternative delivery systems and strategies comes the need for alternative organizational structures which foster the innovation required to both generate and implement these systems and strategies. The status
quo and tradition are no longer suitable organizational
companions. Health care organizations exist in an environment of uncertainty. Ultimate success rests with the ability to respond effectively to the challenges of this environment; to be effective administrators and marketers; to
be innovative.

WHAT IS INNOVATION?

Peter Drucker in his book Innovation and Entrepreneurship
has defined innovation variously as "the search for and the
exploitation of new opportunities for satisfying human
wants and human needs," and "the specific tool of entrepreneurs, the means by which they exploit change as an opportunity for a different business or a different service"
(1983, p. 19). Those organizations which have successfully
mastered the discipline of innovation have leaped beyond
the barriers of tradition and have introduced to the health
care field various "different business(es)" and "different service(s)" that have taken some health care organizations by surprise: 'freestanding' health facilities
(hospices, medical and diagnostic laboratories, maternity
care, ER services, 'walk in' clinics), mobile diagnostic
services, etc.

Innovation includes a healthy dose of intuition. Because
it is being better understood, the role of intuition in the
management process has gained credibility and support in
recent times. Pondy, in his writing, Union of Rationality
and Intuition in Management Action, presents the argument
that "a union of rationality and intuition is possible,

that they are not antithetical, and that each of these primary human processes functions most effectively in combination with the other" (1983, p. 170). Intuition, then, is
not something mystical with a life all its own. It is, as
Federal Express's Fred Smith says, "...the amalgamation of
a lot of stuff from a lot of different places that leads
you to say about an idea that it's a safe bet..not a fool's
bet..the ability to assimilate information from a lot of
different disciplines all at once" (Inc. Magazine, 1986).

H. Ross Perot, founder and chairman of Electronic Data
Systems Corporation, and the richest man in the United
States as recently reported by Forbes magazine, describes
intuition as knowing one's business and being able to bring
to bear on a situation everything a person has seen, felt,
tasted, and experienced in a particular industry (Rowan
1986). This is also the basis of innovation. From this it
becomes obvious that innovation is not the sole province
of a few visionaries, but is a way of thinking and operating which can be disciplined, learned and practiced.

WHAT ARE THE SOURCES OF INNOVATION?

To be innovative, then, an organization needs to have and
be able to develop personnel with sufficient experience,
backgound and knowledge to bring to bear on a challenge,
and sufficient courage of conviction (intuition) to go
into action.

Drucker identifies seven sources of innovation which the
entrepreneurial organization must constantly monitor:

1. The Unexpected - unexpected success, failures, or outside events

2. The Incongruous - differences between the world as it is
and how it 'ought to be'

3. A Process Need - a better way to do a familiar job

4. Unpredicted Changes in an Industry or Market Structure

5. Demographics - population changes

6. Changes in Perception, Mood, Meaning

7. New Knowledge (1985)

Each of these sources represents a seedbed of opportunity
if the organization is prepared to respond in a responsible, proactive manner. The obvious question, then, is
"What is it that makes an organization both sensitive and
responsive to these sources of innovation and opportunity?"

ANATOMY OF AN INNOVATIVE ORGANIZATION

In her book, Change Masters, Kanter presents the persuasive argument that the environment for innovation consists
of a series of positive interactions between four primary
and critical organizational components: structure, culture,
power and rewards (see Figure 1). While these components
are necessarily present in all organizations, the problem
in traditional, highly hierarchical organizations is that

they are used to promote specialization (efficiency), vertical communication systems and an emphasis on "reliability" and predictability while discouraging participation, decentralization and the freer forms of communication necessary for the successful fostering of innovation (Kanter 1983).

Figure 1

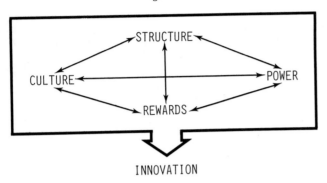

It is Kanter's and the authors' contention that these components must be formed and balanced in such a manner as to encourage and support a participative style of management, free and productive communication, resource sharing, and opportunities for personal development, including the encouragement to try new approaches (i.e., to be innovative) without the fear of reprisal in the event of failure.

An effective, innovative organization fosters entrepreneurship. It manifests confidence in its people and provides them ample opportunity to develop new ideas and approaches. But to truly encourage innovative thought and action, it must also provide the organizational support necessary to allow those individuals to move from concepts into reality. This support means not only the financial resources, but the emotional support and the allocation of time to allow for the nurturing of creative thought and endeavor as well.

By striving to create an environment which provides positive balance between the components of innovation (structure, culture, power and rewards) as presented by Kanter, and one which weaves the catalyst of intuition throughout its fiber, the progressive health care organization can bring the positive potentials of its resources to bear on the challenges of its mission with successful results. It is in this context that this paper will proceed.

ORGANIZATIONAL STRUCTURE

The Traditional Structure

Traditionally, health care institutions have been characterized by segmented and highly hierarchical organizations which emphasize specialization to the extreme. Further, they have been driven by an operations orientation rather than a strategic orientation. This operations orientation is characterized by a rigid breakdown of roles into functional specialties and precise definitions of duties, responsibilities and power. Vertical communication patterns are the norm and are strictly enforced by traditional hierarchical titles/positions, procedures, and policies. And the nature of the activities associated with health care lead to the worship of 'reliability' and the insistence on 'no surprises.'

This segmentalism has provided hospitals with a 'steady course mentality' which has prevented the organization from initiating any substantive internal changes, thus ensuring that its development will consist of a repetition of what it already knows, a promulgation of the status quo. As a consequence, 'turf building' has resulted rather than productive cooperation. We have witnessed generations of experience wherein hospitals dug their moats and aggressively defended themselves from the rest of the health care world. And, internally, hospital personnel have built their own 'organizational castles' which they have defended with a vigor and combative mentality which would put many self-respecting War Lords to shame.

This traditional framework and its fruits prohibit health care organizations from expanding their existing philosophical capacity and corporate mentality in order to innovate and improve. It inhibits the entrepreneurial spirit and makes the organization a slave of its past, a victim, not a master, of change.

The New, Dynamic Structure

In their article, Organizations: New Concepts for New Forms, Miles and Snow indicate that the dynamics of recent years have produced an environment characterized by change which has provoked the development of a new form of organization which they term "a dynamic network." This term suggests that "its major components can be assembled and reassembled in order to meet complex and changing competitive conditions" (1986, p. 64), a characteristic vital to organizational innovation. This type of organization is a combination of structures, processes and interpersonal roles which enhance the potential for innovative development and successful mastery of change.

A "dynamic network" approach to organizational structure begins with the realization that today's environment is far too complex to be dominated effectively by any one or a few organizations; that true innovativeness results from a broad perspective and exposure to one's market forces and components; that perspective and exposure is limited by the 'self-centeredness' of the traditional organizational structure. The network is based on the premise that the synergies of cooperative affiliation with a multiplicity of specialized, highly focused practitioners and/or organizations are more powerful and potentially profitable than the 'efficiencies' of a centralized, inwardly focused and more generalized "do it all ourselves" approach to organizational development. We think it a fair statement that all competent managers appreciate the advantages of specialization and concentrated effort. The dynamic network concept attempts to provide a framework to tap those advantages.

The Miles and Snow network model has four basic characteristics: vertical disaggregation, broker mechanisms, market mechanisms, and full-disclosure information systems.

Vertical Disaggregation. Rather than trying to be 'all things to all people,' a dynamic network approach seeks out relationships in which each 'partner' can concentrate on his area of expertise. One business expert once said that "most businesses would be better off if they would just 'stick to their knitting' and affiliate with other businesses whose 'knitting' complemented and enhanced their own." This is the basis of the dynamic network.

An example of how this might work would be the formation of a PPO product. Although this concept seems simple enough when first viewed, as anyone involved in this area of activity knows, there are a multitude of PPO models, products and complexities. The dynamic network approach would dictate finding specialists to handle the various responsibilities associated with developing and administering this alternative delivery system: an ADS specialist to lead the market analysis and strategic planning; a third party administrator to handle the claims processing and database management functions; a marketing organization to handle the sales and promotion management; and, perhaps, a third party utilization review organization to handle and add credibility to this most important function. And, should the organization become even more aggressive and wish to add an insured PPO product to its arsenal, an insurer would need to be added to the network and its positioning in relation to the other components carefully analyzed.

While this example, as given, is designedly simplistic and, perhaps, obvious, it illustrates the principle of vertical disaggregation. The traditional approach might be to include the strategic planning for this effort in the hospital's operations planning process, in which case the assignment of proper emphasis and appropriate resource allocation might be undermined; the marketing function might be assigned to hospital marketers who, while they could provide valuable input and direction to the marketing effort (and should), would not have the 'sales' orientation, interest or expertise needed to take the effort beyond the first few obvious accounts; and the MIS department might be tempted to add the responsibilities and complexities of the claims/database management functions to its already 'full plate.' Final result: a generalized approach to an effort which deserves specialized expertise and commitment.

This first characteristic of the dynamic network approach might be the one most 'hard to swallow' for the health care sector. Historically, health care organizations have tended to be very self-contained and confident in their ability to 'self-manufacture' virtually all of their needs (vertical aggregation). While the dynamic network approach is distinctly horizontal in nature, when understood and administered properly, it allows an organization to develop and control the expertise it needs to meet the challenges of its marketplace while avoiding the sometimes extremely expensive investments in time, personnel and facilities/equipment associated with the development of new and/or different products and services. In other words, in a very real sense, the real, substantive advantages of vertical aggregation can be maintained and enhanced while eliminating many of the disadvantages. Today's environment dictates such a change in organizational development. And, in fact, we are already seeing this change take place in the more progressive and forward thinking health care organizations.

Broker Mechanisms. Obviously, someone has to form and coordinate the network. This presents an opportunity within the health care organization for someone who is not subject to the 'pride of ownership' syndrome and who has a clear vision of the organization's real mission ('knitting'). The ability to rise above personal prejudice and self-promotion, to recognize opportunity, to locate and build relationships with competent specialists/practitioners, and to maintain those relationships during the inevitable strategic changes and problem solving sessions via effective personal and public relations activities is crucial to the network's success.

Market Mechanisms. The relationships within a dynamic network are not the traditional employer-employee variety. Rather, they are based on carefully constructed and expertly managed contractual arrangements. This too, like all the other aspects of this form of organizational structure, allows for the speedy formation of appropriate alliances as well as speedy disassociation should circumstances so dictate.

The emphasis in a dynamic network is on performance. If the network formed is not working, it can be changed relatively quickly and effectively. Affiliates are paid for their contributions to the network's success. Responsibilities and expectations are clearly spelled out in the affiliation agreements. Affiliates whose contributions are determined to be less than acceptable can be removed from the network and replaced with more suitable 'partners.' It is this flexibility which makes the network dynamic. It is

extremely difficult, practically and politically, to maintain this type of market-driven sensitivity and organizational flexibility in the traditional employer-employee setting.

Full-Disclosure Information Systems. This is perhaps the real key to the success of the network. It has been truly said that "he who controls the information, controls the organization." We have all witnessed this phenomenon.

In the dynamic network, full sharing of information is vital. Each component must be fully integrated into the network and enabled with the necessary resources to support its efforts. And this information flow must go 'both ways.' Through the contractual agreements mentioned earlier and through well-conceived, designed and administered policies and systems, the health care organization must receive, as well as provide, all the information necessary to enhance the successful attainment of the network's goals and objectives.

Although Miles and Snow did not address the health care sector specifically, the rationale for health care organizations to adopt the "dynamic network" is obvious. Unlike the traditional, static bureaucracies with which we are all too familiar, the "dynamic network" is a far more flexible, adaptive structure. It can accommodate a vast amount of complexity while maximizing specialized competence and providing much more effective use of fiscal, organizational and human resources.

And this network approach is not confined to the management of affiliation relationships with outside entities. Dynamic networks can be developed even within the most hierarchical and traditional of organizations, within a department or division.

Matrix management is, in many ways, a form of dynamic network. In this form of management, individuals are given specific responsibilities and authorities within their area of assignment or expertise. Additionally, these people are part of a larger organizational group in which their input is combined with others for specific project developments or task accomplishments. This management approach is participative in nature, an attempt to balance 'top down' and 'bottom up' perspectives, and more effectively utilizes the organization's talent pool.

Matrix management, like all forms of networks, requires that authority be provided along with responsibility. Individuals involved in pseudo-participative management, i.e., condescending management style which picks the participants' brains and distributes responsibility without authority but provides no opportunity for 'real' input into substantive decision making, will end up becoming skeptical of the organization leaderships' motives. Ultimately, they may become agents of strife rather than agents of productive change.

Matrix/network management also requires a project leader or network administrator who can be held accountable by top management, and who possesses well developed conflict resolution skills. The integration of personnel with different backgrounds, personalities and perspectives, while potentially capable of adding significantly to the organization's development, can, and most often will, result in differences of opinions and approaches which, if not well managed, can be divisive. The matrix manager will have to channel these inputs in directions which support and enhance the organization's pursuit of its broader, overriding mission and objectives.

Despite the additional demands on its managements' skills created by the network approach, tomorrow's successful health care organizations will be those which successfully integrate these and similarly sound participative management principles into its structure.

ORGANIZATIONAL CULTURE

To effectively integrate participative management styles and network management into the organization, a culture which is complementary to the management style must be developed. The culture must create a desire for new things, a hunger for new associations. In other words, a culture which develops in its people and supports an addiction to innovation.

An innovative organization provides an environment wherein change is an accepted part of the environment and is welcomed as the seedbed of progress. Each person must be oriented to the fact that there is a certain amount of ambiguity in today's dynamic health care environment and encouraged to embrace change and look for the opportunities it brings with it. In fact, they should be encouraged to bring their own experience and intuition to bear on what seems to be 'established' so that, if appropriate, that too might be examined in the 'looking glass of change,' and refined by the genius of innovative thinking.

While the formal mission of the organization may be the most visible driving force, the informal mission is more important by far. That informal mission should be a commitment to create an environment wherein each of the organization's participants can expand his or her own potential and, thereby, serve the organization and its constituents most effectively. The organizational commitment to this end must be communicated clearly and reinforced frequently. All participants must be willing to change and be changed, both organizationally and personally.

All of this emphasizes the need for talented, committed professionals who have the character and courage to lead the charge in a battle whose end is far from determined. The people of the organization must be made to feel special because they are special. The organization's structure, processes and interpersonal roles must be developed and administered to enhance this feeling of specialness. There is not now nor can there ever be any real organizational success without individual success. The culture must reflect the organization leadership's desire to provide an open environment in which the individual is supreme. The spirit of entrepreneurship must be encouraged, including the inherent risk taking and challenging of the status quo. Leadership responsibilities and authority must be shared to further enhance organizational and personal development and growth. And the pursuit of the spirit and benefits of innovation must, in fact, be the organization's true driving force.

ORGANIZATIONAL POWER

"The vitality of thought is in adventure. Ideas won't keep. Something must be done about them. When the idea is new, its custodians have fervor, live for it, and, if need be, die for it."

Alfred North Whitehead

It is not enough that an organization spawn innovative ideas. The successful innovative organization must also provide means for their development and implementation. The basis for transforming ideas into action plans and results resides in the proper use and distribution of organizational power.

Organizational power can be viewed as being composed of two types: 'power over' and 'power to do.' Traditional organization structure puts an inappropriate emphasis on 'power over.' Even the traditional organization chart places inordinate importance on the 'level' on which one resides. Corporate influence is as much a function of 'what you are' (in terms of title and position) as what you contribute. This type of power is too easily abused, and it can become both a shield behind which incompetency hides and a barrier to organizational progress. The power which is most important in an innovative organization is the 'power to do.'

Kanter presents the case that 'power to do' comes from three sources: access to information, access to organizational support and access to resources (1983, p. 159). If an organization expects its people to produce, it must supply them with the means of production. To take ideas from thought to action requires that all of the above power sources be made readily available to the innovator. And all artificial barriers to communication or resource sharing which might inhibit such power must be systematically eliminated. Further each person should be encouraged to maximize his or her personal 'power to do' through individual skills development, self-education, industry participation, etc.

ORGANIZATIONAL REWARDS

Extrinsic Rewards

People, as previously discussed, are the key ingredient to success. Consequently, the innovative organization must develop a culture which places a heavy emphasis on personal development. Additionally, that culture must be supported and reinforced by a reward system with the same emphasis. While it is not the purpose of this paper to deal in detail with the design of reward and incentive programs, it should be noted that any such program must be designed to avoid the common pitfalls which can undermine its effectiveness: inequity effects, misdirected activity effects and an _exaggerated_ emphasis on extrinsic rewards. While the organization should provide salaries and other extrinsic rewards consistent with its competitive environment, it must also realize that there will always be some other entity willing and able to pay a little more for a skilled professional. To keep its management team productive and committed, the innovative organization must not compete for their loyalty on the basis of dollars alone.

Intrinsic Rewards

The most effective motivation is that which is self-inspired. Management By Objectives offers the opportunity for personnel to interact with top management, to formalize the process of transforming individual vision and drive to practical ends within the context of the organization's mission. As such, it is certainly the most appropriate foundation for developing a functional, motivating reward system for the innovative organization. When utilized properly, in the context of the individual's responsibilities and in combination with management's judgement, MBO can be designed to reward both the acceptable discharge of routine operational responsibilities and the initiation of innovative action and accomplishment.

Personnel should be rewarded verbally and publicly for their accomplishments. They should be encouraged to structure their work patterns in such a way that they provide themselves time for continuing education and personal development. They should be constantly reminded in both formal and informal ways of the value of positive self-worth, self-discipline, pride of accomplishment and other values which serve as the basis for peak performance.

The innovative organization realizes that it has a responsibility which transcends the 'bottom line.' It has a responsibility to society as well. And the primary way it can contribute positively to society is to develop people who are driven from within by a need to participate in worthy pursuits and to excel in that participation. The fruits of dedication and commitment cannot be confined to the workplace. They will, without fail, spill over into all areas of the innovators' lives.

CONCLUSION

Security for an organization in an uncertain, changing environment comes not from domination but from flexibility: the ability to innovate and to master change management. As Kanter states, "It will come not from having everything under control but from quick reaction time, being able to cut across categories to get the best combinations of people and affiliations for the job" (1983, p. 65). For its people, security comes not from building and protecting personal 'turfs,' but from identifying with the whole company, by contributing to an organizational unity of effort based on pride in both organizational and individual growth and progress.

On the surface, an innovative organization may look quite traditional in nature. It has a clear structure; its organizational charts may show a differentiation into departments or functional units; there may be stated reporting relationships; and people may occupy specific jobs with specific job descriptions and bounded responsibilities. But when the need arises, the underlying connections between and across segments become clear: management teams considering decisions together; 'dotted line' reporting relationships with one or more other areas, multidisciplinary project teams; teams of employees pulling together to improve performance; networks of peers who exchange information and support each other's projects.

It is this ability to network individuals, separate divisions, and/or affiliates when the need arises, and the resultant synergies of participation and employee commitment, that gives the organization its capacity for innovation. Integrative, participative mechanisms do not replace the differentiation of defineable segments that carry out clear and limited tasks; they complement and enhance it so that the organization can more effectively deal with the complexities of change and the opportunities of innovation.

Change - rapid, dramatic, change - is the norm today. The traditional organizational framework in which health care has been delivered must be restructured. The greatest obstacle to organizational success will be the outmoded views of what an organization must look like, and the self-imposed and short-sighted constraints within which it must operate. From the traditional 'order' we must perform 'creative destruction,' bringing in a new order of things: new relationships, new obligations and new expectations.

Future organizational models will all feature some of the properties of the dynamic network approach described herein. They will be "characterized by an increasing reliance on self-managed workgroups and a greater willingness to expand organizational boundaries and memberships" (Miles and Snow 1986, p. 73). Although this means trading comfortable routines for new orientations and challenging old habits with new competencies, it will better equip hospitals for effectively meeting the future challenges of the health care environment.

Someone recently said, "Don't count hospitals out. There may be fewer of them in the years to come but they'll become competitive, more efficient and more innovative." The visionary among us will reach out and grasp the present opportunity to change and improve. The myopic will continue to be tossed about by the waves of change...or be drowned by them.

REFERENCES

Drucker, Peter (1985), *Innovation and Entrepreneurship*, New York: Harper & Row.

_____ (1986), "Interview with Fred Smith," *Inc. Magazine* (October).

Kanter, Rosabeth Moss (1983), *The Change Masters*, New York: Simon and Schuster, Inc.

Miles, Raymond E. and Charles C. Snow (1986), "Organizations: New Concepts for New Forms," *California Management Review*, 27:3 (Spring).

Pondy, Louis R. (1983), "Union of Rationality and Intuition in Management Action," *The Executive Mind*, Suresh Srivastva, ed., San Francisco: Jossey-Bass Publishers.

Rowan, Roy (1986), *The Intuitive Manager*, Macmillan Executive Summary Program, Vol. 2, No. 10 (October).

NO MORE TANGLES:
MARKETING THROUGH PRODUCT MANAGEMENT

E. Preston Gee, Sacred Heart General Hospital, Eugene, OR
James C. Folger, Northwest Healthcare Consulting, Eugene, OR

ABSTRACT

Product line management may represent the true conversion of health care organizations to a marketing mindset. Although hospitals that attempt a direct translation of the principles used in consumer packaged goods may experience frustration, the basic principles of decentralized authority and broadly-defined accountability are beneficial if the organization adopts a flexible orientation.

INTRODUCTION

The past five years of turbulence in healthcare marketing have demonstrated to us that a hospital is too complex to manage as a single entity. A hospital is a many-teathered thing with diverse target audiences and a broad range of services. One sound solution is to break the organization into manageable components that are more flexible and can compete more effectively.

The genious of product management exists in its singular focus on the service as a business, and in the assignment of accountability. Pushing power downward, the responsibility for success or failure lies directly on the shoulders of those already bearing the burdens, exactly as it should. Hence individual managers and matrix team members receive customized challenges and subsequently make concerted commitments. The system also provides a clarity of vision to focus on the key elements of an operating entity, namely profitability, revenues, and market share. An added dimension of the concept is the constant challenging of conventional wisdom, asking the question, why can't it be done bigger, better, or differently to meet customers' needs.

BACKGROUND

Originating in consumer packaged goods, the concept of product management has become an effective means to focus on the customer and his/her needs.

The product manager in industry is somewhat like an orchestra conductor, matching the resources of the organization with market needs. In a hospital setting the PM is no less critical in this coordination function. The hospital setting may call for even more creativity, however, because the resources are more limited.

While the concept was first adopted in the early 70s, the process has recently picked up popularity, but still lacks the dimension and comprehension of other applications. Several hospitals that have initiated the concept have been frustrated by its lack of instantaneous results, and have consequently written off the theory, rather than recognizing their own inability to implement it.

Also, many hospitals thought of PM as a "branded" program approach, with the emphasis on advertising and promotion. This fundamental flaw negates the other elements of the product mix, and detours around the value of the system in organizing and monitoring the data aspect of PLM.

Many of the first hospital models were based on accounting systems, or a computer information orientation with the focus on the cost data. While these systems captured the value of the data assessment, they do not constitute the end product. The key for successful product management is to bring together the financial and marketing data in a systematized fashion that considers all constituencies, not just the consumer. This data must be manageable, and must reflect accurate and adequate impact of program implementation. Hence the need for a smooth operational flow between the triumvirate of data systems, fiscal operations and marketing management.

While the fully integrated approach may be the ideal, it is not the only method that has succeeded. Two examples of more narrowly defined approaches are Republic, which has used a branded approach, and NKC, which has chosen individual entities to focus on in its application.

Another example of a singular focus is Northwest Hospital in Seattle, which selected as its primary criteria a product champion who would establish a good precedent for PM, and launch the process with a success.

SETTING UP THE SYSTEM

Hospitals throughout the country have used a variety of approaches in establishing their systems. We mentioned a few examples above, and would suggest the following criteria for consideration in establishing a PLM approach:

1. Data available, hospital-wide and service area specific. 2. Resource focus (i.e. capital expenditures, technology, medical staff, etc.). 3. Competitive response - preemptive, offensive, or defensive. 4. Leadership within personnel ranks - medical, staff, administrative. 5. Consumer orientation of services. 6. Ability to differentiate the service or product offering. 7. Separate/distinctive nature of service area in terms of operations management.

Steps to Setting Up An Effective System

We would suggest the following ten steps:
1. Obtain CEO support--a must.
2. Identify line(s) and methods to measure results.
3. Develop product managers. Internal candidates where possible.
4. Develop matrix teams or task forces to assist product line managers.
5. Educate hospital staff and medical staff at all levels. Marketing department should act as coach/counselor/colleague.
6. Business plans should be drafted as primary task, and should identify meaningful and measureable goals.
7. Business plans should be consistent with the overall hospital strategic planning objectives.
8. Integrate the planning process into the budget system.
9. Establish monthly or periodic review mechanism and accountability reporting process.
10. Focus efforts on a high probability candidate to establish a precedent for success.

Results

The Sacred Heart Adolescent Recovery Program (SHARP) was
able to, for the first time, show a respectable bottom-
line. The volume of the patients seen in the unit increased significantly. The director of the unit received
considerable attention and accolades from community leaders for his involvement with local schools and other organizations where the youth were involved.

Conclusion

In conclusion, we would suggest that the product line
management system can be both an effective organizational
tool, and a way to improve volume and profit performance.
In order to achieve optimal results, we would suggest the
following 6 steps for holding the product manager accountable:

1. Establish goals and objectives that are both reason-
    able and measurable.
2. Establish marketing database reporting system.
3. Facilitate the process of holding people accountable
    by use of flow charts and implementation detail.
4. Require product manager to report periodically on
    status of progress against business plan objectives/
    strategies.
5. The CEO should support the function in words and
    actions - promote those who succeed in meeting goals,
    and remove those who don't.
6. Set up incentive compensation systems that reward
    product managers and product line task force members
    for increased volume or profitability.

CASE STUDIES

Short Stay Unit

The short stay unit at Sacred Heart represented a service area with many attractive variables for launching it as the first product line.

The unit operated as a separate entity; that is, as a separate but contiguous outpatient facility, its data and operations function were self-contained. Therefore, the access to information was easily assembled and easily monitored.

The unit also was well-known for its high technology, thereby representing an area of focus for the hospital, as well as portraying one of its critical strengths.

The doctors operating in the unit (one in particular) had established national reputations, and had operated on nationally prominent athletic personalties. This then became a point of focus for marketing and advertising efforts.

Finally, the type of services performed in the SSU were representative of the trend in medicine to ambulatory surgery, and more of a consumer-oriented process for the delivery of health care. Based on these criteria, the business plan for the Short Stay Unit was developed. The Administrative Director of that unit took the lead in gathering the data and pulling together the relevant details for the business plan. The Marketing Department acted as the facilitator in formatting the plan, editing the information, and helping establish issues of relevance in improving the Unit's performance.

Results

Due to the strategies suggested in the business plan, the Short Stay Unit was able to effectively increase its revenue, market share, and bottom-line. Significantly, the impact of the business planning process had a very favorable ripple effect on other product lines that were being developed and the plans that were being drafted.

Cardiology

The Cardiology Product Line at Sacred Heart represented the first product line developed with a matrix team format. A product manager was hired from outside the hospital. He had a combined background of business and law. The product line matrix team was made up of department representatives ranging from surgery to radiology, with a heavy emphasis on nursing.

The first task of the product line committee was to draft a business plan. The outgrowth of that plan, as well as previous decisions, was an effort to consolidate outpatient cardiology services into one location. Also out of that plan was developed a uniformity of purpose and name, identifying all cardiology services as the Oregon Heart Center. The business plan also identified opportunities for increasing awareness among staff members and the general public. The focus of the plan, however, was dealing with referring physicians.

One of the most important dynamics in this particular case study was the interface with the physicians. An advisory committee of doctors ranging from cardiovascular surgeons to internists was developed to parallel and advise the activities of the hospital product line committee. Eventually this committee would develop its own marketing subcommittee and would place 2 to 3 doctors on the hospital's product line committee.

Results

Chiefly through the efforts of the physician strategies (which included seminars and mailings), the cardiovascular line was able to reverse a declining trend in open heart surgeries and overall inpatient admissions. Importantly, the successes of the matrix team were pivotal in highlighting the value of the product line management system and the impact it can have on a very complex service area which crosses a variety of functions.

Mental Health

Work with the Mental Health product line involved a repositioning of basic services. The unit, which had previously been identified as the Johnson Unit, had a history of poor public perception due to practices in the 60's of accepting mentally disfunctional patients from the local jails. There were also interface problems with the physicians, and a generally poor perception among the community leaders and community residents.

The focus of this business plan effort then was to "repackage" the services in such a fashion that professionals would feel comfortable referring their patients, and patients would feel confident in the services offered.

In this case, the product line manager assigned the task of developing the business plan and implementing its strategies was the medical director, a phychiatrist. Again, the Marketing Department took a major role in facilitating the process, but the medical director remained the key person in interfacing with the physician community. A few of the strategies involved in re-positioning the unit involved a new name, a remodel of the facility (including open houses for physicians and members of the community), the hiring of two new psychiatrists, and the addition of an eating disorders program. The thrust of these open houses was to show that indeed the unit had received a philosophical, as well as a physical, facelift.

Results

The Mental Health Unit was able to reverse a disturbing trend of declining patient days and financial losses. A greater awareness of the facility, as well as confidence in its practitioners, was measured by the research.

Adolescent Recovery Program

The main thrust of this product line development involved a termination of a contract management situation. The Adolescent Recovery area of the hospital had previously been managed by a national firm, but had consistently produced major bottom-line losses. The business plan identified the need to terminate the contract, and bring the services in-house.

Therefore, the thrust of this business planning process was to assist the professional and consumer community in generating awareness of the newly-named, newly-organized facility.

The pivot person on this project was the Administrative Director of the Unit, a social worker by training. He not only became the product champion for the service, but its main proponent in outlying communities. The nature of this service provided opportunities for considerable promotion in a variety of media. Coupled with the national interest in curtailing drug abuse, this program then became a very positive vehicle for representing the hospital in the community.

REORGANIZING AND MOTIVATING STAFF
TO MAKE PRODUCT LINE MANAGEMENT WORK

Tim M. Henderson and Michael S. Leibman
McManis Associates, Inc.
Washington, D.C.

ABSTRACT

Hospitals typically must face the threat of increasingly-competitive market forces, shrinking inpatient revenues, organizational chaos and other crises within their institution before they will consider alternative market driven means for structuring and delivering services. Those that have decided to institute a product line management (PLM) system under such circumstances often have found the process to be unmanageable and ultimately unacceptable. This presentation will focus on the opportunity hospitals have to successfully plan and implement PLM, initially in selective product areas, in times without major turmoil. PLM's evolution in industry and its recent adaption to healthcare will first be reviewed, stressing the benefits and limitations for healthcare organizations. What is essential for creating a supportive and accountable corporate culture will next be outlined and, most importantly, what characteristics, roles and relationships, and incentives are necessary for motivating staff, physicians and the marketing department are examined.

INTRODUCTION

The rapid and continuous evolution of our increasingly competitive healthcare market poses unprecedented challenges to today's providers. In conjunction with progress in medicine and technology, changes in reimbursement methods, and new types of facilities, a market driven by sophisticated and selective consumers has emerged. Within this environment, viability of a healthcare institution is dependent upon targeting and meeting the desires of the healthcare buyer and their intermediaries: the consumer, the employer and even the physician. Product line management (PLM) is a management tool which can help your institution meet those desires. It couples a marketing orientation with a comprehensive accountability system to integrate one or more service or products across functional lines. An institution organized along product lines or strategic business units (SBU), or clusters of related products, results in the flexibility necessary to respond to changes in the market, decentralized accountability, greater employee involvement and a clear picture of profitability.

EVOLUTION AND VALUE OF PLM

PLM has been used to manage businesses since its inception in 1931 at the Proctor & Gamble Company (P&G). P&G implemented PLM in the hope of reversing the unexpectedly poor sales of Lava Soap. Failure of Lava Soap to create healthy competition for another P&G product, Ivory Soap, was attributed to unintentional emphasis on the more well-established product. The introduction of PLM proved successful: it enables independent thinking and marketing not possible under the traditional functional style of management. By identifying market opportunities, relating product development and

orientation to consumer desires, and giving equal attention to each product, PLM responds to market changes and a competitive environment.

Unlike functional management, PLM creates employee loyalty to a product. Through PLM a large number of products can be effectively managed. It emphasizes many of Peters & Waterman's lessons from the best selling book A Search of Excellence -- from encouraging a bias for action to remaining close to the customer. It also provides managers the ability to make clear evaluations of products and their costs and profits.

Despite the potential for internal unrest, which could result from shifts in authority, reporting relations, new culture, incentive or simply the unrest from a transition, many packaged goods companies recognized the clear benefits of PLM and abandoned their strictly functional organizational structures. PLM has now spread to non-packaged goods industries and is being implemented in such diverse industries as banking and healthcare.

Application to Healthcare

Product line management can be useful to any organization that is characterized by fierce competition within its industry, various market segments and the need for proactive marketing. Yet, the adoption of PLM from the packaged goods model to healthcare institutions has its twists and turns. Elements of the model must be altered to accommodate the unique relationship between the product and the person. Whether the product line is cardiology or oncology, the connection to the person's overall health is fundamentally different from that of the person's preference for soap. While industry should discontinue a product that cannot turn lucrative, a healthcare product deemed a financial loss may remain on the market as a necessary service. The second major difference between the traditional industrial PLM model and the healthcare model involves the physician. The physician, except where he/she is an employee of the healthcare institution, functions as an external supply and distribution network. The independent status of the physicians demands unique adaptions of the PLM model.

To date, PLM in the healthcare industry has proven most successful in large (over 400 beds), urban hospitals with many definable product lines. It is especially effective in teaching hospitals. Its implementation is frequently precipitated by a crisis in revenues, followed by lack of significant data. Although implementation has required up to five years, hospitals should aim for a two to three year goal.

We plan to focus on certain organizational aspects of transforming the organization to excel within a PLM orientation. Specifically we will look at developing the proper organizational environment or culture, the role of the PLM manager, the integration of the physicians and the role of the marketing department.

IMPLEMENTING PLM IN HEALTHCARE INSTITUTIONS

Any organization preparing to implement PLM had also be prepared for the turmoil which inevitably accompanies this massive internal change. Typically, there are two reasons for this turmoil: the external stress that caused the institution to consider introducing PLM; and the internal upheaval caused by the institution's total conversion to the PLM model. A methodical and planned approach to implementing PLM can reduce this turmoil.

To maximize organizational effectiveness, we recommend the selective application of product line management. Through effective product research, a number of optimal markets for exploitation can be identified. We suggest that the healthcare institution select only one or two product lines to implement. Lines should be chosen on the basis of the market research, level of staff and physician acceptance, the rapidity for implementation and probability for success. The experience gained from implementing these product lines will benefit future lines. More importantly, the success of these initial lines will encourage enthusiasm among other staff and make subsequent product lines easier to introduce.

CORPORATE CULTURE

Engendering an appropriate corporate culture is an essential step for successful PLM. The promulgated culture establishes values and helps communicate top management's expectations. Clearly defined, shared objectives bind staff to the institution and guide behavior. Since change is often perceived as a threat and reacted to with resistance, the introduction of PLM must be planned and capitalize on those aspects of the existing culture which will foster its acceptance. To introduce PLM, the culture must be characterized by an entrepreneurial spirit, decentralized accountability, a market orientation, and a concern for quality.

The following steps help develop and maintain a corporate culture receptive to PLM:

° **Shape the culture.** The more market sensitive culture must be tailored to the specific institution. Each institution has a tradition and image to draw upon, and each should build that into its culture.

° **Educate the staff.** The nature of the new philosophy, environment and goals, as well as performance expectations, must be clearly communicated. Interest and confidence increase with knowledge and understanding provided in classes and seminars.

° **Encourage participation.** Commitment comes from ownership and ownership from participation. The staff should play a role in structuring the product line and defining the market.

° **Create leadership models.** Words are not sufficient to establish culture. Demonstrated enthusiasm, active commitment and new behavior on the part of senior management will transfer values to all levels of staff.

° **Establish horizontal as well as vertical communication.** Creates ties and formal communication between departments. New accountabilities provide only one dimension among departments that will need to be more closely coordinated. While the acceptance of a new reporting relationship is crucial, it is not sufficient. Teamwork must be fostered.

° **Increasing accountability.** Responsibility must match authority. Interaction between departments must be identifiable so that reporting relationships can be identified.

° **Selecting acceptable nomenclature.** "Product Line Management", "product lines", and "PLM" are viewed by some as popular, hackneyed terminology. Acceptable terminology should be used to both adequately describe the change and instill confidence in the longevity of its organizational structure. Alternatives such as "business unit management", "management centers", and "Centers of excellence" may be more appropriate.

° **Offering incentives.** Monetary and non-monetary performance rewards should be employed to change behavior. Pools of money can be allocated for team performance based on product line organization. Alternatively, personal recognition and free tickets to social events, for example, also serve as incentives to modify behavior. Finally, external publicity, such as favorable news coverage, serves to foster pride in the product line.

THE PRODUCT LINE MANAGER

Duties

The product line manager's first responsibility is to be the product champion. His duties include identifying market opportunities, developing the product to capitalize on these opportunities, creating and implementing marketing strategies and monitoring the product's success. In coordinating all aspects of business relating to the particular line, the product line manager promotes horizontal and vertical communication and develops pricing strategies, profit projections, and staffing and resource allocations. Although responsible for the product line, the manager's duties will remain circumscribed by the overall institutional policies and mission.

Colleague interactions

The product line manager oversees all employees that contribute to the development and delivery of the product line. Product line managers exercise a certain amount of direct authority over functional managers such as lab or pharmacy managers. The product line manager, however, is accountable to senior management.

Skills

Familiarity with both the product line and institution's organizational workings are important considerations when selecting a product line manager. Product line managers should come from within the organization. In this capacity, organizational changes can be affected by building on management staff. The peer struggle among managers should be expected. The product line managers will be the new power brokers of the organization. Disagreement and dissent can be anticipated after appointing the new managers; attrition should be expected for two reasons: (1) disappointment in not being selected; and more importantly, (2) not fitting in with the new orientation. This turnover is not necessarily bad.

The following skills should be possessed by every product line manager.

- ° Familiarity with the product line;
- ° Good communicator, both orally and written;
- ° Persuasive in motivating others;
- ° Achievement-oriented;
- ° Innovative thinker, both broadly and strategically; and
- ° Analytical as data must be interpreted to assist in meeting goals.

PHYSICIAN INTEGRATION

Physician acceptance and participation is necessary for successful product line management, yet physicians are likely to resist its introduction. They foresee the loss of their autonomy and authority from the functional system. Physicians recognize that implementation of PLM can mean that the product line managers will replace the CEO and COO as the physicians immediate contacts. To prevent this resistance, physicians must become involved in the development of the product lines. While not all the physicians may participate in the development of the product line, all should participate in either supplying market information, educational dialogues, and be kept up to date on the product line development. Physicians whose practices are not yet mature will probably be more receptive to hospital innovation than physicians with thriving independent practices. PLM should be structured to promote physician practices, and should be appropriately portrayed.

There are three basic methods to involve physicians. First, administration will decide and develop a product line management structure without a lot of direct physician participation. In this instance, administration should keep physicians informed and where appropriate gather specific intelligence. Second, a group of specialists may approach the institution about developing a product line based on their specialty. Finally, physicians along with nurses, managers, and ancillary personnel, will work together to devise product lines and market strategies.

THE MARKETING DEPARTMENT

The marketing department, headed by an administrative vice-president, will provide the leadership in PLM. This office will interact with other staff offices and product lines. The marketing department, having the best perspective of the hospital's overall market, is responsible for directing the development of the PLM structure and providing overall integration of the marketing strategies for the institution. Specifically, the department develops the marketing plan based on the individual product line market plans; annually updates its three to five year projections; publishes an annual quantitative plan; and compiles reviews and projections on a monthly basis. In addition, it performs market research, places advertisements, and establishes media contacts.

CONCLUSION

Is product line management a viable strategy for your hospital? It can target and attract consumers, provide a comprehensive assessment of products and services, and increase profits or revenues. Its implementation is however costly, time consuming, and potentially stressful. There is no mathematical formula to determine the effectiveness of PLM in your institution. We suggest a carefully planned implementation, preferable before you are in a crisis situation, of no more than two or three product lines. Careful planning will ensure acceptance of the new market-oriented culture.

MARKETING COMMUNICATIONS

While Public Relations is still the major preoccupation
of a large number of health care institutions the focus
of papers in this track reflects a shift from this peren-
nial topic. Two papers by Eudes/Divis and Thalhuber/Clasen
recommend that tools and strategies developed and successfully implemented in the retail industry be more carefully
scrutinized with an eye towards introducing these to the
health care field. They argue that the recognition of
the retailing nature of the health care delivery system
exposes health care managers to a treasure trove of
hitherto untapped marketing communication strategies and
tools.

Klegon and Lyon's paper addresses the need for a systematic evaluation of marketing communication. They present
a strong case for utilizing market research as the key
component of this evaluative process.

AMERICAN MARKETING ASSOCIATION
USING CATALOGING PRINCIPLES TO ATTRACT REFERRALS
TO TERTIARY SERVICES

John A. Eudes, Univ. of Alabama Hospital, Birmingham
Kathy L. Divis, Univ. of Alabama Hospital, Birmingham

ABSTRACT

Health care institutions and physicians can utilize retail
cataloging principles to build referrals, increase revenue
flow and enhance image. This paper and presentation dis-
cusses the compelling reasons for incorporating a cataloging program into your marketing mix, explains the basic
principles of developing an effective cataloging program
and gives examples of retail cataloging principles applied to health care. References will be made to both
printed catalogs and their counterpart electronic versions.

INTRODUCTION

Hospitals and physicians can use cataloging principles,
similar to those routinely used in retailing, to increase
referrals, improve revenue flow and enhance image. These
principles are particularly relevant to tertiary care or
"specialized" services, but can also be effectively applied to primary care hospitals. Catalogs are generally
written for one of two audiences: industrial or domestic
audiences. An industrial catalog is one developed for the
health care professional. A domestic catalog is one
developed for the lay public.

Logically, when making a presentation, results are given
at the end. In order to convey the value of these principles from the onset, however, the results will be
presented first. The University of Alabama Hospital from
1974 to 1981, had seven years of declining census (this
was during the boom years of health care). In 1981, the
Hospital decided it had to do something to reverse this
trend. ONE thing it did was embrace the marketing concept. In 1981, the University's market share ranked 7th;
by 1986, the University ranked first in market share.
Part of this turnaround is due to a comprehensive, integrated marketing program, of which cataloging is a
large part.

Other environmental factors also converged to create an
atmosphere conducive to cataloging, including the fragmentation of the health care system, the emerging importance of women in the health care decision making
process, the consumerism movement and the demand for
price-value equality.

BACKGROUND AND EXAMPLES

Putting together an effective catalog is an immense
task, but effective catalogs are premised on common
sense principles. These principles can be categorized
into five general areas:

- Pre-Production
- Content
- Formatting
- Distribution
- Maintenance

In addition, there are basically two types of catalogs:
full service and specialty, either of which can be
designed for the industrial (professional) audience or
the domestic (lay) audience.

Full Service Catalogs

A full service catalog includes all product lines. In
a full service catalog, equal treatment to all products
should be achieved, if possible. A lesser treatment im-
plies to the buyer that there are secondary lines in your
business. Also, it may cause improper ordering or misconceptions and the buyer may become disillusioned if
he receives something different than he thought he ordered.

One full service, industrial catalog example is a Directory for Referring Physicians. The University of
Alabama Hospital's Directory for Referring Physicians is
a 300 page, full service catalog for the professional
health care market. It is a catalog which outlines all
of the services, physicians and programs of the University of Alabama Hospital.

A second full service catalog example, written for the
domestic market, is called the Guide to UAB Medical
Service. It is a catalog of all the patient care
services provided by UAB which are available to the
general public, including physicians, services, education
and research.

Specialty Catalogs

A specialty catalog concentrates on one or a limited
number of product lines. While a specialty catalog
duplicates some of the information in the full service
catalog, its primary purpose is to supplement it. The
specialty catalog is generally smaller in size but provides more detail or may be seasonal. A retail example
of a specialty catalog is the J.C. Penney's Christmas
catalog or a Big-Tall Men's catalog.

A health care example of a specialty industrial catalog
is the UAB Directory of Cardiac Services. This "cardiac
catalog" details all cardiac-related services available
through the University including cardiology, cardiovascular surgery, pediatric cardiology, and cardiac
education and research. In a full service catalog,
cardiac services would probably only take up a dozen
pages in total. The UAB Directory of Cardiac Services
devotes 90 pages to that single product.

Another health care specialty service catalog example
is a series of plastic surgery catalogs. These catalogs
are the specialty, domestic market example and represent
a series of catalogs on the different types of plastic
surgery. Although possibly used by the professional
market, they are specifically written for a lay audience.

BASIC PRINCIPLES

The basic principles for the development of an effective catalog can be categorized into five general areas:

- Pre-Production
- Content
- Formatting
- Distribution
- Maintenance

Pre-Production Principles

The first category of principles are those connected with pre-production planning. If there is any axiom in cataloging it must be "know your user." To produce a catalog which is effective, the author must:

- define the potential user.
- know the user and be true to the user.
- be prepared. The better prepared one is, the more likely one is to obtain maximum results.
- always try to anticipate the user's needs.
- perform field research.
- pay particular attention to troublesome and weak areas, as identified by research.
- discriminate between essential and non-essential information from the user's viewpoint.
- and finally, determine what user reaction is solicited -- do you want the reader to:

    - request more information?
    - self refer?
    - physician refer?
    - register for a program?

Not all catalogs are designed to sell directly. Sometimes, especially in full service catalogs, the user reaction wanted may simply be to request more information. This is particularly true as the complexity of your product (like tertiary care) increases.

In pre-production one must also consider costs, and the cost of a catalog is affected by many things, including:

1. Cooperation...the more cooperation, the lower the cost of production.
2. Approval Authority...the more people required to approve the catalog, the higher the cost.
3. Accuracy of Source Data...the data must be accurate. If not, additional time is required for verification of facts and statements...this time is expensive.
4. Quality...what quality is desired. The best isn't always practical, but the cheapest isn't necessarily the best route either.
5. Type of Product or Service...if unique, complicated or technical, then specially talented writers are necessary.
6. Status of Product/Service...new services or new technology often require expanded explanations or new photography. Also one must consider the status which should be conveyed through the catalog.

7. Available Literature...all available literature should be gathered and evaluated. If possible, any appropriate information should be used to cut cost. However, use only the information which is compatible with catalog objectives and audience.
8. Special Requirements...during development invariably someone wants to include information that doesn't belong...with the philosophy of "killing two birds with one stone". This can be very dangerous because sales is the function of the catalog. Do not load the catalog with unnecessary technical data or history or anything not needed to complete the sale. When you increase the size, you increase the cost.

And, a poorly prepared and designed catalog, no matter what the cost is expensive when considering lost referrals and opportunities.

Content Principles

The second category of catalog principles are concerned with content. The content and its preparation is really the heart of any catalog. An effective catalog must be: informative, well presented, well organized, in good taste and easy to use. Most of all, the content must be written in a language the reader understands and using accepted trade terms.

Having clear objectives is important during both the planning and content phases. Many decisions and challenges are made during development of a catalog. It is helpful to review objectives when determining answers or responding to challenges.

It is also important to remember that when contact between a user and provider is personal, there is an opportunity to adjust the description or explanation as you go along. One of the drawbacks of a catalog is you don't have that chance, <u>therefore</u>, the catalog must give the best content presentation possible.

Formatting Principles

The third major category of catalog principles is formatting. An effective catalog must be formatted such that it leads the reader to his item of interest in the shortest possible time. The format must be physically attractive and use white space optimally. The typical catalog user knows what he wants; therefore, your job as the catalog producer, is to make finding that information as easy as possible. <u>Sections and indexing helps.</u> Also, make ordering easy and use the front cover and spine to command attention.

In addition, the information provided on the services and physicians must be quick and easy to find. The use of formats which outline information is helpful as is the attractive and functional use of white space so that the reader is led quickly to the necessary information.

Distribution Principles

The fourth major category of general catalog principles is distribution. A catalog, regardless of content or format, can only be as effective as the distribution me-thod. Things to remember as distribution is planned include: 1) in many instances, the first or even only contact a buyer may have with an organization is its catalog. So its important that a catalog stand on its own; 2) a product specified is not necessarily a product sold. For example, even though a physician may decide that your oncology service is the best decision, the author must assist him in implementing this decision by including information on communication systems, transportation options and information to pass on to patients; and 3) the potential "buyers" market is always larger than the number of available catalogs, thus, one must make the most effective distribution of a limited number of catalogs. This means you must prioritize your potential markets and almost "ration" your catalogs to the most frequent user or those with the greatest potential to purchase or refer.

The best way to distribute a catalog is by a sales force. If there are too many to distribute personally, then mail is the most practical alternative. When you lose that personal touch, however, you must consider other ways of stimulating interest, such as:

- a pre-distribution survey, as an announcement
- pre-mailing promotional campaign to announce publication
- envelope or container message

There are, however, advantages of a catalog over a sales-man, such as:

1. Presistence...the catalog is always on the shelf and thus, always present when needed by the reader.
2. More economical than sales...cost of mailing is minor when compared to the cost of a personal sales call.
3. Internally it can be used to orient new employees or doctors.
4. Catalogs can more easily support an advertising program...as an example, "see page 26 of our Directory for Referring Physicians". Also, always support the catalog with an advertising campaign.

Maintenance Principles

The final category of catalog principles is maintenance. Catalog maintenance is a problem that must be considered during preparation of the initial edition. One needs to decide "how long the material will remain valid" and "how rapidly does the information change."

When updating a catalog, there are essentially three options:

1. Revision -- issuing extra or correction pages. The disadvantages are that you impose on your customer the responsibility of making the changes and the binding method must be loose leaf.

2. Reissue -- a reissue is a new catalog. When there are too many changes just to revise... you reissue the total content. This preserves the format and many of the decisions you've already made and is particularly useful if the existing catalog is well received.

    When publishing a reissue, make a significant change on the cover but leave some resemblance so it ties in to the existing one. Also send with the catalog a reissue notice that states that this issue replaces the existing one and make a suggestion to discard the old one to avoid future confusion.

3. New Editions -- a new edition is an opportunity to start over and to reflect field suggestions for improvement on content, format and organization.

The most important thing about catalog maintenance is to make sure that the catalog never becomes so outdated that it is a source of annoyance to your clients.

Catalogs which are isolated in an overall marketing plan lose their tremendous sales potential and weaken the overall marketing effort. So, reference the catalog in every advertisement or direct mail piece. And finally, do follow-up with physicians and other target audiences on such subjects as content, format, organization and use. It may be the only way to accurately judge the catalog's impact.

ELECTRONIC VERSIONS OF CATALOGS

A newly emerging trend in the cataloging industry is the development and utilization of electronic versions of a catalog. These electronic versions can also be applied to health care. The challenge, of course, is to develop a software package which is usable by your target audiences. This will include the use of very user friendly applications and possibly the facilitation of the automation of the referring physicians office in your market place.

SUMMARY

Catalogs, if designed using the basic principles outlined in this paper and if integrated into a comprehensive marketing program, can have a dramatic and positive effect on the revenues, referrals and image of the catalog producer. And although catalogs may be most effective in explaining tertiary or specialized services, they can be effectively implemented by any hospital, health care institution or group practice.

IF SEARS CAN DO IT, SO CAN WE . . .
A RETAIL APPROACH TO HEALTH CARE ADVERTISING

Jim Thalhuber, Courage Center, Minneapolis
Nancy Clasen, Carondelet Community Hospitals, Minneapolis

ABSTRACT

In today's competitive healthcare marketplace, it's no longer a question of whether to advertise, but how to advertise to maximize the return on dollars spent for this purpose. This presentation is a practical case study on how one hospital organization utilized strategies and techniques from the retail industry to hone and shape an ad program that delivered results.

INTRODUCTION

The competitive environment that exists in the healthcare industry today dictates that providers develop and implement aggressive, well-rounded marketing programs. Many include such program elements as physician recruitment and retention, HMO contracting, new service development and patient/guest relations programs. In addition, mass media advertising has become an accepted and increasingly important element of a comprehensive marketing program.

Operating within a highly competitive and innovative local market, hospitals in the Twin Cities of St. Paul and Minneapolis have used advertising as a marketing communications tool since the late 1970s. In recent years, HMOs and other providers have also utilized media extensively in an effort to gain or hold market share. Today the print and broadcast media are cluttered with a wide variety of commercial messages from the entire spectrum of healthcare providers. This presentation focuses on the advertising efforts of one Twin Cities hospital system, Carondelet Community Hospitals, and its success in being heard above the cacophony of competing messages.

For several years prior to their consolidation as Carondelet Community Hospitals (CCH), St. Joseph's Hospital in St. Paul and St. Mary's Hospital in Minneapolis had experimented with mass media advertising. And, while some of these efforts yielded positive results, ads were generally developed outside the context of an overall program or direction. As a result, they were inconsistent in style, limited in number and haphazardly placed.

The union of St. Mary's and St. Joseph's in mid-1985 presented an opportunity to re-evaluate advertising efforts and to set a new direction.

Market research commissioned by CCH indicated that while both hospitals enjoyed a high degree of name recognition within the community, neither scored well in overall consumer preference (as corroborated by a weakening market position). It was clear that the newly formed organization did not have the luxury of time associated with a long-term image building campaign. Instead what was needed was a single, sustained mass media advertising campaign; one that would "make things happen." The Carondelet image would need to be built as a result of a sharply focused, product-specific program.

Consumer research was again used to measure attitudes and preferences for select hospital-based programs/services. Results showed that neither hospital was seen as a provider of choice for many "high tech" services, such as heart surgery. However, the data did reveal that the hospitals ranked high among consumers for select "low tech" services, particularly in the behavioral medicine area. For many other "low tech" services, consumers displayed a minimal level of awareness or preference for any provider.

Research results were then combined with what was already known about a growing number of local healthcare consumers:

- they are becoming more active participants in the management of their healthcare needs. More and more, consumers are selecting providers independently or in partnership with their personal physician.

- that younger, more affluent, better educated females, especially, are more likely to be proactive in making healthcare choices.

- that the less serious the health problem or concern, the more likely they are to make their own decisions regarding the provider or service. Conversely, they tend to rely on their physicians to make decisions about life threatening situations.

Carondelet Community Hospitals now had a general direction and a market focus, but how was it to go about designing a sustained, results-oriented mass media advertising program?

LOOKING TO THE RETAIL INDUSTRY

One of the first steps was to look at the marketplace to determine how other organizations dealt with similar situations. The healthcare industry -- so relatively new -- offered little guidance. But the retail industry provided some clues. Sears, Roebuck & Co. was one interesting case history with some parallels to the Carondelet situation (albeit on a much smaller scale).

Like each of the Carondelet hospitals, Sears had been a presence in its industry for a century. It became a dominant retailer in the United States after World War II, just as each Carondelet hospital was once a leader in its service area.

Over the past two decades, both Sears and the Carondelet hospitals were hit head-on by stiff new competition from emerging mega-providers, while a host of specialty providers nibbled away at market share. Volumes and market positions eroded.

The 1980s brought major changes for each organization. There was new leadership, consolidation of operations and cost controls.

The new leadership at Sears brought new direction and a deceptively simple slogan: "There's more for your life at Sears."

Traditionally the country's most comprehensive retailer, Sears began the process of examining every one of its 800 product lines. Its formula for change was simple: products that didn't sell or increase market penetration were to be dropped or de-emphasized; for products where it was already a leader, new energy was to be given to maintaining dominance; where it was not a market leader, but saw opportunity, it would aggressively introduce new products and approaches.

It went about developing new "signature" lines of merchandise to attract long overlooked audiences, redesigning stores to ease consumer access, opening financial boutiques to broaden its appeal and planning small specialty stores to lure back lost business.

Simply stated, the company's aim was to convince consumers that Sears is THE place to satisfy all their personal needs from work shirts and sabre saws to insurance and real estate.

Many of Sears' strategies were worthy of consideration as Carondelet attempted to design its approach to the marketplace.

Observation of the retail industry also drove home the simple but often ignored (by healthcare providers) principle of advertising sensitivity. To product results, advertising must focus only on those products that are "advertising sensitive" -- products that consumers can understand and access directly.

This principle ruled out consideration of most "high tech" medical services like open heart surgery where physicians, not consumers, determine the service and the provider. Conversely, services like maternity care and behavioral medicine programs would be likely candidates for inclusion in a mass media advertising program.

Further observation of retailers led to the conclusion that effective retail advertising narrowly focused on specific products, promoted with creativity and flair, and contained strong invitations to target audiences to buy or use the product.

GOALS, OBJECTIVES & STRATEGIES

Based on the research findings, the following marketing goals were established for the proposed advertising program:

- To increase awareness of, preference for and market share of advertised services.

- To maximize the return on advertising dollars spent.

- To enhance the overall image, position and name recognition of Carondelet Community Hospitals.

The core marketing strategies spelled out an approach similar to that used by the most successful companies in the retail industry. They were as follows:

- Select services based on their potential to generate consumer self-referrals.

- Focus on services that consumers already associated with CCH and/or services with no clear market leader.

- Target audiences most likely to be involved in health care decision-making.

- Provide a strong "call for action."

- Capture the largely unoccupied "service" position in the marketplace by making it easy for consumers to access services advertised by Carondelet.

- Demonstrate visible support for physicians who are closely affiliated with the hospitals.

Finally, specific annual performance objectives were established for the advertising program:

- To generate 5,000 consumer inquiries.

- To make 500 referrals to physicians affiliated with the Carondelet hospitals.

- To generate 50 hospital admissions.

IMPLEMENTATION

Gaining Management Approval

The scope of the campaign was a radical departure from the hospitals' previous promotional efforts. This coupled with a substantial budget request in the middle of the fiscal year represented an internal "sales" challenge for the Marketing Department.

The advertising concept was first presented to senior management. To allay initial objections or concerns, the marketing staff focused on the purpose of the campaign: to sell "products." It also emphasized that consistency of style and approach (a "family" of advertisements) would strengthen the overall image and name recognition of Carondelet Community Hospitals. Further, it was anticipated that a 12-month, sustained presence in the marketplace vis-a-vis advertising would have a positive cumulative effect, each new month building on the last. Senior management approved.

The next step was intended to expand the base of support. Realizing that broad internal acceptance and support would be critical to the success of the program, the marketing staff identified and presented the concept to key physicians, board members and middle managers in a series of informational sessions conducted over the course of several weeks.

Creative Development

Armed with the necessary approvals, it was time to turn the concept into something tangible, something that would bring patients to Carondelet Community Hospitals. Based on the criteria identified through market research, specific services were earmarked to be included in the ad program. Interviews were held with medical directors, managers and key clinicians of those services who provided technical and operational details critical to accessing their fit with the core marketing strategies. Following these interviews, the final selection of "products" was made:

- Physician Referral Service
- Chemical Dependency Rehabilitation Services
- Obstetrics
- Stress & Depression Management Center
- Osteoporosis Center
- Sleep Diagnostic Center

Drafts of the first two ads, Physician Referral and Chemical Dependency, plus an introductory "catalog" ad were prepared by the agency retained to produce the ads. Creativity and flair were key to their development. Bold headlines and graphics for print and intriguing sound effects for broadcast were combined with a personal copy tone to attract the target audiences. Further, each ad featured a "call to action" and a direct response mechanism.

Customer Services

As the advertising concept evolved, it became increasingly apparent that a critical element was needed. Because of each ad's intent to illicit a consumer response, it was essential that a means be developed that allowed consumers direct access to "product" information.

The tactical approach developed to accomplish this was the creation of a Customer Services Coordinator position. The coordinator -- Paula -- was hired shortly before the campaign began. She was to serve as the conduit between consumers, the services advertised and physicians on staff.

A special telephone number was installed, a line dedicated

exclusively to handle incoming calls generated by specific advertisements. It was further decided that each ad would include a direct reference to Paula, giving callers the name of a specific -- and very real -- person, not simply a switchboard operator. This provided a means of differentiating Carondelet's service from competitive services at the same time reinforcing the "high touch" image consistent with its desired market position as a community hospital.

The Campaign Begins

With all key elements in place, the following advertising schedule was developed and implemented:

Month	1986	Service Advertised
February (10 days)		Introductory "Catalog" Ad
March		Physician Referral Service
April		Chemical Dependency
May		Obstetrics
June		Stress & Depression Management Center
July		Osteoporosis Center
August		Sleep Diagnostic Center
September		Physician Referral Service
October		Obstetrics
November		Stress & Depression Management Center
December		Off

The schedule allocated four weeks for each service, using a combination of major daily metropolitan newspapers and radio. Radio stations were selected based on the demographic profiles of their listeners that match the patient profile of the service advertised. The goal was to reach a level of frequency comparable to what major retailers employ for major sales. (Television advertising was not considered because of cost, lead time and limited flexibility.)

Data Tracking

In order to monitor results, key data elements were identified prior to the beginning of the campaign. Manual data tracking systems were developed that allowed Paula to track the following:

- number, nature and disposition of calls received through the dedicated Customer Services telephone number.

- number of referrals of prospective patients to affiliated physicians, including the actual number of appointments made and kept.

- number of callers who took advantage of special promotional offers associated with the services being advertised (e.g. free assessments, attendance at free seminars, etc.).

- number of callers eventually admitted to the hospital as an inpatient or outpatient.

- demographics of callers, when possible.

RESULTS

All objectives for the year-long advertising campaign were exceeded in just over six months. Results through November of 1986 showed that:

- there was a total of 6,400 consumer inquiries, 1400 more than the annual objective.

- more than 1,600 physician referrals were made, far exceeding the annual projected total of 500. Of those callers leaving their names, more than 40 percent made and kept appointments with physicians to whom they were referred.

- through mid-September, nearly 225 hospital admissions -- more than 4 times the objective set -- could be attributed directly to the advertising campaign.

Because of the single product focus of the campaign, the impact of each ad was unique and the response often unpredictable. Each ad took on a personality of its own, attracting a different audience and resulting in a distinct set of opportunities and problems. Each ad taught the organization something new.

The corporate introductory ad positioned the two affiliated hospitals within the community. It helped promote the general public's understanding of the common ownership of St. Mary's and St. Joseph's by Carondelet Community Hospitals. Further, it served as an introduction to the range of "products" offered through the hospitals.

The physician referral ad marked the introduction of a new service that was designed to serve the needs of both consumers and the hospitals' medical staffs. With traditional patient loyalties being constantly tested, the service was a tangible and highly visible means of supporting the hospitals' respective medical staffs. Referrals that had averaged a handful per month prior to advertising, grew to more than 200 per month, a number that has been equalled or surpassed in every month since the ad was first placed.

The chemical dependency ads generated both national and local media attention, which in turn increased the promotional impact of the advertising. Chemical dependency services saw a significant increase in admissions to their inpatient, outpatient and special adolescent programs.

Advertising for obstetrical services also resulted in patient increases. During the three months following placement of the ad, a record number of deliveries was recorded at one of the hospital's units. This represented a 12 percent increase over the same period of a year before.

The Stress & Depression Management Center, a new service, was publically introduced through mass media advertising. Appearing in June and again in November, the ad generated almost 800 inquiries. In fact, the initial placement was so successful that it was questionable whether it was prudent to run it again due to a continuing backlog of patients.

The consumer response to the osteoporosis advertisements exceeded the most optimistic expectations. In the first six weeks an overwhelming 1,600 calls were received, leading to several hundred outpatient assessments.

The Sleep Diagnostic Center was also a surprise. This small but sophisticated diagnostic service has since tripled its patient load. Second only to osteoporosis, the ad generated over 450 calls in three weeks.

OPPORTUNITIES AND PROBLEMS

Opportunties

Several unanticipated opportunities and problems were identified as the campaign progressed. Ongoing and frequent contact with consumers identified unmet needs that have since been met by expansion of key services within the hospitals. Typical of these opportunities was the addition of an outpatient program within the Stress and Depression Management Center. Also, consumer contact pointed to the need for a program to serve insomniacs, a condition not normally handled at the Sleep Diagnostic Center.

Another opportunity created by the advertising campaign was new sources of patient referral both within the metro

area as well as throughout Minnesota and out-of-state.
Physicians and clinics not previously associated with the
hospitals made referrals as did HMOs, other hospitals, community service organizations and occupational health services.

The advertising campaign has also led to consulting opportunities. The marketing staff provided counsel for the
development of similar programs at other hospitals and is
now exploring other opportunities on a wider scale.

Problems

For the most part, the problems that developed were envi-
able ones. No one anticipated the remarkable level of
response to several of the advertisements. Waiting lists
for services developed. In some cases, hours were extended, more beds added and staffing increased to accommodate
the demand.

Calls to Paula mounted in number, with a record setting
200 inquiries in one eight-hour period! At times all
available department personnel were called upon to assist
with the phone answering detail. Eventually a second
staff person was added to handle the growing volume.

It soon became apparent that the department was in critical
need of an automated system to manage the data generated
by the ad program. The manual tracking systems originally
developed quickly became dinosaurs as the paper mounted.
It was not unusual, for example, for one ad to generate
literally thousands of pieces of paper. The necessary
computer equipment was ordered.

FOLLOW-UP

During the months ahead, a careful review of market share
data will be conducted. Because there is significant lag
time in the compilation of these data by local government
sources, the currently available data do not reflect the
time period of the hospitals' advertising campaign.

The baseline consumer research conducted at the start of
the campaign will be repeated to determine changes in consumer preferences for advertised services. The findings
coupled with the results of internal evaluatory systems
will lay the foundation for future market planning. They
will be vitally important in the selection of services to
be advertised as well as development of new services and
the future enhancement of existing services.

Advertising Health Services - What Works, What Fails

Trevor Fisk
Thomas Jefferson University Hospital, Philadelphia

(This presentation is partly based on a recent book, Advertising Health Services - What Works, What Fails by Trevor A. Fisk and published by Pluribus Press, 160 E. Illinois St., Chicago, IL 60611.)

Hospital advertising has been around now for at least a decade. Indeed, at Jefferson we can trace use of advertising of clinical services back to March 1825.

So why is there still any controversy about hospitals advertising? Americans and American institutions, including hospitals, are remarkably responsive to innovations. They try them and adapt to them rapidly.

The major reason why innovations get rapidly adopted is simple - people see that they work. One of the major reasons why hospital advertising is still in many places controversial is that its practitioners have done a poor job in proving its worth.

The only good ad is one that works. However attractive, however popular <u>within</u> a hospital an ad may be, if it does not work it is a bad ad.

A lot of the hospital ads which you see today are good ads. You see a lot, however, which are bad and some that are ugly. You see very few that have been clearly demonstrated as effective.

So, what does it take to advertise health services effectively and to demonstrate that you are doing so?

The short answer is that it takes action at each of five critical steps in advertising:

- <u>before you start to advertise</u>
- <u>in selecting an agency to work with</u>
- <u>in defining the platform for each ad campaign</u>
- <u>during an ad campaign</u>
- <u>after the fact results analysis.</u>

At each of these steps, you have an opportunity to influence the value of the dollars spent and to demonstrate that you are doing so.

Before You Start To Advertise

Many people start advertising with false expectations about what it can and cannot do and what it takes. Advertising does one thing better than any other form of communication.

<u>It is the most efficient way to convey a relatively simple motivational message to members of a large population whose identity is unknown to you.</u>

There are several components to that statement. An advertising message must be relatively simple. An advertising message must be motivational - its purpose is to influence "consumer" behavior. Advertising is economic when it addresses a large audience but only needs a small minority to respond to be worthwhile. If the audience which you need to address is small, or if it is large but you know by name those most likely to respond, there are better marketing options than advertising - such as sales calls or direct mail.

As you will also see in that definition of advertising, its goal is to motivate action - to influence behavior. Doing that well demands a good understanding of how the target audience currently behaves, makes decisions and takes action to seek health care. Effective advertising rests upon good market research. At Jefferson, for every $10 spent on ads, another $2 is spent on researching public attitudes and behavior. We do so because we do not take it for granted that we already know how people think and act about their health.

Above the door to the oracle at Delphi in ancient Greece was carved the inscription - "know thyself." For a marketing executive that is dangerous advice because you are almost certainly unrepresentative of your customers. Your imperative is to "know thy target audience."

It is also vital to understand the basics of motivation. Behavior modification depends upon repetition and reinforcement. Consequently, an effective ad campaign has to achieve a minimum frequency - or critical mass of repetition - to have any impact. The rule-of-thumb is an absolute minimum of 4 exposures to the target audience within a fairly short time-span (a few weeks at most). Many well-conceived hospital ads currently receive insufficient frequency.

Behavior modification which is voluntary - with no "punishment" for non-response - also demands that you make the desired behavior as easy as possible. Ads for consumer products - like cereals or soaps - have a relatively easy task to perform because the audience is likely to encounter the product when next shopping in a supermarket. The job of the ad is to pre-dispose you to pick up that product when encountered. The processes by which patients get into contact with health care require more deliberate effort and are more complex. Again, many health ads, otherwise excellent, fail at this critical step of making response as easy as possible.

Selecting An Ad Agency

Selecting the "right" ad agency is no substitute for thinking these issues out for yourself. Although hospital advertising is not new, nor is it old enough for a major body of experience to have been acquired by any agency. There are "rules" which can be followed in any sphere of advertising to maximize effectiveness. (For example it has been well demonstrated that headlines under photos are better read than headlines printed above - and so on.) However, each field of advertising also has special "rules" for effectiveness.

In each case, it has taken decades of trial and error and of research, plus multi-million ad programs, to reach such conclusions. No agency has yet acquired comparable hospital experience.

In any event, even in these well-developed fields of advertising, the best ads come from a close partnership between client and agency. There are 4 critical decisions in any ad campaign:

- what message shall we convey
- to what target audience
- using what motivational message(s)
- through which media?

For the first two questions, the client should know best. It is his business. Even so, he should listen openly to the challenges to his assumptions posed by the agency. Even if it

does not know the business as well as the client, it is often in a better position to think like the audience.

For the second two questions - the content of the ad and media selection - the agency should know best. These are its fields of expertise, but a thoughtful client will also question and contribute to ad development and placement decisions.

At Jefferson, our agency is the largest Philadelphia-owned ad agency - Weightman/ Schaefer. Our working relationship with them involves almost daily contact and is characterized by "creative tension." We spend a lot of time arguing back-and-forth with each other but always from a position of mutual respect, and we only ever challenge their judgements based upon our own understanding of advertising principles or our own insights into patient attitudes - never based on unsubstantiated whim.

There is a further key aspect to that relationship. Hospitals have complex governance structures - and university hospitals even more so. An agency willing to negotiate its ideas through your governance structure is an agency with time on its hands and not one that you want. For advertising to be effective you cannot pay for unnecessary agency hours. Nor can you design your ads by committee. One of the key jobs of a hospital marketing executive is to be the interface between the institution and the agency.

Developing A Campaign Platform

Much as you and your agency may resist the self-discipline involved, before you even start designing an ad you should set down a campaign platform in writing. The process compels you to face up to any "fuzziness" in your ideas. It should initially answer the following questions:

-   What specifically are we advertising?

-   Who do we want to motivate, where and why?

-   Which medium will we use and why?

-   What principal benefit is this audience seeking?

-   What are the intrinsic technical advantages?

-   How initially do we think our ad might capture attention?

-   How initially do we think that our ad might create awareness?

-   How initially do we think our ad will create preference?

-   How initially do we think that our ad might motivate action?

At this stage, a further opportunity is present - to test the proposed platform by focus group or by cross-reference to earlier market research findings. Minimally, the platform should be reviewed by formal criteria, not unstructured assessment. We, for instance, refer to Dick Twedt's Theme Test. The platform is critically reviewed for its desirability to the larger audience, its credibility to them and the uniqueness of the theme to us vs. competitors.

Most of my recent book is devoted to setting out and illustrating systematic techniques for reviewing proposed ads for print media, outdoor billboards, radio and television.

Time prohibits summarizing it fully today, but we will take print media ads as an example of its approach.

To be effective, an ad must move a reader through the so-called "hierarchy of effects." It must:

-   Capture attention
-   Create awareness
-   Create preference
-   Motivate action.

If it fails at any one of these steps, an ad cannot be effective. Indeed, it may be worse than no ad at all. One, for instance, that only captures attention and creates awareness of a medical benefit to be obtained may just increase demand for the services of your competitors (if that is where the target audience's pre-disposed preference to turn for service lies).

To achieve these four steps, a print ad can have up to six elements (shown as column headings below):

1.	2.	3. Body Copy	4.	5.	6.
Illustration	Headline	Copy	Offer	Signature	Layout

Capture attention
Create awareness
Create preference
Motivate action

We call this matrix TEAM (Task/Element Ad Matrix). To evaluate a print ad, you take each element and consider how much it contributes to performing each task:

-   If no attempt seems to have been made score a 0. (For instance, the headline may create awareness of a health benefit to be obtained but not attempt to create preference for the sponsor hospital as the place to obtain it.)

-   If the ad seems to contribute positively to performing a task, score it between +1 and +4.

-   If the ad seems to you actually to detract from carrying out the task, score it between -1 and -4.

As you will see, the scoring does call for judgement. What, for instance, is the difference between a headline worth +4 for capturing attention and one worth -4? Even if your experience in evaluating ads is limited, following the matrix will keep you focused on the issues of major importance - as you will see shortly.

Here is a hospital print ad from Florida and the TEAM matrix for it. (To be shown and discussed.)

Here for comparison is an ad from a Massachusetts hospital for a similar service - a place to take a child in an emergency. It emphasizes a different benefit - availability - but could be easily adapted to the idea of concern for the parent. It was a good ad when we first saw it, but the hospital made a few small changes that we recommended. (To be shown and discussed.)

In summary, the eventual effectiveness of an ad is critically dependent upon how early proposals are evaluated. Doing that depends upon experience but also upon being systematic.

During An Ad Campaign

However professional and thoughtful you may be in developing ads, there is still an element of uncertainty in any campaign.

Large-scale advertisers usually, therefore, take care both to pre-test ads and to test two or more versions in the initial phase of a campaign.

Here (to be shown) is the draft of an ad used at Jefferson to promote the hospital as a source of help in selecting a physician. Here is the final version. The differences look subtle, but are, in fact, major - with the addition of the response coupon and the careful selection item of final illustration. (Incidentally, this ad won a 1986 Philadelphia "Addy" for the best black and white ad of the year to appear in the region's media.) We were confident from this review process that we had a strong ad. However, because of Jefferson's location, younger affluent people are also important to us. We had concerns that they might not identify well with the older couple, and that some younger women might actually resent the "subservience" of the wife to the husband.

The two other versions were, therefore, developed emphasizing the "self-interest" of younger women

and men.

The three ads were given equal media placement and frequency through the first 6 weeks of the campaign. We then analyzed in detail the computerized records of all who had responded by mail or phone. "He's My World" had drawn 10 times the response of "What A Difference" and 15 times the response of "I Ask The Experts." Among younger women, "He's My World" had produced 4 times as many inquiries as "I Ask The Experts." Despite being tailored to an older audience, it was much more appealing to them.

Consequently, we dropped "I Ask The Experts" and re-allocated those media dollars to greater frequency for "He's My World," thereby doubling our overall response for the same dollars. We continued to run "What A Difference," as it seemed to have a comparable pull to "He's My World" among younger men.

This example is just one illustration of an ongoing process of monitoring results and adjusting a campaign accordingly.

After The Fact

There are a wide range of methods available for "auditing" the results of advertising.

The most direct and accessible, as the previous example showed, is to track inquiries generated.

To do so, the ad must of course have an inquiry mechanism. It is amazing how many you see that do not.

"Inquiries generated" is the most immediately available measure that ads are having an impact. However, it is an imperfect indication of the pay-off from advertising.

The next most valuable measure is of changed levels of awareness and preference resulting from advertising. There are various services with standardized methodologies to survey ad impact available to large-scale national advertisers. The best known include Starch, NETAPS and Triplex. They are not readily accessible or affordable for smaller-scale local advertisers, but their methodologies can be imitated in other types of surveying.

At Jefferson, our advertising has been paralleled by periodic public surveys. They are used to gather further insights into consumer attitudes as new strategic issues arise within the hospital. They are also used to quantify the level of public awareness of, and preference for, the hospital and services which have been advertised.

Finally, it is also possible to track actual increased usage and to quantify its financial value. To do so depends, however, upon the co-operation of the physician offices/hospital units to which new patients come.

Here is part of a series of ads promoting specific Jefferson services. I cannot, for competitive reasons, disclose to which of these ads the following data relate. It is one of them. The relevant hospital service asked each new patient how he or she had learned of the program.

You will see that the program involved is a small one. So why all the advertising effort? Our marketing strategy at Jefferson is based on promoting both the hospital as a whole and a wide range of specific services, both large and small, but each with potential to enhance patient volumes. As you know, Pete Rose holds the all-time record for hits in baseball, but most of them have been singles. I seems to us that a lot of current hospital advertising strategies swing for home runs and miss the ball completely. Strong marketing performance comes more often from successive small achievements.

The ads for this specific Jefferson program ran for one month in various publications. Prior to that month, new patients had averaged 11 monthly. In the month in which the ads ran and the 2 subsequent months, volume rose to "maximum" capacity of 45 new cases per month.

They identified for us the minimum set of tests and treatments which all new patients received on an outpatient basis. They also identified the admission rate - between 10% and 15% of new patients seen.

We then went to Jefferson's very sophisticated
cost accounting system and identified the
revenue generated by 70 new patients.

The campaign took $21,000 of hospital money
and over a 3 month period paid it back, plus
another $38,650 - a sound "investment" by any
standards.

Conclusion

The major reason why hospital advertising has
proved more controversial is largely because
little effort has been made to prove that it
works too.

Several people who have heard me talk before
or read my book, ask if I literally mean that
the effectiveness of all advertising is
measurable. Aren't there general image ads
which are worth pursuing even if not directly
measurable? Our view is "no." All ads are
measurable, and all ads should be measured,
because no institution can afford to put
infinite resources into advertising. It
must use its dollars wisely. You have all
heard Bill Wrigley's famous statement that
"I know that half of my ad dollars are
wasted, but I don't know which half."
However, he said that 60 years ago, and since
then, to borrow an ad slogan, "we've come a
long way, baby." Like medicine itself,
advertising can and should proceed by
systematic diagnosis, prescription,
treatment and monitoring of an organization's
market communications needs.

EVALUATING MARKET COMMUNICATIONS:
KEY ROLES FOR MARKET RESEARCH IN THE HEALTH CARE SETTING

Douglas A. Klegon, Ph.D.
Karen E. Lyon

ABSTRACT

Well planned and executed market research can provide the
competitive edge, distinguishing effective from ineffective
market communications. Prior to a communications campaign,
market research helps establish business objectives, determine target audiences, and develop promotional themes.
Following a campaign, market research is crucial in multi-
dimensional evaluation and refinement of future campaigns.

I. INTRODUCTION

Much of the current discussion over the applicability of
marketing to the health care industry is really a result of
dissatisfaction with advertising. As such, the debate is
misdirected. As is clear in any classical definition of
marketing, the key to the marketing process is to design a
product or service that meets the needs and expecations of
consumers. There should be little doubt that hospitals and
other providers within the health care industry need to be
responsive to their relevant markets--including physicians,
patients, and purchasers of services such as insurers and
employers.

Furthermore, market communications have been and will
continue to be an important element in the total marketing
effort. Advertising, one element of market communications,
can convey information to relevant markets and influence
attitudes as well as behavior. To frame the question in
terms of whether advertising does or does not "work" is
inappropriate. The more useful question is how to design
various types of market communications that have a high
probability of achieving objectives.

Developing effective market communications is dependent on
careful formation of business objectives, as well as execution and evaluation. In all of those stages, market
research plays a crucial role. This paper presents
specific applications of the use of market research in
development of objectives, targeting communications efforts
and creative themes, and evaluation of effectiveness.

II. FOCUSING THE CREATIVE PROCESS

A. Setting Business Objectives for Advertising

The value of a marketing communications campaign can only
be evaluated in relationship to predetermined business
objectives. Without a clear understanding of the objectives to be achieved, the effort will lack appropriate
focus. It is clear that objectives are not always readily
quantifiable, particularly for an institution with minimal
previous experience in communications. However, overall
expectations should be clear.

Characteristics of the product itself constitute one
variable likely to influence strategy. For example, a
minor emergency service will involve business objectives
very different from those of tertiary care for cardiovascular disease. Minor emergency care is a price sensitive
localized market. At any given time, a significant portion of the target market may have use of the services
available. However, need for the service may be of limited duration, since some potential users will have self
limiting conditions. For these reasons, advertising for an

urgent care center should focus on quick response, immediate volume increases. Incentives to immediate action
(e.g., special pricing or premiums) are likely to be very
important in such a situation.

At the other extreme is tertiary care activity. The
market is more geographically dispersed, conditions are
not likely to be self-limiting, there are fewer people in
need of the service at any one point in time, and there
frequently is a intermediary customer affecting choice of
tertiary care providers (i.e., the referring physician).
In such a situation, promotion of tertiary cardiovascular
services should not be based on an objective of immediate
volume increases. Instead the goal is more likely to
revolve around long term positioning of the service among
both the lay and referring physician markets. Furthermore, calls to immediate action through price incentives
or premiums are less relevant than a comprehensive advertising, sales, and public relations strategy.

Given any overall strategy appropriate for the product,
market research can then serve to refine the business
objectives. In the case of the urgent care center with
its focus on immediate volume, this may take the form of
an analysis of past visit trends, patient origin data
relating to market share, and new patient percentages.
From such an analysis, volume expectations can be developed. In the case of tertiary care, market research
might take the form of a base line consumer and/or referring physician survey to determine perceptual market position. Changes in image and top-of-mind awareness could
then be measured after the campaign to determine if objectives were met.

B. Determining the Target Audiences

As in other aspects of the marketing process, market
segmentation is also important in communications. The
target market for an advertising campaign must be consistent with the business objectives for the product or
service, and must be clearly articulated. Otherwise, even
the most innovative creative effort is likely to fail.

In identifying the target audience for market communications, traditional market segmentation variables should be
considered, including demographic, geographic, life style
and attitudinal variables. In addition, the specific
aspects of health care decision-making and the existing
patterns of care need to be examined.

For example, consider the health care decision-making
process for the particular service or program that is the
focus of the advertising campaign. Traditionally, the
personal physician or the specialist played the most important role in determining what health services were
needed and what health care provider would be used. While
this remains true, today health care consumers and their
family members are increasingly becoming health care
decision-makers. In addition, third party payors are
decision-makers regarding the use of health care services.
Therefore, it typically is necessary to develop market
communications plans for a variety of audiences, specifically focusing on those products and services for which
the audience has some role in the decision-making process.

The demographic characteristics of the decision-maker
should be considered when designing the campaign and eval-

uation strategy. For patients these may include: age, health care status, income, primary source of information about health care, and third party payor. For physicians, these may include: specialty, staff or non-staff status, patient load related to the service program, and high/low admitter status.

It is particularly important to keep in mind that the characteristics of the decision-maker are not always the same as the user of the service. For example, decision-makers regarding use of a nursing home are often the sons and daughters of the users. Advertising targeted directly at the elderly person may not be effective. Similarly, it remains true that women are the predominant decision-makers regarding their family's health care. Thus, advertising is often disproportionately targeted at them.

The geographic characteristics of the target audience should also be defined for the campaign. This will be particularly important in making choices about media placement. Media vary significantly in geographic bredth and selectivity, and the goal should be to be as focused as possible. For a single site service with a limited geographic draw, television is frequently inappropriate. However, if the distribution system for the service is more widespread, then television can be a cost-effective medium.

The target audience may also have special life style characteristics that need to be considered when designing the campaign and its evaluation. For example, communications for an obstetrics program targeted at professional women who have delayed child birth could not be promoted through appearances on local day-time talk shows. The target audience would be at work--not listening to the show.

Existing patterns of health care should be considered at this stage of the project. What health care providers are currently being used, what services are currently being used, the likelihood of patients changing providers, the likelihood of physicians changing referral patterns, the presence of HMO's, and the perceived reputation of the hospital and its competitors should be considered in relation to the target audiences. In other words, to what extent do market communiations have to overcome existing patterns versus create new demand?

C. Developing Market Communication Themes

The purpose of advertising and other forms of market communications is to motivate the desired reponse in the target audience. Setting business objectives determines the "desired response," and identifying the target market determines the "audience." Then those responsible for the creative process have the job of figuring out the best way to elicit that response from the audience. Market research can be crucial in guiding the creative process by determining which themes are most important to the target audience, as well as by testing the ability of proposed creative approaches to communicate those themes.

Survey research is often the most appropriate approach for initial investigation of the themes that are relevant to the target audience. For example, telephone surveys have been successfully used by Henry Ford Hospital to determine salient attributes in the choice of ambulatory care providers. The hospital operates seventeen ambulatory care centers in southeast Michigan. Prior to engaging in major advertising efforts, the traits most influencing choice of provider needed to be investigated. The creative approach could then mirror the themes determined during the market research process. In this case, the research indicated the need to stress factors such as the nature of the physician relationship, a personal atmosphere, and the quality of care. Themes often stressed in promoting ambulatory care centers, such as the range of services and the existence of extended hours, were judged to have less of an impact.

As another example, Henry Ford Health Care Corporation operates Health Maintenance Organizations in a variety of environments, ranging from relatively mature HMO markets to those in which HMOs were only recently introduced. Advertising approaches in such varied markets must differ significantly. Existing perceptions in the marketplace vary, as does the nature of competition. Therefore, market research was used in the newer market to determine which issues were perceived as barriers to joining an HMO, as well as the weaknesses of traditional indemnity insurance.

Given the initial development of the market communications approach, market research can also help assure that the creative effort is perceived as intended. That is, has the desired strategy been effectively translated into a advertisement in which the target market receives the desired message? For this purpose, focus groups are likely to be the most useful. For more than a year Henry Ford Hospital has been engaging in an aggressive television advertising campaign to promote tertiary care services. As part of the development process, multiple advertisement concepts are tested with consumer groups.

The focus groups are typically presented with an inexpensive mock-up of the commercial. Story boards are video-taped, with narration and limited music. Although very rough depictions of finished commercials, the focus groups provide valuable information about the impact and clarity of various graphic and script concepts.

In sum, effective advertising must first be based on knowledge of what will motivate the target audience, and second, on sound execution that successfully communicates desired messages. In both cases, well constructed market research is crucial. An advertising agency, no matter how good creatively, cannot be expected to produce effective advertising if the client has failed to investigate what is salient to the audience, and worked closely with the agency in translating that knowledge into advertising that meets business objectives.

III. THE CHALLENGE OF EVALUATING EFFECTIVENESS

Even the best market researchers working together with the most creative advertising team cannot assure success every time. It is always necessary to evaluate major market communication campaigns, and to learn new ways to enhance future efforts for a product or service. In this section some of the methodological difficulties in evaluating advertising are discussed, as well as ways to minimize those difficulties. Then in the following section, examples of various types of evaluation are discussed.

A. Difficulties in Evaluating the Effects of Market Communications

Numerous difficulties arise when attempts are made to evaluate the effectiveness of an advertising campaign. These problems can be simply categorized as: internal, external, and methodological challenges.

1. Internal Challenges

Internal challenges are the difficulties within the health care organization that can impede the evaluation process. One common internal challenge is the need for personnel and financial resources for evaluation. A health care provider may not have staff with the skills required to conduct market research and may not have a relationship with a high quality market research firm. Furthermore, the health care provider may have budgeted for the production of the advertising campaign, not for its evaluation.

The evaluation of market communications is frequently an after-thought and, as such, time becomes an internal challenge. The health care provider and advertising agency may become so involved in the production of an advertising campaign, that little attention is devoted to the prior design of the evaluation phase of the project.

Another internal challenge is the lack of baseline information about the service or product being marketed. For example, if the purpose of a campaign is to increase consumer awareness and image of a hospital's perinatal services, it is necessary to have a benchmark study of the target audience prior to implementation of the campaign. Thus, the baseline which is used to set business objectives should also provide a comparison for the evaluation of results.

2. External Challenges

Since the delivery and marketing of health care services does not take place in isolation, intervening factors need to be considered during design and evaluation of the advertising campaign. Where there is intense competition among health care providers, it seems that the external variables become even more difficult to determine and isolate. These factors may include the marketing communications of competitors, news items about new treatment modes or other breakthoughs, and other events which occur and are beyond the control of those implementing the advertising campaign and its evaluation.

There is no easy solution to the problem of external events. A "pure" efffect of market communications efforts will not likely be determined. However, time series data (e.g., periodic measurements of volume and/or attitude changes) can provide rough indicators. Whereas single measurements are very sensitive to a unique external occurrence, repeated longitundinal measurment is more likely to be informative.

3. Methodological Challenges

The type of marketing communications being planned and the audiences to be reached create their own unique challenges related to evaluating the effectiveness of the campaign. For example, there can be difficulty obtaining objective evaluative information from the desired populations and samples.

Difficulties may arise in constructing the survey instrument so that it is both valid and reliable. Technical words that may be appropriate for a survey of physicians can be misunderstood or not interpreted the same way when used in a survey of health care consumers.

One common difficulty when evaluating the effects of market communications is deciding what data collection method to use. As will be discussed in the next section, the choice of a data collection method will contribute to the outcome of the evaluation. The allowable time frame, financial resources, type of data needed, and the types of target audiences all affect the method of data collection chosen.

Depending on the research skills of the staff or consultant and the quality of the survey instrument and data collection, data analysis can be viewed as either very productive or another "challenge." A survey instrument that contains many open-ended questions may result in data that are not easily interpreted. The meaning of the phrase "garbage in/garbage out" becomes apparent during the data analysis phase.

Reporting the results of the evaluation can be as challenging as the design of the advertising campaign. Final reports have limited value if they do not concisely summarize findings, or are not clearly related to business objectives and future strategies. When this is the case, the results of the evaluation are forgotten, and marketing and administrative personnel tend to use intuition rather than objective data for future decision-making. Intuition,

although a valuable input into decision-making, is by itself a dangerous basis on which to risk the success of marketing communications efforts.

B. Ways to Minimize Evaluation Difficulties

Even the most experienced researcher evaluating the best designed advertising campaign can be faced with difficulties. However, careful planning, the implementation of high quality research methods, and adequate personnel and financial resources can minimize evaluation difficulties. Some suggestions are discussed below.

Attention to the evaluation of the advertising campaign early in the project is important. The design of the evaluation strategy can begin as soon as the business objectives and target audience are determined. Throughout the project, it is critical that those evaluating the campaign work closely with other marketing staff and the advertising agency. These people are key resources for identifying the types of information to be obtained and coordinating the timing of the evaluation phase.

To obtain information that is generalizable to the target audiences, several sampling issues must be addressed. Complete population lists must be obtained; appropriate sample sizes and types of samples must be selected; and, the desired levels of confidence and accuracy of the data must be determined.

In most cases, measurement of changes in consumer perceptions will be part of the evaluation. The design of the survey instrument should be a group process involving key persons, particularly those who are designing the advertising campaign and will be using the data. Careful attention must be devoted to constructing reliable and valid questions. We recommend pretesting the survey instrument with members of the target audience; however, we recognize that with some advertising campaigns this is not always possible.

The method of data collection selected must match the need for information and the target audience. A variety of methods for collecting data can be used in one study. The importance of obtaining a high response rate must be recognized and nonresponse bias needs to be minimized. Where appropriate, confidentiality for both the health care provider and the respondent must be preserved.

The analysis of the data and presentation of results must be useful and easy to understand. High quality tables and graphics can enhance the written findings and can increase understanding. In addition, results should clearly relate to business objectives and implications for future decision-making.

IV. ELEMENTS OF SUCCESS: WHAT TO EVALUATE

The business objectives of a market communications campaign will guide the evaluation process. However, there are four potential elements of success that are important to consider:

1. Patients (Volume and Profitability)
2. Performance (Service)
3. Promotional Message (Creative Approach)
4. Perceptions (Image Change)

In essence, there are "four P's" of evaluation. Which are most important for any given product or service will depend on the overall strategy that has been adopted.

A. Patients

"Patients" refers to volume changes (and associated

profitability) that occur as a result of a market communications campaign. As indicated earlier, it is generally difficult to isolate the effect of advertising--other events occur in the environment at the same time. However, trending of volume changes is generally helpful.

One approach that has been used by Henry Ford Hospital is to monitor ambulatory care visit volume before and after advertising efforts. The results have then been subjected to "dummy variable" regression analysis, with the dummy variable corresponding to pre versus post campaign months. Such an approach not only measures the size of the change in volume, but also indicates results in a predictive model for future growth.

B. Performance

"Performance" refers to the ability to meet expectations raised by advertising. Objections to advertising in health care are often related to misguided perceptions that advertising necessarily promises more than is delivered. In fact, health care advertising that promises the "best" care or gives an impression of universal "cures" is not legitimate. Well intentioned advertising must be backed by a product or service that delivers as promised. For this reason, part of the evaluation of advertising should include an assessment of performance.

There are a variety of methods available to monitor performance. In terms of subjective measures, two of the most common at Henry Ford Hospital are satisfaction surveys, and "mystery shopping." Satisfaction surveys are routinely done, and include evaluations of specific physicians. Formal departmental reviews often include the results of satisfaction surveys. Mystery shopping has also become increasingly common. For example, a caller might play the role of a nurse in a physician's office inquiring regarding an appointment with a consultant. The reponse to the caller will be formally evaluated, with appropriate feedback. Finally, objective measures of performance are also used. Waiting times, appointment access, and other relevant measures are objectively monitored.

C. Promotional Message

"Promotional message" refers to the effectiveness of the creative approach in communicating the intended message. If an inappropriate promotional theme has been chosen, then having it perceived accurately will be of little consequence. However, assuming an appropriate theme has been chosen, then its effective communication is crucial.

Just as focus groups can be used to pretest commercials, they can also be used to retrospectively evaluate the impact of a commercial. Henry Ford Hospital has tested final commercials for its own services, as well as those of competitors. In that way it is possible to evaluate the relative merits of various creative approaches for similar products.

Surveys also have a role in evaluating creative approaches. A telephone survey was done following a direct mail campaign for an ambulatory care center. The creative material was to communicate the personal nature of care received at the center, as well as a strong patient-physician relationship. The post-test revealed that consumer perceptions towards the ambulatory care center changed positively on those dimensions. Thus, the creative material was successful in communicating the intended message.

D. Perceptions

"Perceptions" refers to the impact of the market communications on the positioning of the product or service within the mind of the consumer. Top-of-mind awareness, as well as positioning on specific attributes affecting behavior, are frequent goals of advertising.

In the discussion of setting business objectives, it was noted that perceptions may be particularly important for tertiary care services. Therefore, in conjunction with the promotion of tertiary services, Henry Ford Hospital conducts periodic consumer telephone surveys. In evaluating the impact of market communications, overall changes in position vis-a-vis competitors are measured. In addition, recall of advertisements is explored. In particular, those with recall versus without recall of advertising are compared in terms of perceived image of various tertiary services offered by the hospital.

E. Choosing the Appropriate Methodology

The choice of an approach to evaluating an advertising campaign depends on research objectives, resources, and respondent considerations. Regarding research considerations, the decision to measure patients, performance, promotional message, and perceptions affects the decision about methodology. The need for qualitative data requires one type of method; in contrast, the need for quantitative data requires another. In addition, the types of target audiences for the campaign must be considered because they affect the type of methodology chosen.

One resource consideration is the budget for the evaluation portion of the project. Compared to a telephone survey, a well-designed mail survey can obtain the desired information and be less expensive. Face-to-face interviews, of course, are the most costly. Another resource consideration is personnel. Whether the health care provider has the personnel to design and implement the evaluation study or chooses to hire a consultant is a major consideration when planning the evaluation of an advertising campaign. The time frame within which data are needed is also an important resource consideration. More time must be allowed for mail and face-to-face surveys; telephone surveys can be completed in a shorter period of time.

Considerations related to the respondents or target audiences also affect the choice of evaluation methodology. The need for respondent confidentiality or anonymity of the sponsoring health care organization affects the method. Finally, personal characteristics, such as literacy, physical disabilities, and availability should be considered to insure that an appropriate methodology is selected.

Thus, there is no single correct methodology. Just as marketing involves appropriate matching of the product to the needs of the target market, so too evaluation is a question of matching the methodolgy to the specific characteristics and objectives of the market communications campaign.

V. CONCLUSION

As the health care industry has responded to changes in the external environment by becoming more competitive, marketing and market communications have new significance. To assure effective market communications, market research is essential. Careful market analysis helps set business objectives, target markets, and develop promotional themes. In particular, market research can provide knowledge about the appropriate decision-maker for the service being promoted, the messages that will motivate those decision-makers, and how to convey those messages. Finally, market communications campaigns should include a well designed evaluation stage. The effectiveness of a campaign can be judged in terms of patients (volume), performance (service), promotional message (creative approach), and perceptions (image change). Without adequate evaluation, it is not possible to enhance the effectiveness of future promotional strategies, and gain a competitive advantage.

MARKETING INNOVATIONS AND CASE STUDIES

The increasingly privatized and highly competitive health
care market has led health care providers to unbundle
their services and more narrowly segment their target
markets. This has unleashed creative energies in the
development of new services or repackaging of spin-offs
by a growing number of hospitals and health care systems.

This section provides further evidence of this trend.
The authors provide insights into the development and
marketing of innovative health services - mental health
and chemical dependency programs (Yost); rehabilitation
facilities (Matthew); indigent care (Kinney); and consumer
information referral systems (Plumlee).

MARKETING STRATEGIES FOR REHABILITATION FACILITIES

Cindy B. Matthews, Baylor Institute for Rehabilitation, Dallas, Texas

ABSTRACT

Rehabilitation is currently a "hot" topic among health care providers. Because of the DRG-exempt status, many hospital administrators are turning to rehabilitation units to fill empty beds. Since the rehabilitation industry is growing rapidly, health care marketing professionals should be aware of strategies to use in marketing rehabilitation programs.

This case study will describe a practical marketing model which was utilized by the management team at Baylor Institute for Rehabilitation in Dallas, Texas. By setting specific objectives and implementing an aggressive marketing program, management was able to dramatically shift the hospital's patient and payor source mix. (This case study was awarded the Gold Award for Achievement for Marketing Communications, Total Expenditures over $50,000, by the Academy for Health Services Marketing, March, 1986.)

INTRODUCTION

Baylor Institute for Rehabilitation is a 74-bed, free-standing rehabilitation hospital serving patients who have suffered traumatic head injury, spinal cord injury, stroke or other neurologic and orthopedic disorders. The hospital, located in Dallas, Texas, is an affiliate of the Baylor Health Care System, a 1509-bed not-for-profit, multi-hospital system.

In spring, 1984, Baylor Rehab was functioning with an average daily census of 64.5 and an occupancy rate of 87.2%. The majority of patients (40.5% of patient days) were older stroke victims with the primary payor source being Medicare and Medicaid (53% of patient days). In planning for fiscal year 1985, the management team saw the need for strategic market planning and goal setting. In an increasingly competitive environment, management needed to better position the hospital in the marketplace. A Marketing Department and budget were formulated, and a Marketing Director was employed by the hospital in September, 1984, to assist in planning and to direct all marketing activities.

In developing market strategy for the hospital, a simple marketing model, adapted form Hillestad and Berkowitz (1984), was utilized. The model outlines each step taken in reacing targeted objectives.

FIGURE 1

```
        ┌─────────────────────────┐
        │ Organizational Mission  │
        └─────────────────────────┘
                    ↓
Internal Organization Analysis        External Analysis

        ┌─────────────────────────────┐
        │ Establish Goals and Objectives │
        └─────────────────────────────┘
                    ↓
      Strategy Development and Integration

              ┌────────┐
              │ Action │
              └────────┘
                    ↓
               Evaluate

↑
│
└──────────── Dynamic Process
```

The model begins with the organization's mission which defines the specific business in which the organization functions and the scope of services offered. Having determined the hospital's mission, management at Baylor Rehab proceded toward an internal and external situational analysis.

SITUATIONAL ANALYSIS

Knowing that the situation analysis is the foundation of all market planning, a detailed external and internal analysis was completed. All research was secondary; no primary research was completed at this time.

External Analysis. In performing an external analysis, a number of issues were researched:
- The overall rehabilitation delivery system
- Services already provided or needed in the rehabilitation marketplace
- The competitive environment
- Current and potential purchasers of rehabilitation services
- Service area perceptions

The analysis determined that rehabilitation services were being provided on both an inpatient and outpatient basis and at both freestanding rehabilitation hospitals and in units of acute care hospitals. In Baylor's market area, a number of rehabilitation services were already provided; however, a significant need was determined for additional rehabilitation services for head injured and spinal cord injured patients. Because of the area's neurotrauma centers and the improved technology in saving these patients in the emergency room, there was a growing population of head injured and spinal cord injured patients needing rehabilitation.

The external analysis also showed that the competition was well aware of this growing need for rehabilitation services. Baylor Rehab's primary competitor, another freestanding, investor-owned rehabilitation hospital in Dallas, was building a new 120-bed facility, expanding it's present capacity by 80 beds. Additionally, a number of acute care hospitals were opening rehabilitation units. Because of the DRG-exempt status of rehabilitation units, many hospitals were opening units as a way to fill their empty beds. The external analysis indicated proposed addition of 300 rehabilitation beds for Texas in 1985. It was obvious to management that Baylor Rehab needed to become well positioned in the marketplace before the onslaught of competition.

One of the purchaser of rehabilitation, as shown by the external analysis, was Medicare. Although presently DRG-exeempt, HCFA has been studying the question of reimbursement to rehabilitation providers for quite some time. It is widely believed in the rehabilitation industry that the DRG system will eventually be implemented for rehabilitation providers. Therefore, the management team chose to take a pro-active, rather than re-active, approach to DRG's while formulating marketing objectives.

Internal Organizational Analysis

A number of issues were analyzed in the internal organizational analysis:
   °Strengths and weaknesses of current programs
   °Current referral sources
   °Program development
   °Pricing strategy
   °Promotional activities

In completing the internal analysis, the management team looked briefly at the history of the hospital and its impact on future marketing. Baylor Institute for Rehabilitation was established in December, 1981, as a free-standing rehabilitation hospital affiliated with the Baylor Health Care System. The hospital was initially named Swiss Avenue Hospital. At the time of establishment, it was felt that insurance reimbursement might be difficult to obtain for a rehabilitation institute, thus the hospital was named for the street on which it resides. In June, 1984, the name of the hospital was changed to better describe the hospital's services and to reflect its affiliation with the Baylor Health Care System, a highly reputable name for health care in Texas. Although Baylor Institute for Rehabilitation was a more appropriate name, the change presented a challenge to the Marketing Department to establish name recognition with referral sources and the consuming public.

Through June, 1984, the programs at Baylor Rehab were geared primarily toward stroke patients.

The hospital's patient mix was as follows:

Stroke	40.5%
Head Injury	10.7%
Spinal Injury	20.1%
Other Neurologic/	
Orthopedic	28.7%

(Based on total patient days, calendar year 1983 data.)

Patient days by payor source was as follows:

Medicare	48.2%
Medicaid	2.8%
Blue Cross	3.8%
Other Pay	45.2%

(Based on calendar year 1983 data; other pay includes insurance, private, state agencies and charity.)

Average occupancy rate for fiscal year 1984 was 87.2%. Most patients were directly referred by physicians with many patients coming from the acute care affiliate, Baylor University Medical Center.

GOALS AND OBJECTIVES

Following the Situational Analysis, broad-based goals were established for the hospital by the Executive Director and Board of Trustees. These goals were general guidelines upon which to base management decisions. The overall hospital goals were as follows:
1. Provide for a sound financial future;
2. Maintain a competitively low charge structure;
3. Protect human resource management (i.e. "keep your staff happy");
4. Insure the integrity of a comprehensive Rehabilitation Program.

With these goals in mind, and with consideration of the situational analysis described earlier, specific marketing objectives were developed. The marketing objectives emphasized the desire of the management team to deal effectively (in a pro-active manner) with the possibility of

an impending DRG reimbursement system for rehabilitation. The decision was made to change patient mix by decreasing Medicare/Medicaid patient days and increasing market share of the disorders traumatic head injury and spinal cord injury. Services for head and spinal injured patients were in shortage in Baylor's market area. These disorders were also primarily insurance paying patients which were more desireable finacially. The marketing objectives also addressed the problem of name recognition with the recent hospital name change.

Marketing Objectives:

1. Decrease percentage of Medicare/Medicaid patient days.

2. Increase market share of the disorders Traumatic Head Injury (THI) and Spinal Cord Injury (SCI).

3. Increase awareness of prospective users and potential referral sources to Baylor Rehab and services provided. Measurement of effectiveness:

    a). Number of new physician referrals;
    b). Increased number of patients from various north Texas counties.

STRATEGY DEVELOPMENT AND ACTION

To reach the stated objectives, specific strategy was developed. Initially, new program development was necessary to improve and refine services for head injured and spinal cord injured patients. Consultants were brought in to assist the clinical teams with program development. Additionally, a coordinator for Head Trauma Services was hired to direct the efforts of the head trauma team. Next, an aggressive marketing program was developed to inform referral sources and the consuming public about Baylor Rehab's new services.

Target markets were determined by looking at the referral process and profile of a typical head injured and spinal cord injured patient. The injured individual is usually male, between the ages of 18 and 24. A head injury generally takes place through a motor vehicle accident, often as a result of drunken driving. Spinal injuries generally occur due to a fall, diving accident or automobile accident. Head and spinal cord injured patients usually spend a month or longer in an acute care hospital before being transferred to a rehabilitation facility. The referral can come from a physician, social worker, insurance representative or state vocational counselor. Frequently, the family members tour many rehabilitation facilities before choosing where to send their loved one. Some families "shop" for services only in the Dallas area; others tour all rehabilitation facilities in Texas, and others look nation-wide.

Promotional strategy included a combination of sales and advertising activities. Direct sales activities generally consisted of exhibits at various conferences targeted toward specific referral sources. Direct mail activities were also used to inform targeted referral sources of Baylor Rehab's services. Personalized "update" letters as well as brochures were periodically sent to referral sources to remind them about Baylor Rehab. Print advertisements were placed in professional journals to further draw interest for Baylor's head injury and spinal cord injury programs. Radio advertising was utilized to establish public name recognition. All radio advertisements were PSA in nature. Billboards were also utilized for name recognition and image building.

EVALUATION:RESULTS

After nine months (September, 1984 to June, 1985), the results of the marketing program were measured. In a short period of time, great strides were made in reaching the marketing objectives.

Objective I: Decrease Medicare/Medicaid patient days

Results:

Payor Source by Patient Day

	CY 1983	FY 1985
Medicare/Medicaid	51.0%	39.3%
Blue Cross	3.8%	8.6%
Other Pay	45.2%	52.1%

The average percentage of Medicare/Medicaid patient days at the end of the fiscal year was a significant decrease from the year before.

Objective II: Increase market share of the disorders Traumatic Head Injury and Spinal Cord Injury

Results:

Patient Mix by Disease Category

	CY 1983	FY 1985
Stroke	40.5%	25.2%
Head Injury	10.7%	24.7%
Spinal Cord Injury	20.1%	22.0%
Other Neurological/ Orthopedic	28.7%	28.1%

A dramatic increase was seen in the hospital's population of head trauma patients. This population grew to approximately 25% of patient days based on an average percentage at the end of the fiscal year.

Objective III: Increase awareness of prospective users and potential referral sources to Baylor Rehab and services provided.

Results:

a). From January to June, 1985, a total of 93 new physicians began referring to the hospital. This was in addition to the physicians who historically referred to Baylor Rehab;

b). In 1982, Baylor Rehab received patients from 49 Texas counties. By the end of fiscal year 1985, Baylor Rehab received patients from 70 Texas counties as well as from eight surrounding states.

Additional results: Average occupancy rate for the hospital rose to 91% for fiscal year 1985 from 87.2% the previous year.

CONCLUSION:A DYNAMIC PROCESS

The use of the marketing model described earlier enabled the management team to be systematic about the marketing changes desired at Baylor Rehab. The process was logical, goal-oriented and understandable by all members of the management team. The marketing model is a dynamic process. Constant evaluation of the environment, goal setting and measuring of results are needed to establish and maintain a successful position in a constantly changing health care environment.

In this case study, in addition to accomplishing the stated objectives, the marketing program established a reputation of Baylor Institute for Rehabilitation as a "center of excellence" for catastrophically injured patients. The management team and staff members made a concerted effort to project this image to the community. With the competitor's opening of a new hospital and the addition of new rehabilitation beds in the market place, it was imperative for changes in Baylor Rehab's services and patient/payor mix to be made immediately. The successes of the marketing program well-positioned the hospital to meet the competition head-on and to stand as a leader in rehabilitation services

REFERENCE

Hillestad, Steven G. and Eric N. Berkowitz (1984), Health Care Marketing Plans:From Strategy to Action, Homewood, IL:Dow Jones-Irwin.

BEYOND PHYSICIAN REFERRAL:
CONSUMER INFORMATION AND REFERRAL SYSTEMS
AS A PRIMARY MARKETING STRATEGY

by Ken B. Plumlee, Adventist Health System/West

ABSTRACT

Innovative, sophisticated consumer information and referral systems and other telemarketing applications are increasingly being used to effectively — and efficiently — market a wide range of hospital services and programs.

This paper will look at the shortcomings of traditional physician referral programs and how the addition of hospital and community resources with telemarketing concepts has created an integrated program which answers a basic consumer need while enabling hospitals to cross-sell and aggressively market themselves. Consumer research findings which identify attitudes toward and requirements for hospital-based information and referral programs will also be discussed.

Models of the health care decision making process as it exists in both types of programs will be defined, as well as the marketing strategy that re-shapes the process to the hospital's favor. A point-by-point program comparison will detail capabilities and limitations.

A brief review of how hospitals have implemented integrated information and referral programs will be followed by a case history detailing the experience of a non-affiliated multi-hospital network that co-sponsors such a program.

INTRODUCTION – THE TRADITIONAL PHYSICIAN REFERRAL APPROACH

With varying degrees of success, many hospitals have attempted to increase the use of their facilities by offering consumers free referrals to their staff physicians. The service is designed to eliminate some of the confusion inherent in trying to find a doctor on their own. As one consumer put it: "It's better than picking from the Yellow Pages!" But have you looked under "physicians" in the book lately? You'll probably find ads from numerous physician referral programs.

One survey indicated that the establishment of physician referral programs is currently a high priority among administrators. Indeed, the number of these programs has recently increased substantially, creating a "me too" effect in the marketplace. When almost all hospitals offer the same undifferentiated service, the result is little — if any — competitive advantage.

Traditional physician referral programs seem to work best for the well educated, medically-savvy consumer who has made an initial self-diagnosis and is aware of exactly what kind of specialist he needs and which facility he desires. They are less effective in capturing the consumer who hasn't yet decided that the selection of a physician is the best way to solve their health care problem.

What's the difference? Simply put, a physician referral program is just one of the consumer's many health care access options — not all of which will lead to your door. That's where many referral programs fail.

Obstacles to success

For a traditional physician referral program, one of the greatest obstacles to success is having too narrow a focus; not taking an integrated approach to what a hospital has to offer the prospective patient. By focusing only on physician referral, many hospitals ignore the opportunity to refer directly to other hospital services, e.g., emergency room, specialized clinics, health ed programs, residential programs, and others. There is little emphasis on cross-selling.

Opinion research among consumers indicates several negative aspects typical of many programs:

- A non-holistic approach. Consumers want and need more than just a physician referral program. They want a reliable, dependable and convenient source of health care information and advice, as well as information about the resources available to them from the hospital and the community. Existing programs do not reflect a true marketing approach, that is, to identify a consumer's need and find a solution — not to stop short by considering just one approach or solution.

- Responsiveness. Consumers are frustrated with the inability and unwillingness of the traditional referral programs to answer even basic health care questions.

- Physician quality. Consumers often view physicians affiliated with a referral program as being sub-standard.

- Lack of individualized assistance. Cited was the unwillingness of traditional programs to help the consumer choose from among several physicians.

- The inability to act. Consumers dislike the fact that traditional referral programs are unable to act on the patient's behalf in arranging for health care and "entering the system."

- Advertising overload. Too many competing programs with little differentiation is a factor.

Lastly, the referral program is directly competing against the consumer's informal referral network — the physician recommendations received from friends or other sources.

ADVENTIST HEALTH SYSTEM – FROM SEARCH TO SOLUTION

Our own experience

Because these shortcomings held implications for our own network of Adventist hospitals, we undertook an exhaustive study to determine what improvements could be made. We examined referral procedures in our own hospitals, and many others of all types — metropolitan, rural, large and small. We conducted research with physicians, consumers and administrators and learned their frustrations and their desires.

It soon became apparent that there existed a vast and unanswered need for health care information. Within our own hospitals, we discovered that some were receiving literally hundreds of calls a day, to a variety of departments, from consumers looking for help with health care information. We found that large emergency rooms were averaging 75-150 calls a day for health care information. These calls were largely viewed as a nuisance, rather than as a selling opportunity.

The referral "wish list"

What did consumer's really want? What was needed? What would an ideal program be? The list was extensive.

- Consumers wanted the personal touch. They wanted a "face" to the hospital. It was clear they identified with individual physicians and nurses, rather than the facility itself. They asked for access to a qualified professional who could give them specialized knowledge and refer them to exactly the right person, service or facility. And that had to be someone who was easy to talk to, reliable and compassionate.

  They wanted a "doorway to the health care network." A single point of access for, and proper direction to, all of their health care options.

- They wanted a sympathetic, compassionate person, willing to take the time to listen and discuss issues other than medical intervention, e.g., nutrition, prevention, holistic health.

- Consumers needed a referral program to be able to make immediate referrals for care along with callback and follow up services.

- Finally, they thought that an information and referral program should be available to everyone, regardless of insurance carrier.

BEYOND PHYSICIAN REFERRAL: OVERLOOKED MARKETING OPPORTUNITY REQUIRES NEW TELEMARKETING STRATEGY AND TOOL

The tremendous consumer demand for information beyond physician referral and the desirability of a central, hospital-based telephone resource/contact point identified the potential for an innovative marketing opportunity. The door was open to using telemarketing techniques not only to market hospital services, but to actually exert a significant measure of control in the way that consumers select providers from among their various health care options.

The model below illustrates the role that a traditional referral program plays in the consumer's health care selection process. The role of a traditional referral program is reactive — waiting for the consumer to identify the need for a physician and seek the program's help in making a selection. This approach puts you in communication with the consumer only after they have made a decision about health care, and too late to direct the decision-making process. Selecting a physician is only one of several ways the consumer may choose to solve a health care problem. If he chooses your referral program, he may utilize your hospital.

The Health Care Access Model

```
                    Health
                     Care          Starting Point:
                    Concern        Health Care
                                   Problem or
                                   Question
                         └── etc.

Urgent Care  Emergency  Self Help  Physician  Alternative  Personal    Consumer Options
  Centers      Rooms                  Care        Care       Advice     for Care
                                                                 └── etc.

Advertising  Yellow    Walk-in    Personal   MD Referral  MD Referral  Physician Referral
             Pages     Clinic     Referral   Program A    Program B    Options
                                                                 └── etc.

            Hospital A  Hospital B  Hospital C  Hospital D   Hospital Selection
                                                             Options
```

Our objective was to design a means of access to consumers early in the decision making process that would allow us to control the referral choices and direct the consumer to a particular hospital's staff physicians, services and programs.

The solution: An integrated information and referral "super program"

We created a sophisticated consumer information and referral program that emphasized health information to function as a centralized, integrated "information broker" to assist the consumer and, using telemarketing applications, direct them to a variety of hospital-affiliated resources. Staffed by specially-trained registered nurses, we called this resource program "Ask-A-Nurse™."

Using the program, the health care access and referral model now looks like this:

The Ask-A-Nurse™ Concept

The program is both a triage for health care options and a resource of general health care and community resource information. By eliminating the two decision-making layers in the access model, this kind of program provides a direct line to a hospital's entire offering of services and facilities.

Bearing in mind the results of our research, Ask-A-Nurse™ was developed as a free, 24-hour, nurse-staffed information and referral program that would proactively cross-sell hospital services and generate revenue through increased facility usage.

The core of the concept is the "resource nurse" — the logical choice of a qualified person best able to assess a caller's need, provide personalized information and "next step" advice to direct health care choices.

Another important function is its ability to be a contact point for consumers who may be experiencing problems — in following after-care instructions, with drug reactions, insurance coverage questions, or with the hospital itself. The nurse serves as the consumer's primary link to the health care system.

Results generated

How is such an information and referral program received by the public? Hospitals used to receiving 15-20 calls a day for physician referral are now receiving up to 160-200 calls a day from consumers who are being referred to a broad range of hospital services. One hospital in Hawaii received over 800 calls in 24 hours after television ads for its Ask-A-Nurse™ program appeared. Clearly a need is being served.

Because the program emphasizes health information from a registered nurse, many referrals are made to callers who would not have called a physician referral program. These hospitals are experiencing significant and measurable increases in referrals to their emergency room, specialized services such as substance abuse or women's medicine and other residential programs — in addition to significant increases in physician referrals.

They also find this type of program a convenient and pre-established marketing vehicle for the introduction of new products and services. The data base of demographic information that accumulates with the handling of each call is a valuable resource which can be used in strategic planning and market analysis.

Comparing traditional physician referral with integrated resource referral programs

The differences between the services offered and the results generated by the two types of programs becomes clear with a side-by-side comparison:

Traditional Referral	vs.	Integrated Resource

Functions

Traditional Referral	Integrated Resource
1. Physician referral	1. Physician referral
	2. ER referrals
	3. Referrals to other hospital services
	4. Referrals to community services
	5. Answers health care questions
	6. ER visit follow-ups
	7. Outbound follow-up and other telemarketing appli-cations

Revenue Generation

Traditional Referral	Integrated Resource
1. Generates revenue through physician referrals only	1. Generates revenue through physician referrals
	2. Generates revenue through referrals to ER
	3. Generates revenue through referrals to hospital services and programs

Staffing

Traditional Referral	Integrated Resource
1. Staffed by clerical personnel	1. Staffed by RNs
2. Not qualified to make assessments & referrals	2. Qualified to make assessments and recommendations

Marketing Value

1. Relies on consumer to call in for referral

2. Refers callers to physician

1. Proactively contacts new residents to offer referrals
2. Refers to entire range of hospital services
3. Cross-sells other appropriate services
4. Positions hospitals as community health expert

THE DEVELOPMENT OF AN INTEGRATED RESOURCE REFERRAL PROGRAM

Developing a multi-function information and referral program required a team effort of specialists from several disciplines, and a commitment of both time and money. In the case of Ask-A-Nurse™, the process began with extensive research to determine the needs and desires of the three groups who would depend on the program — consumers, physicians and administrators.

After determining the optimal format and structure of the program, the work began:

- Computer Software — The software package was designed to organize the many functions of the program. Adventist Health System worked in partnership with Travenol Management Services in creating a "nurse friendly" software program that provides easy access to the data base information. Based on Travenol's "HEALTH-MATCH" physician referral program, the Ask-A-Nurse™ program enabled the assessment, referral and documentation of all calls.

    A caller documentation function enables the nurse to keep a record of each caller request or inquiry, responses to protocol questions, and the follow-up options suggested. Documentation also tracks nurse-generated calls to consumers to follow-up on referral services and emergency room visits.

- Policies/Procedures — Standardized operational policies and procedures were established to provide users with recommendations concerning several areas including physician referral, handling of emergency calls, nurse practice, quality assurance and office management. The policy and procedural guidelines were designed to be accepted as is or customized by individual hospitals, and adopted according to their own standards.

- Nursing Assessment Protocols. Extensive effort was involved in the development of protocols that enable the resource nurse to reliably and professionally assess a caller's needs.

- Risk Management Review. A nationally-recognized medical director and risk management specialists thoroughly reviewed and refined all protocols to ensure safety and adherence to accepted procedures.

- Manuals — Comprehensive manuals were produced for each aspect and function of the program, and serve as a backup to the software program. They include Operations, Nurse Inservice, Protocol, Community Resource, and Hospital Services manuals and documentation forms.

- Training — Three formal training programs were developed, including a thorough four-day session of operations training for the product manager, nurse inservice training including telephone assessment and marketing/sales techniques and complete software orientation and operation.

- Field Testing — Ask-A-Nurse™ was field tested at Highline Community Hospital in Seattle, Washington, where a prototype program was in operation. Many of the policies and protocols were developed in conjunction with Highline before being introduced and implemented nationally at other hospitals.

- Marketing and Promotion Components — A full complement of marketing and promotional materials was developed to provide hospitals with the means to inform their communities about the program's services. Program components included:

- Advertising campaign, including TV, radio, print, outdoor and yellow pages ads

- A publicity guide

- A Point-of-Purchase program, which can be co-sponsored by community merchants

- A physician and staff marketing package, to ensure that hospital personnel understand and support the program

- Ongoing creative materials, to keep promotional efforts fresh and effective.

The cost commitment over the two-year research and development period was approximately $3/4 million.

APPLICATION MODELS

Integrated information and referral programs have been established in many hospitals, with each facility's individual situation and objectives, market area size and demographics, affiliation, and other factors determining how the program was set up — individually as a stand-alone (single-hospital), or as part of a network (multi-hospital). Both options had their benefits.

Stand-Alone

Being the only hospital in your service area to offer an integrated information and referral program clearly makes your facility the easiest — and therefore the most likely — to be called. In highly competitive metropolitan areas, offering a program like Ask-A-Nurse™ helps to gain market share as well as reach a highly mobile population — an estimated 18 percent of whom move each year. In rural communities, offering a program positions your facility as the caring and reliable health care provider.

Networks

A group of hospitals, regardless of affiliation status, co-sponsoring a program enjoys an additional advantage in the strategic value of a network: more thorough coverage and extension of their service areas; natural market fit and more resources available to satisfy demand; and economy of scale in sharing operational and promotional expenses.

Approximately 30 hospitals are currently utilizing the Ask-A-Nurse™ program, as stand-alones or networks. These include Adventist Health System hospitals and non-competitive hospitals not members of Adventist Health System. The following case study looks at how Mercy Health Care Organization of Sacramento (now part of Catholic Healthcare West) formed a network of non-affiliated hospitals to form a regional information and referral program.

A CASE STUDY: SACRAMENTO-AREA HOSPITALS JOIN FORCES TO OBTAIN REGIONAL REFERRAL ADVANTAGE

The market

The greater Sacramento, California metro area spans a 50 mile radius with a population around the 1 million mark — growing rapidly. Health Maintenance Organizations claim approximately 40 percent of the market, with Kaiser and FHP serving about 30 and 10 percent, respectively. Major providers in the market include three Sutter Hospitals, three affiliated Mercy Hospitals, and the University of California/Davis Medical Center. More than a dozen other hospitals are located within the regional service area.

Network formation

Doug Bruce, chief operating officer and Morley Robbins, vice president of marketing for Catholic Healthcare West, operator of Mercy Hospital and Mercy San Juan Hospital in Sacramento and Mercy Hospital in nearby Folsom, wanted to create a competitive regional network to capture a greater share of the referral market. Last Fall, they selected Ask-A-Nurse™ as the tool and initiated the formation of an 8-hospital network to share sponsorship of the integrated information and referral program.

The objectives were to establish a viable network for contracting purposes; to provide communications resources to the community; and to augment the hospitals' referral base to their physicians and facilities.

Five of the outlying area hospitals were invited to participate. This combination of facilities would provide referral coverage to fully one-half of the entire metro area. Negotiations were concluded last November and actual program operation began in late January.

In addition to the three Catholic Healthcare West facilities, the network will include Auburn Faith Hospital, Auburn; Marshall Hospital, Placerville; Lodi Memorial Hospital, Lodi; Woodland Memorial Hospital, Woodland and North Bay Medical Center, Fairfield.

Benefits and potentials

In addition to the program's immediate benefits, the participating hospital administrators saw its potential for future growth and flexibility pertaining to overlay opportunities such as:

- Using Ask-A-Nurse™ as a credible and established marketing "pipeline" for new specialized hospital offerings like senior programs or women's health.

- Obtaining new patients from any future HMO or PPO contracts and providing informational and referral service to those consumers.

Network logistics

The network's shared program headquarters is located in Mercy San Juan Hospital. Resource nurses have access to information on all physicians, hospital services and community resources the eight facilities offer. Callers are referred on the basis of location, service or facility needed and other factors that best fit their need.

Formation issues

The network faced a number of issues to consider during the formation and implementation stage. These included:

1. Managing each party's objectives. Determining what each participant wanted to achieve.

2. Referral territories. Determining which facilities would receive referrals from which geographic areas.

3. Protocol for referring callers from "non-claimed" areas. How to refer callers who didn't fall in any hospital's predetermined geographic service area.

4. Specialist referral procedures and referral boundaries.

5. Accountability. Evaluating program effectiveness.

6. Division of program operation and promotional costs. Should participants share costs according to hospital size, on a per capita or referral basis, or equally share the cost of staffing and equipment?

7. Staffing. Determining who is responsible for hiring, paying nursing staff.

CONCLUSION — A VISION FOR THE FUTURE

The growing trend among consumers not to claim a primary doctor, their continuing mobility and the increasing impact of HMOs and PPOs are all factors contributing to the erosion of the traditional doctor-patient relationship.

Where doctors once had sole responsibility for managing patient care, it appears that hospitals will increasingly move into this role — meaning that there will be a sharp focus on the new hospital-patient relationship.

Hospitals will be perceived as the health care experts; the place consumers will turn to first. Consequently, hospitals will be called to exercise the role of health care access controllers, placing new priority on utilization management.

Operational and marketing tools like integrated information and referral programs will significantly assist hospitals in this process and in taking their place as the consumer's entree to the entire health care system.

CORPORATE HEALTH AS A PROFITABLE
DIVERSIFICATION ACTIVITY

David A. Kantor, Bethesda, Inc., Cincinnati

ABSTRACT

As hospitals seek ways of maintaining their current business portfolio and look for new opportunities to generate additional revenue and profits, developing a corporate health services product line has become an item of great interest to many health-care providers. The definition of corporate health services is provided, and the financial and other benefits of successfully developing this product line is explored. Elements of a comprehensive product line are then enumerated, and potential methods for segmenting the market are discussed. Finally, one organization's approach to this market, and their results, are reviewed.

INTRODUCTION

It's old news by now--Medicare's Prospective Payment System, combined with increasing market penetration by various managed care plans (HMOs, PPOs, etc.), has produced decreasing hospital occupancy rates, increased competition, and, for many health-care providers, shrinking profit margins on hospital inpatient-related activities and smaller overall bottom lines. Virtually all hospitals, therefore, are looking for ways to maintain their current business portfolio and are seeking new opportunities to generate additional revenues and profits. Developing and marketing a Corporate Health Services product line is one vehicle to help achieve both of these goals.

WHAT ARE CORPORATE HEALTH SERVICES?

Let's start with things that are not considered Corporate Health Services for purposes of this discussion. It is not "traditional" hospital inpatient and outpatient services for which the individual receiving the service happens to be covered by an employee's group health insurance plan. It also is not any form of alternative delivery system, be it HMO, PPO, or some adaptation thereof. These may very well be extremely important items to pursue--they just aren't part of this topic.

Corporate Health Services is a whole range of health-related services directed at the corporate market to improve a company's profitability through reduced absenteeism and lost time, increased productivity, and lower costs. Employees are frequently the direct beneficiary of these services. Some examples of Corporate Health Services include:

1. Employee Assistance Programs (EAP), which provide an employee with short-term counseling to help the individual deal with personal problems before they affect job performance.

2. Occupational Health Systems, which provide a firm with an on-site health care professional (usually either a physician or nurse) to assist with a variety of health related items, including treatment of on-the-job injuries, first aid training, worker's compensation case management, follow-up with absent employees, personal health/safety training, etc.

3. Treatment of On-the-Job Injuries, either in a specialized occupational health center or at the hospital.

Many other services can be incorporated into a Corporate Health Services product line. A more comprehensive list of services will be noted later in this discussion.

BENEFITS OF A CORPORATE HEALTH SERVICES PRODUCT LINE

There are a number of benefits to be accrued from the successful development and promotion of this product line. Among them are:

1. Make Money

   Corporate Health Services can be a profitable product line, given reasonable investments of time and money. For example, Bethesda's Employee Assistance Program was profitable in only its second full year, as were a couple of our occupational health centers. Of course, Bethesda also has several other programs which, because of their early stages of development, are not expected to be profitable in their own right for several years.

2. Generate Referrals

   On the other hand, even programs which won't be profitable on a stand-alone basis for several years can be profitable to the overall organization in the first year if the indirect benefits of the programs are considered.

   Primary among these indirect benefits is the generation of referrals from corporate health programs to the hospital. Examples of this include the referrals from an employee assistance program to a substance abuse treatment program and referrals for diagnostic testing from an occupational health center. One cautionary note: if you're going to be referring within your own system, you must provide services that are perceived as top quality to avoid any suspicion of conflict of interest. This is particularly true for EAP referrals to your substance abuse treatment program.

   In addition to referrals to the hospital, corporate health services can generate a significant volume of referrals to hospital-affiliated physicians. For example, many on-the-job injuries treated by an occupational health center may require follow-up by a specialist. If the patient does not have a physician for this condition (most don't), referrals can easily be made to physicians loyal to your hospital. (Bethesda currently generates over 100 physician referrals per month in this fashion). If the patient eventually requires hospitalization, it's reasonable to expect that the patient will be admitted to your hospital. But, regardless of the admissions issue, this form of referral generation can be a key component of the "bonding" strategy which many hospitals are now attempting to execute to foster a stronger relationship with their medical staff.

3. Develop On-Going Relationships with Business

   Successful introduction of a corporate health services product line will result in the establishment of long-term relationships and the reinforcement of a positive image with businesses in your community. This can be a key component in the execution of a successful alternative delivery system strategy. If the corporate community has a good image of your organization, they are more likely to buy either your managed care plan or the plans in which you participate. This factor will make you more appealing as managed care plans develop their provider networks, giving you a potential negotiating advantage.

4. Enhance Awareness/Image with Employees

Many corporate health services, such as an EAP or occupational health services, provide health-care organizations with a vehicle for maintaining an on-going presence and continuous contact in a positive manner with a firm's employees. For example, Bethesda's EAP, to ensure employee awareness of the program so that all who need it will use it, incorporates a significant promotion element, including posters at the worksite, direct mail to the employee's home, payroll stuffers, etc. In this fashion, the program helps promote positive community awareness and image of Bethesda.

5. Fulfill Mission

If your organization's mission includes the provision of health care services to address unmet community needs, the development of corporate health services is a logical activity, since this will support the process of developing an integrated health-care system. Employers and employees typically have major occupational health and safety needs that are poorly met at best and not addressed at all in many instances. Development of a corporate health services product line can correct this situation.

MARKET NEEDS

What does the market need? This can vary greatly from market to market, based upon the composition of the employer population and the existing providers of various corporate health programs. For example, the greater the percentage of employment in the manufacturing sector, the higher the number of on-the-job injuries and the greater the importance of providing injury treatment services as part of the product line. Given the transition from a manufacturing to a service economy in this country, obtaining knowledge concerning your market's specific composition and needs is imperative.

Regardless of the specific circumstances of any market, it is safe to say that the business community wants the most productive work force it can get at the lowest possible cost. However, health-related issues can prevent a firm from approaching these ideal circumstances, including:

1. Employee personal problems such as substance abuse, legal issues, troubles with an adolescent offspring or aging parent, financial problems, etc.

2. On-the-job injuries.

3. Potentially unsafe work environment/poor safety practices.

4. Poor employee personal health practices, including smoking, overweight/poor diet, excess stress, lack of exercise.

5. Worker's compensation related items such as inaccurately matching an employee's physical capabilities with job requirements, not validating the extent of an employee's disability as a result of an on-the-job injury, and inefficient rehabilitation of injured employees.

These health-related issues have a significant negative impact on productivity since they produce greater absenteeism and tardiness, poorer on-the-job concentration, slower work speed, more on-the-job accidents, and more lost time due to injury. Moreover, they directly impact employer expenses due to increased worker's compensation costs and health insurance premium expenses.

DEFINING THE PRODUCT LINE

There is a wide variety of services that health-care organizations can provide to address the health needs of the corporate community, and any number of ways to categorize these programs. A listing of some of the services which may be considered for inclusion in a corporate health services product line, along with one method of categorizing them, may be found below.

1. Employment-Related Services

    a. Physical Examinations--Pre-employment, periodic, and executive physicals can be a mainstay of the product line. Depending on the customer's requirements, these exams can range from very rudimentary to comprehensive, half-day physicals for senior executives.

    b. Substance Abuse Screening--Is one of the most rapidly growing products in the corporate health services arena. The health care provider may serve merely as a collection conduit for samples which are sent to an independent lab for testing, or can actually perform the tests in its own lab.

    c. Ergonomic Job Analysis--Evaluates the physical requirements for specific jobs and recommends potential job modifications to minimize the potential for on-the-job injury. This service is most meaningful as part of a thrust to assist companies in addressing their worker's compensation issues.

    d. Work Capacity Analysis--Determines an individual's physical capacity and compares it to the physical requirements of a specific job to minimize the potential for on-the-job injury.

    e. Child Care Services--For either healthy or ill children, located at either the hospital, a company's site, or some freestanding location.

2. Work Site Health & Safety

    a. On-Site Health Professional--Acts as the company's health-care consultant, on either a full-time or part-time basis. The professional is typically a nurse, though some firms may request a physician. An occupational health system which revolves around this professional is generally developed, to provide the other services noted in this section as well as some of the other listed programs, including follow-up with sick or injured employees and worker's compensation case management. In essence, this service provides for the contract management of the firm's occupational health needs.

    b. First Aid Training--Provides training to selected company employees in dealing with on-the-job injuries and provision of first aid.

    c. Health Screenings--For either job-related or seasonal illnesses on a periodic basis.

d. Personal Health/Safety Education--Uses health-care professionals to provide individualized direction to an organization's employees on matters related to their health and on-the-job safety habits.

e. Medical Review of the Worksite--To identify potential job-related health and safety problems resulting from normal organizational operations.

f. Toxicology Programs--Typically include "right to know" programs for employees who work with hazardous materials, emergency procedures, and protocols for use in in case of industrial accidents, etc.

3. On-the-Job Injury and Illness

a. Treatment--Can be handled on-site for the most minor cases. More serious cases can be treated at occupational health centers developed primarily to deal with on-the-job injuries, or at a hospital emergency room. Caution must be exercised in considering the use of the emergency room as the primary location for injury treatment since it is highly unusual to find an emergency room which is prepared to provide the level of service which the industrial customer expects.

b. Follow-Up--With sick and injured employees to ensure that the employee understands and follows a prescribed course of treatment and is not unnecessarily absent from work. This service is typically offered as part of an occupational health system.

4. Personalized Employee Programs

a. Employee Assistance Program (EAP)--Provides short-term counseling assistance to individual employees to help the individual deal with personal problems before they affect job performance. Many people consider assistance with substance abuse problems to be the sole purpose of an EAP. In fact, it may be far wiser to consider providing a "broad brush" EAP which deals with a wide range of personal problems beyond substance abuse (i.e., familial, legal, financial), since substance abuse problems affect 10% of the average workforce, while other personal problems can impact 40% of the typical employee population.

b. Health Promotion Programs--Are those which many health-care providers first offer to the corporate market, frequently as an offshoot of community-directed health awareness efforts. Included in this product segment are smoking cessation, weight management, stress management, physical fitness classes, and computerized risk factor analysis, which identifies an individual's areas of health risk based on medical history, lifestyle, diet, and exercise pattern. There are many opportunities available for segmenting the market for these programs based on sex, age, and level of fitness.

c. Fitness Center--Can either be developed and managed for a specific company or a group of companies. In the latter case, the actual customer may very well be the developer of an industrial park who considers a fitness center to be a good amenity to offer to attract and retain tenants.

5. Worker's Compensation Related Services

Several worker's compensation related services have previously been mentioned. Among the others to be considered are:

a. Case Management--Expedites worker's compensation cases quickly and at lowest cost by ensuring the validity of compensation claims, monitoring time off the job, and facilitating the rehabilitation process.

b. Disability Evaluations--Determine the degree to which an employee is disabled due to an on-the-job injury.

c. Rehabilitation Services--Efficiently and effectively restore an individual's physical capabilities to the highest possible level of functioning.

d. Work Hardening Programs--Follow rehabilitation to enhance the individual's physical capacity to enable the employee to return to work.

e. Return to Work Examinations--Verify that the physical capacity of an individual is sufficient to permit the individual to return to work.

6. Health Care Administration

a. Utilization Monitoring and Control--Establishes and implements protocols to ensure appropriate use by employees of company health-care benefits.

b. Claims Administration and Management--Processes employee claims for health benefits and/or worker's compensation claims.

These and other corporate health services may, in many instances, be offered at either the company's work site, the hospital, or at a different off-site location. In some cases, location won't really matter; in others, it is of critical importance. For example, for maximum utilization of an EAP, it is generally advisable to provide the service at a convenient, off-site location so that the individual can easily maintain confidentiality. On the other hand, an occupational health system which revolves around a health professional on site at the company's location will by definition deliver services at the work site.

SEGMENTING THE CORPORATE HEALTH MARKET

As in most other markets, the market for corporate health services can and should be segmented as different types of firms require different services. It is a rare bank, indeed, which requires a toxicology program.

Here are some of the factors to consider in segmenting this market:

1. Size of Operation--Either in terms of number of employees or dollar volume in your local area. The former is strongly preferred since it provides a better measure of the scope of the service to be provided. Local size is key except as noted below--IBM may be in your town but their thousands of employees nation-wide are irrelevant in determining the needs of the local 100 person branch office.

2. Type of Organization--Is the organization in the manufacturing or service sector? Some find it useful to divide the service sector further into "heavy"service, such as mining and warehousing, which tends to have many of the attributes and needs of a manufacturing firm, and "light" service, including such industries as banking and insurance.

3. Location--In which part of the metropolitan area is the firm located? If the firm's employees have to pass other health-care providers to get to you, the odds are good that you won't get much of their on-the-job injury treatment business.

4. Corporate Office vs. Regional Operation--This delineation is likely to determine the number of employees ultimately affected by a sale and the decision-making process to be used. Making a sale to IBM's corporate office may ultimately impact the entire IBM organization. The sale can be larger but can potentially take years to conclude. In contrast, depending on the service and its cost, the local IBM office may be able to decide on a program far more quickly. Of course, in this case, the size of the sale will be much smaller.

Of course, segmenting the market based on demographics will only provide some initial clues regarding a firm's likely corporate health needs. Additional research to identify a particular organization's specific needs must be undertaken.

A MARKETING APPROACH TO
CORPORATE HEALTH SERVICES

Bethesda, Inc. is a two-hospital, 800-bed system located in Cincinnati, one of the 30 largest metropolitan areas in the country and one of the 10 largest metro areas for manufacturing. Bethesda is the largest provider of hospital services in the Greater Cincinnati area.

Bethesda's first active involvement in the area of corporate health was the provision to industry of various health-promotion and wellness programs in the late 1970s, an offshoot of the organization's community-directed health-promotion activities. The organization acquired its first occupational health center in 1982, and has subsequently acquired or developed four additional centers. The EAP and occupational health system marketed by Bethesda were developed during the 1984-85 period.

A major market research study to more definitively identify the needs of the corporate market was undertaken in 1986 using both qualitative and quantitative approaches. Among the key findings were:

-Not surprisingly, larger companies use more services.

-The market trend is to add services if they can be proven to be cost-effective.

-There tended to be significant fragmentation and market awareness levels of providers.

Following completion of this market research, a formal marketing plan was developed and is in the implementation process.

A primary target market was identified for the product line; however, it was recognized that specific services might be directed at a subset or expanded version of the primary target group. The product line incorporates most of the elements of the previously noted product listing, with the most notable exceptions being child care and health-care administration. In essence, given the services already developed or in the process of development, Bethesda was in a position to offer some services to all firms. Since most organizations will not have this depth of services at the outset, selection of the proper target market and development of the correct initial services are key considerations.

Pricing varies by product, depending on the product and our market position. For example, Bethesda's EAP is clearly the best program in town, and the organization now holds a significant market share advantage. Hence, Bethesda is marketing the value of its EAP and has raised the price to more competitive levels from its lower introductory price. In contrast, routine physical exams are virtually a commodity and are priced competitively.

Promotion for the product line is strong, varied, and integrated, incorporating a variety of both advertising and public relations activities. A specialized sales force was also developed to directly sell these services to the corporate market.

From a distribution perspective, a key strategy for this product line has been to make services readily accessible to the customer. Hence, Bethesda operates five occupational health centers throughout the metropolitan area, has EAP counseling offices in multiple locations in the area, and provides health promotion programs both at a company's work site and at convenient locations in the community.

RESULTS

Many of the services in this product line have become profitable within two to three years of their initial start-up while others are projected to take more time to become profitable. Beyond these direct results, the programs are generating significant referral business for Bethesda and its physicians. For example, the EAP is generating a significant number of referrals to our substance abuse treatment and psychiatric programs, and the occupational health centers and on-site health professionals are referring a continuous stream of patients to Bethesda-affiliated physicians each year.

In addition to this positive financial impact, the corporate health services product line appears to be contributing to the positive development of Bethesda's image in the corporate community and the public at large as a progressive health care corporation.

CONCLUSION

Successful development and implementation of a corporate health services product line can enable a health-care provider to achieve many of the desired benefits of diversified activity, including the generation of incremental revenue and profits from non-hospital related activity, support of hospital related activity, and the fulfillment of many institutions' missions to address unmet health-care needs. Identification of the market's needs, effective segmentation of the market, development of the appropriate products, and implementation of a comprehensive marketing plan are the key elements to succeed in this effort.

MARKETING PRINCIPLES APPLIED TO INDIGENT CARE:
AN INNOVATIVE AND EFFECTIVE PERSPECTIVE

Catherine F. Kinney, Catherine McAuley Health Center, Ann Arbor

ABSTRACT

Strategies for the provision of health care to the
indigent are a major concern for health care insurers,
providers, and consumers. A long-term approach must be
designed which responds to the needs of the disadvantaged, provides an adequate financial base, and
encourages appropriate utilization. In the short-term,
health care providers must devise manageable responses
in their local contexts. The purposes of this paper are
the following:

1. Describe the importance of indigent care to the
   overall market image of a health care provider;

2. Propose a process through which marketing principles can be applied to the planning, delivery,
   promotion, and evaluation of services to the
   indigent;

3. Provide examples of the application of that process
   to a large private non-profit health care provider.

BACKGROUND

The indigent population was estimated in 1985 by the AHA
Council on Research and Development to include 45.3
million persons who were "the uninsured, underinsured,
and otherwise medically disadvantaged." This disadvantaged population is growing; the Senate Special
Committee on Aging reports a 20% increase in the number
of uninsured Americans since 1979. These unsponsored
individuals fall into several major categories. Nearly
65% of them are employed adults and/or their dependents;
4.1 million are the uninsured dependents of insured
employed individuals. Other significant subgroups are
early retirees; persons aged 55 to 64 are, in fact, the
group most likely to be underinsured. Unmarried women,
especially divorced individuals who have not remarried,
are also particularly vulnerable. Finally, the uninsured group is more likely to be chronically ill and
non-white than the insured population.

What has been the response of the health care system to
these needs? The AHA Office of Public Policy estimates
that in 1984, $6.9 billion in uncompensated care was
provided by hospitals, an increase of almost 100%
between 1980 and 1984. These unreimbursed costs represent less than 6% of total hospital costs but are not
equally distributed across hospitals. The AHA Council
on Research and Development estimates that 55.4% of
charity care (exclusive of bad debt) is provided by
public hospitals, 44.1% by private not-for-profit
hospitals, and .5% by investor-owned hospitals. This
trend to increased charity care in state and local
government hospitals is expected to increase, according
to a panel of health care experts polled in Health Care
in the 1990's: Trends and Strategies. Little change in
the level of charity care is predicted for not-for-
profit hospitals, but panelists expect investor-owned
facilities to decrease the level of charity care
currently provided. A slight decrease in the percentage
of uninsured people during the next decade, from 13% in
1980 to 12% by 1990, and 11% by 1995, is also predicted.

Proposed solutions to this challenge to health care have
been summarized in a recent AHA report, Cost and
Compassion:

- Increase public awareness.
- Strengthen tax incentives for employers to extend
  health insurance coverage to employees' dependents.
- Require employers to continue coverage for laid-off
  workers for a period of time.
- Encourage states and insurers to find ways to make
  health insurance more affordable for small employers.
- Halt efforts to reduce Medicaid entitlement and
  levels of federal and state funding available to
  state Medicaid programs.
- Establish a pool of funds available to providers
  that care for the uninsured.
- Increase federal responsibility for Medicaid, with
  financing through a payroll tax.

Several of these and other strategies are currently
being pursued. State legislative approaches have
included assessments or surcharges on hospitals; state
risk pools for uninsurable people; statewide sales or
per-capita taxes for indigent health care; expansion of
Medicaid eligibility or services; provision of prenatal
care for pregnant women; offering of catastrophic
insurance coverage. The recent federal COBRA legislation requires that employers provide access to health
care benefits at group rates to terminated employees and
their dependents for 18 months. The Community Programs
in Affordable Health Care project, funded by the Robert
Wood Johnson Foundation, the AHA, and the Blue Cross and
Blue Shield Associations, is developing community
coalitions of hospitals, employers, unions, and government to contain local health care costs while ensuring
quality of care and expanding access for the vulnerable.

Until more systematic responses to this challenge are
devised, it is critical that hospitals develop appropriate, managed strategies for responding to the health
care needs of the disadvantaged in their service
areas. There are several reasons for the salience of
this issue:

The maintenance of not-for-profit status by hospitals
is being increasingly related to the provision of
indigent care. This connection was discussed during
the recent federal tax revisions, and the National
Association of Counties has recommended that maintenance of tax-exempt status by hospitals be explicitly tied to the provision of indigent care.

Needed public sector support on such issues as
Certificates of Need can be enhanced by assisting
state and local governments who are pressured to serve
as the payor of last resort.

The interest of area employers in this issue is
increased by the national policy emphasis on the
financing of indigent care through the private sector,
as exemplified by the COBRA legislation. Collaboration between area employers and the hospital on
this issue will enhance the hospital's linkages with
employers who are making decisions regarding HMO and
PPO affiliations.

Future health services for this market segment may be reimburseable. For the working poor without coverage, future jobs may bring health insurance. The uninsured aged 55 to 64 will be eligible for Medicare payment in a few years.

The public expects hospitals to participate in the solution to this problem. A 1985 study by Professional Research Consultants, Inc. found that 84.5% of respondents agreed that "...all hospitals should admit patients who might not be able to pay." As Emily Friedman observed in Care of the Medically Indigent, "...there is a growing expectation on the part of American society that hospitals will find a solution to the problem (of care of the poor). It is an expectation that hospitals would be well advised to address, before it is addressed for them."

In sum, then, health care for the indigent is a significant and highly visible issue to policy makers and individual and group purchasers of health care. Also, many members of the current indigent pool may be purchasers of health care in the future, representing future market potential.

CLARIFICATION OF HOSPITAL'S STRATEGIC POSITION

A strategic position statement which is grounded in the hospital's identity and history is a critical first step in preparing an appropriate strategy for addressing the needs of this market segment. Organizational mission statements and other formal statements of organizational direction such as governing board actions, charity care policies, financial reports, and other records can provide some historical perspective on the hospital's self-definition of its role with regard to indigent care. Community relations or fundraising materials often include statements regarding the organization's accountability to the community, with some implicit commitments regarding levels of service to those unable to pay.

In many religiously-sponsored or community-based hospitals, these mission statements will explicitly mention care of the indigent. In the case study hospital, the statements of philosophy, role, and goals explicitly identify the disadvantaged as an area of attention:

"We embrace the opportunity to extend compassionate service, especially to the suffering, the lonely, the marginal, and the poor...."
"Role implementation is characterized by special concern for the needy and elderly persons...."
"To enhance mission effectiveness...special programs will be developed that will respond to the health-care needs of the disadvantaged."

These organizational documents can yield a set of assumptions regarding the hospital's strategic position on disadvantaged care. Then, a strategic position statement can be drafted, which would outline a posture which recognizes the hospital's community identity, financial status, political agendas, and future interest in subgroups of these patients. Within the position statement, criteria should be defined for assessing various approaches to serving the indigent, such as:

- Community visibility as a hospital concerned with the poor;
- Limitation on financial exposure for indigent care;
- Opportunity to collaborate among area hospitals;
- Consistency with other organizational directions;
- Availability of appropriate settings and personnel;
- Ability to document costs to preserve not-for-profit status;
- Opportunity to develop innovative strategies for this population;
- Emphasis on certain segments of indigent market or certain types of services.

This strategic position statement, with its historical background and set of criteria, must be discussed with executive management and the governing board, to insure common understanding of the position and its implications. In the case study hospital, the governing board approved a policy for charity care write-offs which was explicitly aimed to maximize efforts to gain third-party payment and assure access to inpatient care. In addition, the board established a commitment of 10% of the net income (after charity care) for non-inpatient services to the disadvantaged, to develop innovative, cost-effective services specifically targeted for the poor.

MARKET ASSESSMENT

Once there is a common understanding among executive management, governance, and the marketing/planning function regarding strategic direction and criteria for specific indigent care initiatives, a market assessment should be conducted. Secondary data regarding this market segment should first be reviewed, beginning with a careful review of census statistics. State departments of social services and local community service agencies and public health departments can provide additional information regarding their service populations. Hospital patient account data bases will yield some information regarding the current inpatient and emergency room charity care population, including type of admission, diagnosis, and type of discharge. The purpose of this analysis is to identify geographic, demographic, or service delivery "clusters" that can focus more indepth study and then direct design of services.

As this market segment has not been perceived as financially attractive, commercially available market research has not generally addressed the needs and desires of this group. Sponsored academic research can provide some helpful insights into the healthcare utilization patterns and perceptions of this population. One major source of research studies is the Robert Wood Johnson primary care clinic initiative funded in the 1970's to increase access to health care. Many of these studies address health care utilization patterns and may be helpful in raising questions for further study in the hospital's service area. The University of Michigan study on Black Americans led by James Johnson is one example of relevant academic research.

Primary research strategies can use standard market research techniques by key informant studies, focus groups, and consumer surveys, if appropriate adaptations of the methodologies are made. The sample and methodology selection for the primary research should allow for distinction among the various subgroups identified by secondary data analysis, as the variance among these groups may be highly significant and suggest different strategies for different subgroups. Key types of data to be gathered include the following:

- Reasons for going for medical care (e.g., seriousness of illness, timing);
- Choices of location and type of care (e.g., emergency room, private physician, clinic);
- Perceptions regarding providers;
- Current health status;
- Current utilization patterns;
- Perceived community and individual needs (distinguishing between the two);
- Barriers to use of health care;

- Strategies to increase accessibility and attractiveness of lower cost health care options;
- Predictions regarding utilization patterns of targeted services.

The study methodology should ideally seek out direct consumer input. Existing community groups may provide natural settings for focus groups, but may reflect a bias toward more active community members. A random household sample can provide a more representative sample. However, the low availability of personal telephones with listed numbers among the indigent strongly suggests use of face-to-face interviews. Selection of surveyors is also extremely important, as surveyors new to the targeted population may not be able to gain access to residents. Use of known community members as interviewers may greatly improve the response rate, while possibly skewing some responses. Data-gathering from key informants, either individually or in groups, provides another valuable perspective. These leaders have a special track on the pulse in the community, but also have their own interests as community agencies or power-brokers in those communities. Therefore, key informants should be drawn from many roles, particularly indigenous leadership among ministers, community agency leadership, politicians, residents, school personnel, attorneys, and health care providers.

The case study hospital conducted a comprehensive market survey of the low income population in two targeted areas of its primary service area. One targeted area was a minority neighborhood with many public housing units and the lowest economic level in the county. Another targeted area was a lower class, older neighborhood near auto plants. The study was designed to identify health care needs and barriers to the use of health care services. Interviews with 293 households were completed, utilizing a one hour interview schedule conducted by trained interviewers who were often accompanied by (or who were themselves) well-known neighborhood residents. In addition, 20 key informants were interviewed, including health care providers, social service personnel, and church and community leaders. Key findings from this extensive market study included the following:

- Dissatisfaction with the health care system is centered around the costs of health care and treatment by health care personnel.

- With a population that smokes, drinks, and rarely exercises, health programs in stress management, exercise, parent education, and alcohol and drugs are desired.

- Home care for the elderly is an identified need in both neighborhoods.

- Schools, clinics, and churches should be more widely utilized for health education classes.

- The critical link to health care is available transportation.

- Cost is cited as the critical factor in over-utilization of emergency rooms, lack of follow-up care, and low compliance with physician recommendations.

- For minority respondents in this population, medical care is perceived as demeaning and unsatisfying because of poor communication patterns and inaccessible services, both in location and in waiting times.

- The case study hospital is the hospital of choice for minority group members in one target neighborhood, while another hospital is the choice for the minority residents of the second target neighborhood; the white working poor prefer a third hospital.

- Services should be focused on two high-risk populations: youth/young families and the elderly.

- Frequently cited health care problems include hypertension, diabetes, and chemical dependency.

SERVICE OPTIONS

This type of market assessment information can indicate a broad variety of services and strategies that can be developed in a focused, cost-effective manner, with specific outcome criteria and financial investment levels identified. Service strategies could include the following:

Patient Relations:

Financial assessment procedures for hospital bills may be streamlined, clarified, and delivered in a manner which communicates respect and sensitivity to the special needs of the indigent patient while maximizing pursuit of all coverage options.

Staff sensitivity to cultural differences may be enhanced by educational offerings regarding cultures with different norms regarding health care.

Screening and Education Services:

Sickle cell, hypertension, and diabetes screening, all diseases of particular concern to minority populations, can be provided in schools, community centers, and other accessible locations.

Weight reduction modules can be developed that recognize the dietary habits and financial limitations in menu planning of various groups.

Prenatal and postnatal health education classes can be delivered in conjunction with medical care visits at obstetric and pediatric clinics, providing volunteer babysitting.

Diabetes, hypertension, and medication misuse classes emphasizing visual rather than written messages can be delivered in senior meal sites, churches, and other accessible locations.

Youth-focused education offerings, including "Just Say No" modules relevant to chemical dependency, sexual abuse, and premarital pregnancy, can be delivered in school or in afterschool settings.

Outpatient Services:

Primary care clinics, located in targeted neighborhoods and developed in collaboration with community leadership, can be instrumental in encouraging use of primary care in managing chronic healthcare problems, rather than reliance on emergency room care.

Academic training clinics can utilize nursing and other personnel proactively, following up with patients to coordinate services and enhance patient compliance.

Chemical dependency and mental health outpatient services can utilize counselors who are familiar with the life situations of the disadvantaged, emphasizing daily coping and behavior modification skills more than long-term intrapsychic approaches.

Affordable access to immunizations and medications can be arranged through collaboration with local public health officials and hospital pharmacies.

Inpatient Services:

When an indigent admission from the emergency room occurs, the discharge plan should link the patient with a primary care clinic accessible and acceptable to the patient and his/her family.

Inpatient treatment planning should include early consultation with the nutritionist, as the length of stay of many indigent patients is extended due to poor pre-admission nutrition.

At the case study hospital, many of these strategies were utilized. Based on the market assessment described above, an annual plan for services was developed, which identified specific program areas and financial commitment levels. These included the following:

1. Within the Patient Accounts department, a few designated individuals were trained as financial counselors for the indigent. This approach insured consistency in the application of hospital policies and accountability for maximizing alternative reimbursement sources. Internal and external referrals for financial counseling were greatly simplified, with very positive feedback from consumers and referrers. Prescription bills, which represent a modest investment in increasing patient compliance, represent the type of non-inpatient bill most frequently written off.

2. A primary care clinic was established in the highest risk neighborhood, one of the two areas studied in the market survey. Before opening the clinic, extensive discussions were held with area ministers and opinion leaders. A Community Advisory Council, including key ministerial, political, community, and agency representatives from the area, was very active in clinic planning. The Medical Director is trusted by the neighborhood; her private office is utilized currently in the evening for the clinic. A Medical Advisory Committee provides important visibility for the clinic with the hospital's private practice medical staff.

3. At the short-term residential chemical dependency program, one adult bed and one adolescent bed are made available for indigent patients. At the long-term, non-reimburseable residential program for adolescents, fees are assessed on a sliding scale. The hospital committed its own resources and the outcome of a highly successful community fundraising drive to assure access to these two chemical dependency programs, which were then matched by the state legislature to serve additional indigent patients.

4. The purchase of 140 home-based emergency response units was funded by a hospital-sponsored philanthropic effort, and then by grant funding. The hospital assumes responsibility for operating costs and utilizes a sliding scale for monthly rental fees.

5. A sickle cell education and screening program is very active through black student associations in

area schools. Screenings are also conducted at the local black heritage fair and the Neighborhood Health Clinic.

6. A seniors health education and screening program sought out low-income seniors in such existing social groups as free lunch programs and subsidized senior high rise buildings.

7. A seniors day-care program was developed in one community in collaboration with another hospital and the Salvation Army, with the Army assuming operating and fundraising obligations.

8. Values clarification exercises and skill building classes have been conducted for hospital staff by representatives of various cultures, to improve personal understanding and program design skills.

9. Health promotion staff with extensive community backgrounds were recruited to serve as internal consultants and to liaison with indigent groups.

10. An assessment by patients and caregivers of the patient experience in the academic obstetric clinic led to the design of health education modules on smoking cessation, breastfeeding, and parenting skills consistent with the needs of the clinic population and the clinic format.

11. Within the home care services and equipment subsidiaries, a specific level of disadvantaged care was recognized as an appropriate offset to revenue.

In the case study hospital, these activities were funded through the governing board policy requiring application of 10% of the hospital net income for targeted, non-inpatient services for the disadvantaged, at an annual cost of approximately $800,000.

Outcome measures for these services can provide extremely valuable information in adjusting activities and in directing future efforts. One essential long-term outcome measure for this target market is change in health care utilization patterns to more cost-effective types of care. Short-term measures, therefore, should analyze patterns of utilization of and satisfaction with the more proactive, non-inpatient services.

In the case study hospital, examples of outcome measures for several of the initiatives include the following:

1. Neighborhood Health Clinic: pattern of Clinic use by neighborhood residents; patient satisfaction with care and interactions; decreased inappropriate utilization of the emergency room by Clinic patients; decreased inpatient length of stay for Clinic patients compared to other indigent patients with similar conditions.

2. Sickle cell screening program: number of target population persons screened for the first time; frequency of detection of carriers of the trait; number of additional family members screened after detection of a carrier.

3 Seniors health education modules: number of participants; satisfaction and behavior change.

4. Patient Accounts function: internal and external referring groups' knowledge of and satisfaction with the system; patient satisfaction with staff sensitivity and responsiveness; frequency of identification by hospital of alternative reimbursement sources.

Promotional strategies for services targeted for the disadvantaged have two separate purposes: to connect patients to the service, and to increase community recognition of the hospital's contribution to this challenge. In promoting services to the target market, a key tactic is reliance on credible sources to promote the service. The opinions of these community influentials will heavily influence utilization patterns through informal gatekeeping and community opinion-setting dynamics. Designation of advisory roles can complicate usual decision-making patterns, but the gain is often well worth the potential risks, if well structured and utilized. Hospital recognition for its contributions can be obtained through annual reports, newspaper coverage, and presentations to community leaders. With these audiences, the purpose of the promotion is to increase support for the hospital, not to increase utilization of the targeted services.

The planning of the Neighborhood Health Clinic by the case study hospital followed several years of involvement in the target community. During that time, information about the institution's mission and goals was shared with key community members. As the Clinic concept was first considered, many meetings were held with area clergy and other key individuals in the neighborhood. Then, a Community Advisory Committee was formed six months before Clinic opening. They designed the brochure, the opening ceremony, and the promotional strategy for the Clinic, using a well-known community skeptic as the cover model for the brochure, and involving three neighborhood clergy in the opening ceremonies, to represent all religious constituencies. To enhance the hospital's image, governing board members, key public officials, substantial donors, and community employers were invited to the opening ceremony and tours. In addition, the hospital's annual report to the community features many of the services for the indigent.

FINANCING OPTIONS

Current private health care financing strategies do not fully recognize the hospital's role in responding to the indigent care challenge. The cost for unreimbursed care, either to prevent or treat illness among the disadvantaged, is not an accepted component of costs in most HMO/PPO/Blue Cross/Blue Shield calculations. Until public policy addresses this issue, hospitals can educate local employers and policy-makers to the consequences of the current non-system: weakening of the community hospital's financial base and/or increasing federally-mandated pressures on the private sector, such as the COBRA legislation. Local pilot projects can also demonstrate the potential for collaboration of financers and providers from the public and private sector.

The case study hospital is participating with other area hospitals, the county, and the state in piloting a capitation approach to health care for General Assistance patients, one medically underserved subgroup. Previously, the state department of social services paid for pre-authorized ambulatory care for these clients, while the legislated county responsibility for inpatient bills was limited to an annual county appropriation of no set level. Over the last three years, the county had appropriated nothing, and the area hospitals had absorbed millions of dollars of uncompensated care. In this pilot program, drafted by consultants Walter McNerney and Sandra Lichty, state funding and new county funding will be joined to provide a monthly capitated payment of $30 for all medical services to the hospital of the patient's choice. The hospital, then, has a financial incentive to deliver outpatient care to

these patients. Implementation issues, of course, are many and complex, including physician contracts, inter-hospital transfers, scope of services, risk management, and distribution of patients. Nonetheless, the concept represents an exciting partnership of public and health-care interests to structure the limited reimbursement now available to provide care in the most cost-effective settings.

CONCLUSION

Responsibility for the financing of health care services for the indigent population is a major health care policy challenge. Until long-term directions are clear, local hospitals can take concrete action to respond to the widespread expectation to participate in devising solutions. Concrete actions can include the following:

1. Become familiar with the nature of the problem nationally and in the community by gathering quantitative data and talking with opinion leaders and indigent community residents.

2. Learn about service strategies which have been tested in other communities for these populations.

3. Adopt an organizational position statement on the hospital's role in care of the indigent.

4. Design, implement, promote, and evaluate some non-inpatient care strategies for specific indigent subgroups, relying heavily on community input throughout the process.

5. Participate in the formulation of local, state, and national financing strategies which are attempting to create system incentives for caring for the indigent.

REFERENCES

Anderson, Arthur and Co. and American College of Hospital Administrators (1984), Health Care in the 1990s: Trends and Strategies, Chicago: Arthur Anderson and Co.

American Hospital Association, Special Committee on Care for the Indigent (1986), Cost and Compassion, Chicago: American Hospital Association.

Friedman, Emily (1986), Care of the Medically Indigent, Chicago: Society for Hospital Planning and Marketing of the American Hospital Association.

MARKETING MENTAL HEALTH AND CHEMICAL DEPENDENCY PROGRAMS:
A SYSTEMS APPROACH

Sandra L. Yost, Vice President of Marketing
Recovery Centers of America

ABSTRACT

The following is an overview of the basic marketing functions necessary to create and maintain a successful census. Each function is process-oriented and integrated in a systems approach to census building. Although each function operates independently, any one function will not in itself have significant impact on the overall goal. Therefore it is necessary to maintain all marketing functions. The emphasis on any give function will vary in response to market needs, maturity of the program, and the training and skills of the staff.

The six basic marketing functions that are necessary to manage are:

1) Planning - developing the basic framework for sales and communications activities.

2) Foundation - building the basic internal systems necessary to receive business and assure success of subsequent activity.

3) Sales - personalizing the one-to-one contact activity necessary to identify potential referral sources and the development or conversion of those into active business.

4) Communications - developing a variety of visual, audio and/or written material to support the sales and service efforts.

5) Collateral Services - developing and maintaining patient/consumer access services to assure non-direct availability to the program.

6) Maintenance - Activity to assure consistent repeat business and a high level of customer satisfaction.

Within each function a variety of smaller components exists to create a network of activities and systems. Equal commitment and management of each function is an all-hands-on proposition. The administration, marketing, and clinical staff, working as a team, share the responsibility of the development, implementation and maintenance of quality services, responsible marketing, and professional delivery.

BASIC PHILOSOPHY

Marketing, defined as meeting the needs of the client (both the self referral and the referral source) before, during and after utilization of services is a team effort, although much of the responsibility for planning and implementation of marketing rests on the marketing director. The administrator or director must make a clear and verbal commitment to marketing as an integral part of clinical care, financial management, and daily operations. He or she is a marketing role model for the entire staff.

Marketing never operates in a vacuum within the program or facility. Involvement according to skill, position, and desire on a consistent level by each and every member of the staff is critical for a balanced, quality marketing effort. Generally, psychiatric and chemical dependency programs offer the same therapeutic values as their competitors. Specialized programs are rarely unique, espicially in metropolitan and suburban areas. Adult chemical dependency programs, for instance, deliver basically the same components with few variations. Adolescent psychiatric programs provide similar treatment.

The only thing that will distinguish us from our competitors is our individual commitment in the communication, delivery and customer service activity of our own program. Our distinctive competencies are our human resources. Our competitive edge is simply our commitment to do everything a little bit better.

In his book A Passion for Excellence, Tom Peters speaks about customer loyalty. "Excellence is a game of inches, or millimeters. No one act is, per se, clinching. But a thousand things, a thousand thousand things, each done a tiny bit better, do add up to memorable responsiveness and distinction - loyalty (repeat business) and slightly higher margins."

Pride, enthusiasm for the service we provide, and a passion for customer service is fostered and encouraged every hour, every day. It is the norm and is expected from each member of the team. It is nurtured internally and readiates externally.

PLANNING

The development and implementation of an active, balanced marketing effort begins with the Planning function. There are several components to the Planning function which need to be in place: a) staff understanding and support of marketing, b) identification of external market needs, c) thorough knowledge of competitive programs, d) the development of distinctive product lines and e) a written marketing plan.

Staff Understanding and Support: To begin, an objective assessment is necessary of our internal attitude and understanding of marketing; the delivery of our programs and current customer service efforts. How does our staff perceive our services and their individual and collective role? Are they currently involved in any marketing activity? What are the roadblocks to involvement? How do they perceive their program in relation to consumer needs and customer service? Setting the stage with an orientation and awareness program to gain understanding and support is basic.

Identification of External Market Needs: Since marketing is simply meeting the needs of the consumer (whether the self referred patient or the professional as a referral source) we first need to identify those specific needs. Who is the customer base? What is the catchment area? Where does the consumer seek services currently? What kind of services do the want? Are they aware of the services they need? Who are the potential referral sources and gate keepers? Are there services which are provided, and which services are they? Are they happy utilizing them? What is our perceived reputation in the community? Are the referral sources aware of our services? What are our strengths and weaknesses as seen by the referral sources?

Competition: It is imperative to have a current understanding and working knowledge of not only who our competitors are, but specifically what their services are; how they "sell" their services; and how they are perceived in the community. Doing a comparative benefits study on a quarterly or bi-annual basis is recommended. After completing our investigation we can ask ourselves: Are our competitors providing services or benefits that we should provide? Is our cost for services comparable to the benefits provided? Do we have a competitive edge in providing services our competitors do not? Beyone the benefits of our competitors that we should be aware of, how do they handle marketing? In what organizations are they active? Do they advertise? Where? How much do they spend? Do they have an active referral development program? Who are the marketing personnel? What is the competitors reputation? Who are their major referral sources? What do their capabilities materials look like? How do they communicate their program and services in writing?

Developing Product Lines: Once we understand our market and our competitors, we can develop distinctive product lines or services which can be marketed and promoted individually and collectively. For example, a psychiatric hospital may have an adult psychiatric program, an adolescent psychiatric program, an adolescent or adult chemical dependency program, an acute care unit, a geriatric program and an eating disorders program. These can be considered separate product lines. An adult chemical dependency program can also have product lines: A cocaine track, a young adult tract, a women's tract, a 24 hour hotline or referral service, a community education program and/or family intervention services. Communicate the availibility and accessability of such services to both the referral sources and the general public in sales activity, written pieces and/or publicity.

A Written Marketing Plan: The process of writing a marketing plan is as much an internal marketing activity as it is a strategic guideline for planned future activity. Developing the marketing plan is a team effort. A synergistic approach to planning who to target and what strategy to implement, as well as the goals and expected outcome, will invest the staff in successful accomplishment of the overall goal/goals. A basic marketing plan includes a) census projections, b) number of admissions required to reach census projections, c) identification of the key market groups to be targeted, d) specific marketing strategy and activity (one-to-one contacts, education program, questionaire mailings, open houses, advertising in a trade journal, etc.), e) who is responsible for which activities, f) time frame for each activity and g) measurable objectives for each activity (what we want from the activity).

Marketing plans can plan for 3 to 6 months for action plans and for one year for general strategic plans. Action plans should be as specific as possible with realistic, obtainable goals.

FOUNDATION

In order to assure that the measurable objectives of sales and other collateral marketing activity are realized, it is important that an internal foundation be in place. Components to the function of the Foundation include a) referral development team, b) referral source customer service program, c) inquiry system, d) information and referral system, e) physical plant readiness, and f) reporting and data gathering system.

Referral Development Team: Developing a potential referral source into active business is a process typically requiring several steps, each tailored to meet the needs and wants of the referral source. Rarely does one face-to-face visit to a referral source, or a brochure, result in a referring relationship. A referral source may require a preferred provider arrangement; a tour of the facility; a meeting with the clinical staff or medical director; a service agreement; staff privileges. A first contact with a potential referral source is an information exchange. We find out what the referral source needs, what we have that meets those needs, and what we need to do next to develop an active referral relationship. Because a combination of actions is necessary to remove all roadblocks to referring, a referral development team is essential to coordinate the activity necessary to get the active

business.

The referral development team is a select committee who meets on a regular basis to communicate all marketing and related activity and plan "next step" activity. Attention to detail and synergism are the key words. The committee coordinates all steps and activities and who will be involved in implementing the plan. The committee is also responsible for the bulk of the one-to-one contacts. Regular members of the committee are the administrator or director (the chairperson), the marketing director (the co-chairperson), other marketing personnel, any department heads, the medical director, the inquiry or admissions person and selected clinical staff, nursing and support personnel. The frequency of meetings reinforces the commitment to marketing and follow-up.

Inquiry System: Sales or contact activity, advertising, public relations activity, word of mouth produce inquiries about our services. A system to handle the calls and an identified inquiry person or persons trained specifically to convert appropriate calls into business is a critical component. Back up personnel, usually the clinical staff, is also trained to take calls.

The inquiry system is the gate keeper component of our business. Without an adequate system and trained personnel we are missing a vital link in the marketing process. Call which are handled with professional concern, timely follow-up and disposition will assure that potential business is realized.

Information and Referral System: Since many calls generated by advertising and publicity are not appropriate for the services we provide it is necessary to have current information about community resources for every cal regardless of their individual problem or their ability to pay. A community referral network book, compiled by our program explains this in more detail in the Services section.

Referral Source Customer Service Program: Since our treatment programs do not operate to the exclusive wellness of most patients, but are instead part of a continuum of care shared by other professionals, a guarantee and exchange of information between ourselves and a referral source will provide a high quality of care and client satisfaction. Many referral sources require specific information and communication from our programs in order to provide good client care.

The provision of a system which guarantees that the referring professional gets the specific feedback, written information, and desired level of involvement in the referred patient's treatment is basic and necessary to customer service.

Converting potential referral sources into active business includes the offer of a service agreement in which the referral source can specifically outline all preferred written and verbal information required while we are treating their patient. That service agreement then becomes a checklist, which can go on the patient's chart and be monitored during their stay in the program. As specifics of the agreement become due (i.e. written progress report) it is completed and signed off by the person responsible. All criteria is reviewed at the time of discharge and a "How did we do?" questionaire is forwarded to the referral source.

Physical Plant Readiness: Our physical plant is our "package". It exemplifies what our services are; how we feel about the services; how they will be delivered; what we think about our two most important assets - ourselves and our customers.

Our package should reflect the positive, professional, caring, warm atmosphere we describe in our capabilities brochures. Our package should mirror our values and philosophy of treatment.

A obsessive attention to detail- awareness and pride instilled in the team about how our unit or facility appears can and will make a difference. A sparkling clean and neat plant says,"We care about you, we care about quality."

Reporting and Data Gathering System: Just as planning and strategizing where we are going is important, so is analyzing and measuring our efforts. A simple marketing report should be designed which is cumulative, shows the relationship between contacts, inquiries and the resulting admissions and breaks down target market groups. This gives us invaluable information. Are we staying on target? Are the contacts resulting in expected business? Are we getting inquiries and admissions from areas we are not currently marketing, but need to? Is too much effort going into areas with too little return? Is our advertising getting the desired results? Are we converting an acceptable number of calls to admissions?

SALES

The sales function involves all the personalized marketing activity which revolves around developing the referral sources into active referral relationships. Initial contacts determine the potential for referral and follow-up activity develops the referral relationship. One-to-one contacts can and should be done by all members of the referral development team. Specific goals are set for accountability and focus. Training and support are given on an ongoing basis to enhance skills and level of enthusiasm. Matching professional to professional is also advantageous (i.e. director of nurses meeting with emergency room nurses; medical director meeting with other physicians). There is a direct relationship between the level of sales and the admissions from referral sources. It is important that this level of activity be consistent, even in times of high census. The sales activity is the heart of referral development. Quality of contacts, attention to detail in planned follow-up and customer service will assure expected results.

COMMUNICATIONS

In order to promote our name, position ourselves, support the active sales effort and to reach the general public who might not otherwise be referred by a community professional, it is necessary to develop effective written and visual communication on a variety of levels. Components of the function of Communications should be a similar strategy of message.

Advertising: Depending upon financial resources, budget and market advertising can enhance all other marketing activity. Advertising can produce "icing for the cake" or it can be an unnecessary drain on the bottom line. It is a support component of marketing, not a basis for census. Questions which are addressed prior to making a decision about whether or not to use advertising; which mediums to use; and how much to spend are a) What is the objective of advertising (name recognition, education, community awareness, direct business)? b) Is the budget for production adequate in order to produce a quality representative of the services we provide? c) Are there affordable mediums we can use in our community which will meet our objective and fit within our budget? d) What does the competition do in the area of advertising, and is it effective for them? e) Can the same budget be put to use in other ways which will produce better results (a newsletter, a direct mail piece, etc.)?

Advertising should never be used solely to aquire census goals, but instead to support and enhance those goals and to reach a population not reached through referral development. Otherwise success is short lived and dependent on an ever increasing budget. Cost effectiveness decreases.

Publicity: Actively seeking favorable publicity both for our facility and for mental health/chemical dependency awareness in general, can be done on a regular basis. Getting to know your local news and feature story people both in television and newspapers and submitting to them a healthy list of possible story lines which are of community interest and paralell internal expertise is very valuable. Additionally, news releases about items of interest within our facility or about current related issues many times can spark story ideas for the local media.

Public Relations Activities: Another component to communications is "soft" or collateral activity which positions the program, increases visability and enhances image. Those activities, although not sales, can also provide an opportunity for leads to future contacts. There are limitless possibilities to be involved in public relations activities - such as health fairs, sponsored athletic programs/events, speaking engagements, trade shows, fund raisers, seminars, exhibits. A good support component and a necessary part of a balanced marketing effort, a public relations program alone is rarely an adequate return on investment and should be kept in perspective.

Direct Mail: Direct mail campaigns are an excellent way of getting tailored messages to specific target groups. A quarterly newsletter sent to target markets, professionals in the community, alumni, and referral sources can result in inquiries about your facility, foster good image and act as a reminder that your program is active and energetic.

Speakers Bureau: In order to position ourselves in the field as knowledgeable on a variety of pertinent issues related to our area, offering an organized set of topics and using staff to present is another component to communications to enhance overall marketing efforts.

Capabilities Materials: Brochures, professionally produced which communicates who we are and what we do acts as a tool used in sales, public relations, publicity, and information for the general public. Emphasis is placed, not on what we provide but the benefits of what we provide.

Care should be taken not to communicate in "field gargon." Like our physical plant, the brochure or capabilities material is our package and directly reflects who we are. Xeroxed copies, typographical errors, bad sentenance structure can hurt the overall message.

COLLATERAL SERVICES

Collateral services to our primary program or programs are necessary to position our facility as the place to call for help; to assure that we keep prospective patients in our system until they make the necessary decision; and to assure supportive help to adjunctive professionals who deal directly with prospective patients but cannot provide the service themselves. Components in this area can be expanded depending on human resources and budget.

Community Network System: Our experience has shown us that advertising, public relations activities and publicity creates many inquiry calls which are not appropriate to the services we offer. It is our ethical and professional responsibility to assess what the caller needs and refer him or her to the most appropriate service available in the community. Investigating our community resources and developing a community network system is a team effort.

Family Intervention Services: A critical component for chemical dependency programs is a Family Intervention service. Because a high percentage of family members call needing assistance to motivate the prospective patient to seek help, providing Family Intervention classes is a valuable service. The program should be conducted by internal staff.

Crisis Intervention/Hotlines: In mental health and psychiatric programs a crisis hotline can enhance the helping image and produce a high percentage of admissions from people in acute conditions. The referral network book is used in this service for those callers not admitted.

Professional-to-Professional Services: There are many professionals in our respective communities who deal with clients appropriate for our programs but out of the scope of the services they provide. For example, emergency rooms see many psychiatric and chemical dependency clients who seek help in a medical setting because of physical trauma. The emergency room team, after completing medical triage do not readily deal with behavioral, emotional or psychiatric issues. Many times they recognize the needs but have no resources from which to draw. Offering on-site assessment and referral services to specific professional groups can be highly effective in increasing our referral base. Other professional-to-professional services include but are not limited to employee assistance services, student assistance services, professional consulting hotlines, physician consulting services, rotating internship programs, inhouse volunteer programs/ services, marketing training programs for private practtice professionals.

Assessment and Counseling Services: Face to face assessment of prospective clients provided free is essential to bridge the gap between the caller and therapeutic services offered by our programs. It is uncommon to make a determination about treatment over the phone, therefore it is an automatic system to schedule assessment/counseling interviews is necessary in order not to loose the client. Anyone taking an inquiry who determines that an assessment is appropriate should have easy access to a pre-planned appointment book. Timing is critical. The appointment should be offered during the initial call by whoever takes the inquiry. Scheduling in the same day or not longer than 24 hours will assure a high percentage of clients who keep the appointment.

MAINTENANCE

In order to maintain the two most valuable assets for referrals - the former patient and the active referral source - it is necessary to support and provide special services to these groups in particular. Patients are not a commodity and therefore we can never take for granted that business will walk in the door just because we have a quality facility or program. We must rely, in part, on the satisfied customer to maintain the business we have, and encourage positive word of mouth from former patients. There are five critical components of this function.

Maintenance Contacts: Once a referral relationship is developed we must continue a planned contact strategy to assure repeat use of our programs. Seeing an active referral source on a regular basis to obtain feedback, to hear ideas for improvement of services and to foster continued relationships can be done by everyone on staff. Communicating the feedback obtained can be discussed in the referral development committee meeting and then acted on in a timely manner. Positive feedback is always welcomed and should be shared with the entire staff. Emphasizing their continued support and involvement in the patients they refer, and the program itself can foster strong loyalty.

Patient Satisfaction Surveys: Another component of maintenance is to directly ask the patient to give us feedback about the program, staff, physical plant, etc. Almost all other service industries ask their clientele for such feedback and use the information to improve those services, compliment employees, validate the effectiveness of what they provide. Tom Peters in A Passion for Excellence calls it Management By Walking Around (MBWA). This can and is achieved in three ways, a) written questionaire at the time of discharge, b)face to face interviews with patients and families toward the end of treatment and c) informally anytime, anywhere in the facility.

Alumni Organizations: Although more common in chemical dependency programs an organized alumni group (separate from clinical aftercare or AA) this fellowship can by one of our best source of referrals. Some programs account for up to 40% of their admissions from referrals from their alumni.

Volunteer Services: A program involving "civilians" who volunteer time and energy to a facility or program is a valuable way of reducing the myths, stigma and fear of psychiatric or chemical dependency programs in the community. Many times former patients or their family members want to be active involved in the program that was of value to them. It can enhance the quality of services within the facility itself by its synergestic nature.

Focus Groups: Involving a variety of professionals, leaders in the community, former patients, staff, and referral sources is a component which can lend better knowledge and understanding of the needs of the community which we serve.

What we are doing right, what we need to improve upon, new concepts and ideas, keener sensitivity of the needs and wants of our service area enhances our allready balanced, active marketing and treatment efforts. Holding focus groups on a regular basis is simple and enlightening.

CONCULSION

As our industry grows and matures and competition becomes keener a balanced marketing effort which is consumer sensitive and customer service oriented will provide the needed competitive edge.

Providing for a referral base which is broad and consistent, without relying on any major referral source for our business will insure long term success.

Managing the marketing efforts daily, knowing when and where to put the emphasis in relation to the functions outlined, and being consistent with our commitment both internally and externally guarantees that we can meet the challenge before us.

SENIOR HEALTH CONSUMERS

The presence of a growing geriatric health care consumer
segment has long been recognized by health care providers.
To successfully target and effectively serve this market
the health care provider must have an intimate understanding of the health needs of the elderly as well as a
meticulously well planned approach. The three papers in
this section present insights into how the different
needs of this consumer group has been successfully met in
a variety of settings - a community-based whole person
wellness program (Boyd/Gibbs); a hospital based long term
care program (Gross); and a comprehensive array of
clinical and non-clinical health related services package
(Jacques).

SENIORS ARE SPECIAL: A COMMUNITY-BASED WHOLE PERSON WELLNESS PROGRAM

Sheryl H. Boyd, Texas Tech University Health Sciences Center, Lubbock
Eileen E. Gibbs, Lubbock General Hospital, Lubbock

ABSTRACT

To address the burgeoning whole-person wellness needs of our aging society, it is imperative that communities develop private and public partnerships for identifying, coordinating, and communicating senior health care services. This case study workshop is designed to assist healthcare professionals with the development of a community-based seniors-oriented wellness program.

INTRODUCTION

Suddenly, seniors are everywhere! Reports on aging, baby-boomers, and senior health-care issues appear as lead topics in all types of medical and consumer produced publications, advertisements, and media presentations. In the 1980's it has become popular and in vogue to be recognized as an individual who is: a "Post World War II Baby Product," a "Silver-Haired Senior," or a "Card-Carrying Medicare Beneficiary." This group of individuals represent the fastest growing age brackets in the U. S. population and also are easily identifiable as the largest potential consumer-purchasing segment for health-care related products, services, and facilities. Further, in many families or even shared households, it is not uncommon to have three generations of "boomers plus" (a 45, 65, and 85 year-old) reviewing information and ideas regarding the "How-To's" for aging gracefully, enhancing one's personal total vitality, and making arrangements for enjoying life's retirement years with dignity, quality and independence.

With these thoughts in mind, the opportunity for a teaching hospital and a health sciences center to develop and co-sponsor a whole-person wellness program targeted to this market niche seemed to present a natural marriage. Further, if coordinated appropriately, it appeared that the human resource teaching talent between Texas Tech University Health Sciences Center and colleges of the main campus and the service facilities of Lubbock General Hospital needed to accommodate a whole-person wellness educational program were already in place to support such an activity.

Hence, in November, 1985, Dr. Boyd began developing an outline for a series of whole-person wellness seminar topics which would include both life-style and medical-care update issues. The whole-person wellness orientation for a senior's program evolved from her years of research and interest in the field of consumer health education and a belief that human health must be viewed as a multi-dimensional unity which involves addressing aspects of the whole person in his total environment and includes: physical fitness, mental health, social and financial well-being, and spiritual faith.

Prior to designing the proposal outline, several marketing research methods were used to gain "real-life" data to support the literature findings regarding whole-person wellness topics for seniors. Through a method dubbed "Project ALERT[3]" by Dr. Boyd, 100 seniors were given the opportunity to reply both in person and through questionnaires about their priority medical-care and life-style issue concerns. The five steps involved in the "ALERT[3]" process are: 1) Ask, 2) Listen, 3) Educate (self), 4) Respond, and 5) Target Transferable Tools.

The title "Seniors Are Special" (S.A.S.) was selected as the theme for the program and the slogan "A Tribute to Yesterday's Youth, Today's Wisdom, and Tomorrow's Future" was chosen to reflect the comprehensive orientation of the program's goals. Both at its inception and in all on-going activities associated with S.A.S., the program has been marketed both to and for seniors, their caregivers, and their health professionals. All sessions of the program are offered free of charge.

OVERVIEW: "S.A.S." SERVICE AREA AND MARKET PROFILE

Lubbock, Texas, population 200,000 is located in the plains of West Texas and has evolved as the major medical industrial complex for West Texas and Eastern New Mexico. The nearest cities with a population of over 100,000 are Amarillo, which lies 90 miles to the north; Midland-Odessa, 136 miles to the South; Albuquerque, New Mexico, 315 miles to the West; and Fort Worth, 291 miles to the East. Small rural communities which are largely agricultural or energy industry related constitute the employment bases for those individuals living between Lubbock and these other major cities. Lubbock's employment base is diversified among agriculture, the University, retailing, medical services, energy, banking, and small business operations.

In Lubbock, there are eight hospitals - three of which are large not for profit plus five smaller proprietary facilities. By the end of 1986, these hospitals provided in excess of 1900 beds, a capacity which is greater than one would normally expect to find in a city the size of Lubbock. As a result, a strong competitive challenge has arisen among these hospitals and especially among the big three of which Lubbock General Hospital is the third largest with 300 beds.

As the primary care and tertiary referral center for the TTUHSC, LGH offers acute care services plus the following specialty services: Level III Neonatal and Pediatric Intensive Care, a Burn Center, a Kidney Transplant Center, an Eating Disorders Program, a High Risk Obstetrical Unit, a Pain Center, a Level I Trauma Unit, an Oncology Center, and a Gastrointestinal Unit. Capital expansion programs for 1987 include a $2.5 million Radiation Therapy Center plus major renovations in other clinical and surgical areas.

Since the eight medical facilities employ over 4300 people which translates into an annual payroll in excess of $101 million, their economic impact in the community is tremendous and they rank as the fourth largest employment category in the city. As a result of the vast economics associated with Lubbock's hospital industry, area consumers have witnessed a major escalation in new services and product developments as well as ongoing program promotionals at all of the Lubbock hospitals in the past twelve months. Extensive use of newspaper copy, TV advertisements, direct mailings, and telemarketing activities have been initiated by all of the hospitals in the past year.

It is interesting to note that the S.A.S. program was the first seniors oriented hospital program to hit the Lubbock market. However, within sixty days of its initial October 1986 five-part pilot series, both of the two larger hospitals came out with medical club packages targeted to Medicare beneficiaries. At this point, community seniors are delighting in the attention, recognition, and courtship promotionals that are being showered upon them by the hospitals.

A look at the demographics of the senior population in the fifteen counties surrounding Lubbock which constitute the primary service area for TTUHSC/LGH helps validate the potential opportunities which exist for targeting health-related programs to seniors in West Texas. Currently, statistics report that nationally persons 60 and over account for about 12% of the total U. S. population, but this segment's explosive growth due to baby-boomers maturing will account for 25% of the U.S. population by the year 2020. The South Plains regional average for persons 60 and over was 13% according to 1980 census data. However, in eleven of the fifteen counties in this region, persons 60+ already account for 15% or more of the population base. In three counties, persons in the 60+ age group in 1980 accounted for 20%, 28% and 30% of their county's total population. Again, it is important to recall that agriculture and energy related employment have been the major industries in most of these counties. As tough economic times have reduced employment opportunities in rural communities, young people have moved to larger cities to seek work leaving parents and grandparents to maintain the rural economies.

"S.A.S." PROGRAM IMPLEMENTATION

Initial presentations to TTUHSC chairmen and deans and LGH administrators to explain the concept of, need for, and potential positive outcomes of a S.A.S. program began in January, 1986. In these presentations, Dr. Boyd stressed the natural opportunities which existed between the two organizations for joint co-sponsorship of the S.A.S. series.

Knowing that seniors are sincere advocates of remaining well informed about whole-person wellness issues, especially as it assists them in stretching their disposable income, an educational focus was intentionally selected as the primary design for each session. Speakers for each topic would be selected based on their medical or professional expertise on a subject. Naturally, this approach would provide medical school faculty with the opportunity to be featured on each program. Since no other hospital organization was conducting a senior's health education program, Dr. Boyd stressed the need to take the "Hertz" approach and be number one in offering this educationally focused community service series. Further, by hosting the programs in the cafeteria of LGH, a room that is located midpoint between the TTUHSC and LGH, attendees would have the opportunity to visit and become familiar with the layout and facilities of both organizations. Additionally, the educational focus of the series provided a very low-key and non-exploitive sales tool via which both organizations could introduce their programs, services, and people.

After four or five repeat "sales calls" to the leaders at both TTUHSC and LGH to review the S.A.S. concept, it was concluded by both organizations that the program should be done but the logistical and financial "How To's" for offering the series remained in question.

Finally, the idea emerged that it seemed only logical that a program designed for seniors should be produced by seniors. At this point, the LGH administrator over volunteers and the LGH Auxiliary President, Mrs. Gibbs, were contacted for help. Yeah for the talent and insight possessed by the senior volunteers! Mrs. Gibbs immediately acknowledged the positive need for the series and after visiting with her Auxiliary Board Members announced to Dr. Boyd and the LGH administrators that the 185 member Auxiliary Organization of LGH had voted to officially adopt and sponsor the S.A.S. Program. The hospital administration enthusiastically endorsed the volunteers' sponsorship and pledged to offer clerical and support assistance as well as contribute $5000. for printing and publicity expenses for this series.

Because the initial thrust of the S.A.S. Program was to provide a high quality whole-person wellness community education service project for seniors, the next step in the program design was the development of a committee of key advisory experts who had current expertise in the management and delivery of senior lifestyle and healthrelated issues. The group of community individuals selected included representation from professional, lay, and volunteer groups that work with some component of a whole-person wellness issue as it affects seniors. In July, the twenty-five member advisory group was hosted to a lunch visit at LGH to introduce them to the S.A.S. program concept and format and to request their advice and input as well as to encourage their active participation in and support of the pilot series.

In addition to supplying valuable input and ideas, the initiation and implementation of the advisory committee approach succeeded in generating much positive goodwill and gratis community promotion for the S.A.S. series. Their comments and willingness to assist where possible enabled instant liaison entries for the S.A.S. program coordinators and have resulted in providing an informal community network for promoting ongoing S.A.S. program developments.

The following topics note the priority subjects which were selected for the 5-part pilot series: Lifestyle (1) Aging with a Positive Attitude - Planning Ahead - A Family Affair, (2) Financial Planning Strategies for Retirement Security and Medicare, Assignment: What does that mean, (3) Exploring Alternative Living Arrangements and Understanding Home Health Services, (4) Looking at the Whole Issue of Diet and Nutrition and Understanding Drug Interactions, (5) Activities for Seniors - Identifying Community Opportunities; and Medical Care (1) The Aging Brain: Alzheimer's and Parkinson's Disease, (2) Advances in the Treatment of Arthritis and Rheumatism, (3) Updates on Managing Hypertension and Heart Disease, (4) Diabetes Update, (5) Progress in the Treatment of Cancer.

SENIOR VOLUNTEERS' COMMITTEE ACTIVITIES

Next, in August, a volunteer chairman was elected to organize S.A.S. committee activities with the auxiliary members who had volunteered to serve as committee chairmen for the series. In total, 40-45 volunteers worked on the 10 committees that were active components of the S.A.S. series. The chairmen met weekly during August and September with committee members, the program coordinators, and key hospital administrative staff to outline, implement, and check-up on the progress of committee assignments.

The following committees were appointed: Publicity, Information Packets, Medical Screening, Home-Bound

Transportation, Valet Parking, In-Hospital Transportation, Nutrition-Breaks, Informational Handouts and Incentive Gifts, Hosts, and Audio-Visual. Each committee chairman was a member of the Lubbock General Hospital Auxiliary or the Lubbock General Hospital Foundation.

A brief outline of the activities of each committee follows. As you will see, resources from the community, TTUHSC, LGH, and the main campus of Texas Tech University were actively involved with the program:

1. Publicity - 200 posters were distributed by a local Lions Club and 5000 brochures were used either in mailings to local and county wide groups or as handouts to Seniors groups at churches, Senior Citizens centers, clinics and libraries. The Community Relations Department of the Lubbock General Hospital was responsible for media coverage. Press releases to the local newspaper, commercial ads placed in the Avalanche-Journal, and live presentations on local T.V. stations were initiated. The content of all posters, brochures, and ads simply served to invite citizens to the free program and to identify topics, location, and time.

2. Information Packets - This committee was responsible for obtaining medical care and lifestyle related printed materials from various agencies and organizations that would be of value to seniors. Organizations contacted included: Nursing services, Home health care services, LTC agencies, Citibus (sent 1000 schedules), State Committee for the Blind, State/County/City agencies, Meals-on-Wheels, Retirement homes, and national groups such as ADA, ACS, and the AHA, etc. A LGH/S.A.S. labelled packet was given to each participant. New materials were distributed on a weekly basis to supplement the topics for the day's programs.

3. Hosts - This group was kept busy before and after sessions directing people around the hospital to the meeting rooms and back to the front entrance. The members of this committee and the valet parking committee were easily distinguished. In addition to wearing their auxiliary uniforms they all sported black top-hats. Guides were placed at intervals along the corridors. This was essential since many of the guests had never been inside our facilities.

4. Transportation - Auxiliary members volunteered for this service which provided residential pick-up for individuals who without it would have been unable to attend the seminars. At least six volunteers picked up 4-6 Seniors for each session. As often as was possible the drivers transported the same passengers each time. A warm relationship developed between the drivers and passengers.

5. Valet Parking - Valet parking was offered in order to avoid the long walks from the hospital parking lots. Spaces were reserved in the Doctor's parking lot for this purpose. The chairman of this committee was a spry, tennis playing 70+ gentleman, who was also past Chairman of the Board at LGH. Assisting him were security guards, hospital staff, and volunteers. As our guests became aware of this convenience, the requests for residential pick-up service declined.

6. In-Hospital Transportation - One of the local country clubs loaned us two golf carts each week. The LGH E.M.S. technicians picked them up each week, operated them during the sessions, and returned them to the country club. This was a very welcome and valuable service since many of the seniors were unable to walk the considerable distance from the hospital front door to the cafeteria location. Everyone enjoyed this experience as they glided through the corridors.

7. Nutrition Breaks - One of the most popular segments of each session was the nutrition break. The Food Services Department did an outstanding job of providing tasty, nutritious, and attractively prepared refreshments. For certain sessions special foods were served such as sugar-free items for the session on diabetes and low cholesterol snacks for the session on heart disease. The significance of these special foods was not lost on the audience. Auxiliary members served the refreshments and acted as hostesses.

8. Information Handouts and Incentive Gifts - The ladies who served on this committee had a variety of duties. They arranged tables at the entrance to the cafeterias and displayed information pertinent to that day's topics. Also at each session a small gift was given to each guest. The gifts were all labelled "Lubbock General Hospital -- Seniors are Special." Such things as sewing kits, flashlights, pens and jar lid grippers were distributed and for the Christmas program gift packs of potpourri were handed out. Another of the duties of this committee was to try to ensure that each guest signed a roster and to tally the sign-in sheets after each session. This activity enabled us to compile a mailing list for future S.A.S. programs, newsletters, etc., and to keep records for data analysis to present to our administrations.

9. Medical Screenings - At each session a specific medical screening was offered with blood pressures being checked at every session. The screenings included hearing, glaucoma, diabetes, colon cancer stools, and pulmonary function. Professionals from the medical school, hospital nursing service, the speech and hearing clinic at Texas Tech and one commercial hearing center in town volunteered their services to perform these tests.

10. Audio-Visuals - One volunteer in cooperation with the TTUHSC media department arranged for microphones, speakers and visual aid equipment. Each session was taped and the tapes were sold at cost to participants. To date, over 200 tapes have been mailed out.

Currently, the L.G.H. Auxiliary has 185 active members. They range in age from students at the university to very senior citizens. The oldest active member is 86. The occupations of the members are equally diverse. They represent students, housewives, retirees (of both sexes), teachers, artists, nurses and many other professions. LGH's auxiliary motto best describes the motivation which propels this this super-charged crew -- "Touching Lives Through Loving Service"-- the perfect description of their exemplary contributions to the S.A.S. series.

"S.A.S." PROGRAM REVIEWS AND OUTCOMES

"Overwhelming success" and "exhilarating experience" are the best descriptors for the five-part S.A.S. pilot series! For each session, the audience-size averaged 300-350 people with the average age of the attendees being 70+ years. The participants for each session began arriving about 1:00 P.M. for each program which started at 2:00 P.M.--they wanted front-row seats! By 1:30 P.M. on each session day, the cafeteria was fifty percent filled by seniors.

A zip code analysis of the attendees by address revealed that participants travelled to the S.A.S. series from varying locations both inside and outside of Lubbock County. Two-thirds of all attendees came to three or more of the five sessions. About 10 percent of the attendees averaged a round trip drive of between 60-100 miles which included representatives from ten counties outside of Lubbock County. Analysis also showed that about 35-40% of the S.A.S. attendees had never used the facilities or services at either LGH or TTUHSC prior to these visits. The complimentary medical screenings were part of each session. Weekly, at least 50-100 people remained after a program to partake of the free screenings. On-site requests for assistance with obtaining a physician appointment also occurred.

Administrators and faculty from both TTUHSC and LGH viewed with wide-eyed amazement and happy amusement the glowing vitality and genuine quest for knowledge expressed facially, verbally, and in attitude by this group. Both presenters and program coordinators commented on the fact that participation in this program stood out as one of the most gratifying highlights of their professional careers.

As a community service project, the S.A.S. series really gained incredible momentum. Seniors, community leaders, and presenters applauded openly and in the media the value of this whole-person wellness series as a greatly needed community service activity. The series also served to introduce many citizens to both facilities and gave them an opportunity to discover that they could maneuver about in a large medical complex. TTUHSC and LGH are attached structures and encompass over 1,111,131 square feet. The fact that health care professionals from competing organizations attended each session was viewed as a super compliment. Further, after the first program, the Vice-Presidents for Marketing at each of the two other big hospitals commented that "TTUHSC and LGH had hit a home-run with the S.A.S. program."

At each session, evaluation forms were distributed to attendees so that they could rate the topics, the speakers, the facilities, and the snacks as well as offer additional suggestions for future programs. Program coordinators and committee chairmen were thoroughly pleased with the consistently outstanding reviews given by attendees for all aspects of the series.

Although the pilot program was designed almost a year prior to its inception, Dr. Boyd, Mrs. Gibbs and other key S.A.S. coordinators remained firm believers that the pilot series was just the beginning for S.A.S. So,

as you can imagine, with the repeated weekly success of each new program, strong believers were made out of even the staunchest of cynics prior to the October series. When the participants began to express remorse that the series would soon end, administrators immediately decided to coordinate efforts so that the series could be offered on a monthly basis beginning in January. Based on the attendees comments and suggestions, Dr. Boyd summarized and outlined a twelve month series for S.A.S. for 1987. Additionally, special discount coupons for services available in the TTUHSC ambulatory clinics or at LGH are being devised.

Tracking efforts to measure both new patient clinic visits and requests for LGH special services are being initiated. In the Internal Medicine Clinic alone, at least 5-7 new weekly clinic visits were cited for S.A.S. attendees in November and December. In early November, a S.A.S. gentleman chose LGH for a prostate surgery which generated $3392.60 in billings for the hospital. He noted that he had never used LGH before but now felt comfortable with the facility since his S.A.S. visits to the hospital.

As a result of the sign-in sheets generated from each S.A.S. session, a computerized mailing list of over 600 different senior names was compiled. Monthly newsletters to S.A.S. attendees were initiated in December prior to the special Christmas program and will continue on a monthly basis. Further, S.A.S. participants age 55 and above will be extended the opportunity to join at a nominal charge of $5.00 the S.A.S. Club. This club will afford them a well-defined package of comprehensive benefits, service discounts for medical and ancillary services both at LGH and in the ambulatory clinics of TTUHSC, and on-going whole-person wellness educational programs. A S.A.S. card will be issued to each participant which will designate his membership in this club.

CONCLUSION

As a marketing tool and community service image builder to enhance and expose the general public to TTUHSC and LGH, the S.A.S. series has been a winner on all fronts. The educational thrust of the series provides a medium for presenting and show-casing people, facilities, resources, and ideas that is non-threatening and non-commercialized in format. To date, S.A.S. has resulted in bringing in more than 600 different guests for over 1800 visits to our institutions -- consider the multiplier effect as they relate these sessions with friends! Also, this pilot series and Christmas Special have created new opportunities for mutually beneficial team-building professional relationships among the faculty, administration, volunteers, and staff of both organizations. Moreover, the decision to give ownership of the S.A.S. program to the auxiliary group truly resulted in the origination of a superb program that was both created for and produced by seniors -- a winning combination.

As we approach the 1987 S.A.S. series, participants, presenters, and volunteers alike recognize that this program has opened doors for communication, education, caring, and service delivery as it touches the lives of seniors, their caregivers, and other health professionals living in the 125 mile radius of Lubbock, Texas. Indeed, "Seniors Are Special" and they deserve to be recognized, honored, and kept well-informed. After all, whole-person wellness for America's tomorrows begins with enhancing her seniors' health status today!

LONG TERM CARE IN THE HOSPITAL SETTING

Arthur E. Gross
Johnson County Memorial Hospital, Franklin, Indiana

ABSTRACT

Many hospitals are looking at alternative ways of using excess acute care patient units. Much is being written about the aging of America and how hospitals need to develop programs oriented toward the needs of older adults. This paper describes how one hospital converted a vacant patient unit to a skilled nursing facility and launched a successful introductory marketing campaign.

INTRODUCTION

There are a number of events shaping the direction of health care, and hospitals in particular. Two of them are our aging population and the Medicare Prospective Payment System. The nation's aging trend is creating demand for extended care services oriented toward chronic conditions. The Prospective Payment System has created vacant beds in our hospitals.

Hospital CEO's and Marketers are looking at new ways of using vacant space to generate revenue. One area receiving much attention is long term care within the hospital setting. Although it seems simple, it is not as easy as it looks. Long term care within the hospital must be viewed as a new business venture, it is different than acute inpatient care. The development of such a program involves many diverse elements which must be addressed.

PROJECT DEVELOPMENT

The 1986 marketing plan for Johnson County Memorial Hospital, Franklin, Indiana, contained strategies related to positioning the Hospital at competitive advantage among older adults in their market area. In particular, one of the enabling strategies employed was the development of a long term care unit (skilled nursing facility) in the Hospital.

The decision to develop a skilled nursing facility within the Hospital was based on several considerations:

** A strong acute care market share of area residents age 65 and over;
** Market research results showing high unaided awareness and preference levels along with very high effectiveness ratings for Johnson County Memorial among residents age 55 and over;
** A significant older adult population in the county, particularly in the Hospital's core market area where nearly 18 percent of the population was over age 65;
** The growing demand for post hospital care fostered by the Prospective Payment System;
** A competitor analysis of other long term care facilities in the area, looking at such items as level of care provided, historical census data, and potential competitor responses.

Early in the program's planning the Hospital's executive management group concluded that assistance with long term care expertise was needed. Accordingly, a firm with management experience in the long term care business was sought. A management contract was subsequently made with a company specializing in retirement living and long term care facilities. Through this contract, assistance was gained in facility design, program development, equipment and furnishings selection, market planning, and project implementation management.

The facility remodeling involved numerous issues specifically related to long term care facilities. Though located within the Hospital, the unit had to comply with Indiana's requirements for free-standing facilities. Issues involved:

** The suitability of the acute care patient room for long term care. Such problems as additional lighting, access to the toilet, additional storage space for personal belongings, and furniture arrangement had to be resolved;
** Allowance for dining, lounge, and recreational space on the unit;
** The development of an attractive and appealing decor;
** The selection of appropriate furnishings attuned to the needs of the infirmed older adult;
** Traffic flow into and within the unit;
** The planning for nursing support space in conformance with regulations.

Ultimately the skilled nursing unit was located in a vacant 50 bed acute care unit. The resulting remodeling project created a 39 bed unit.

On the regulatory side, several departments at the State Board of Health had to be dealt with. Those agencies included the Offices of Health Planning, Hospital Licensure, Health Facilities, and the Hospital Section of the Division of Sanitary Engineering.

In the program's early stages it was necessary to gain Certificate of Need Approval to obtain Medicare and Medicaid certification. An obstacle facing the project was the State Board of Health's long term care bed projections forecasting no need for such additional beds in the county. Although the initial efforts to gain CON approval were denied, the Hospital was able to undertake the project on a private pay basis as permitted under the State's Health Planning Law. Following amendments to the State's Health Planning Law in the Winter of 1986, Medicare and Medicaid certification became accessible.

PROGRAM MARKETING

Early in the project's development, efforts were concentrated on attracting the private pay patient and their family. A comprehensive marketing plan was written addressing competitor analysis, target market segments, marketing themes, referral sources, promotional tactics, media schedule, and marketing budget.

The target audiences for this marketing effort included older adults, grown children of older adults, family practice and internal medicine physicians, discharge planners at area hospitals, intermediate care facilities, clergy, and trust officers at financial institutions.

Two primary marketing themes were developed; one emphasized the rehabilitative nature of the services while the other discussed the unit's physical closeness to the Hospital. Promotional materials were created to convey sensitivity and professionalism.

A print advertising campaign was created supporting the two themes with the following ad titles: "For older adults, the first step in getting well is getting well informed" and "In an emergency we can get her to the hospital in 30 seconds." Each ad had three different pictorial images, producing a combination of six advertisements.

Specific marketing tactics employed to create awareness of and referrals for the skilled nursing facility included the following.

** Creation of a promotional brochure intended to reinforce the marketing themes. The brochure was distributed prior to the unit's opening to referral sources, older adult groups, and prospective clientele.
** An introductory letter announcing the unit's coming was sent to the targeted referral sources three months prior to opening.
** The initial print advertising campaign was placed in local newspapers for twelve weeks, from four weeks before opening to eight weeks after. The first ad flight consisted of 48 ad placements.
** The facility was featured in the Hospital's "Focus On Health" newspaper in early April, four weeks prior to opening. The paper is published quarterly and distributed to 49,000 households in the area.
** An information kit featuring articles about the skilled nursing facility was sent to area news media three weeks prior to opening.
** Special open house events were held the two weeks before opening for physicians and their office staffs, discharge planners at neighboring hospitals, financial trust officers, Hospital employees and volunteers, and the public.
** A second ad flight was planned for the Fall, once census development needs were determined. The second flight ran from early November to just before Christmas, during the family oriented holiday period. The print ads were placed in five local newspapers in communities neighboring the Hospital for a total of 30 ad placements.

WHAT WAS THE OUTCOME OF THE MARKETING EFFORT?

The marketing effort was intended to raise community awareness of the skilled nursing facility, demonstrate Johnson County Memorial's commitment to older adults, and generate admissions to the new unit. All three objectives were accomplished.

The initial promotional tactics generated 50 telephone inquiries, resulting in eight admissions to the unit. The public open house attracted 500 people to see the skilled nursing facility.

The initial occupancy projections were based on three admissions per month, building to a 90 percent occupancy level at the end of the first year. Through the first six months of operation, the admission rate far exceeded projections while the length of stay was lower than expected. Admissions numbered 73, with 48 discharges and a length of stay averaging 31.1 days. The patient mix objectives were achieved, as 42 percent were private pay and 53 percent were Medicare.

The high admission rate has indicated to us a high level of satisfaction derived from our initial clientele, which in turn has generated positive word-of-mouth promotion of the unit.

WHAT WAS LEARNED?

The long term care business is quite different from acute care inpatient services.

Long term care is highly regulated and is under intense public scrutiny by olderr adult advocacy groups.

The certification process for Medicare and Medicaid is extremely lengthy and quite subjective.

Remodeling an acute care unit to long term care requires an appreciation for the residents' extended care needs. One particular problem is that many older acute care rooms are undersized for long term care purposes.

Although extensive efforts have been made to develop a separate environment for the skilled nursing facility, the physicians and Hospital staff perceive it as another nursing unit.

In comparison to a free-standing facility, the unit within the Hospital is invisible to passers-by on the highway.

The hospital culture operates at a more hurried pace than the long term care culture.

In regard to skilled care, the hospital connection is a competitive advantage upon which to build.

Developing a long term care unit within the hospital can be a profitable way to use vacant space. However, the pitfalls are many and hospital executives need outside assistance to help chart the way.

THE SENIOR CIRCLE-
A SUCCESSFUL MARKETING EFFORT

Henry T. Jacques
Fairview General Hospital, Cleveland

ABSTRACT

Fairview General Hospital's Senior Circle of Care is a comprehensive array of services for persons over-65 and others eligible for Medicare benefits. The program combines services of a more clinical nature, such as a specialized inpatient unit for the elderly, an outpatient geriatric assessment clinic, and an active schedule of off-site health screenings, with a range of services appealing primarily to the well-elderly, such as discounts on parking and meals at the hospital, free subscriptions to health-related publications and price breaks on purchases at more than 200 stores of all types in the community. Extensive market research conducted by a national firm during the development of this program indicated that approximately 6,000 persons could be expected to apply for membership--to date the number enrolled is approaching 15,000, or 43 percent of the over-65 population living within Fairview General's primary service area.

HOSPITAL BACKGROUND

Fairview General Hospital is the fourth largest hospital in Greater Cleveland in terms of annual inpatient admissions. At the same time, current data shows 18 of 24 local hospitals with average costs per case higher than Fairview General's.

Fairview General is the dominant health provider on the city's West Side, serving more patients from Western Cleveland and its suburbs than any other hospital. More than 23,500 patients were admitted to the hospital's 519 beds during 1986. The hospital also maintains a large-scale outpatient program, which recorded a total of nearly 175,000 visits last year.

Fairview General provides a full range of primary medical care services, and a growing number of secondary and tertiary level programs. It is the leading maternity hospital in Northeastern Ohio and is also particularly well known for its services in cardiology, oncology, pediatrics and geriatrics.

Fairview General has 500 physicians on its Medical Staff; is a teaching hospital with residencies in Surgery and Family Practice and a School of Nursing; and also operates the area's premier health education center in a free-standing facility which is currently registering approximately 40,000 visits per year.

COMPETITIVE SITUATION

Hospital competition, as it is now commonly defined, is relatively new to the Greater Cleveland area. Serious advertising of services by Cleveland hospitals dates back only two to three years, and, in fact, many local hospitals still only advertise sporadically. Competition here is in its infancy, but it is growing rapidly and programs designed to influence physician and patient choices for one hospital over another are coming onto the scene with a regularity not heretofore observed.

There are several basic causes underlying this increased interest in and use of marketing techniques by Cleveland hospitals. All are related to declining inpatient usage patterns.

One reason lies in the fact that Cleveland suffers from the same forces affecting many old, northern industrial giants-- loss of industry, outmigration of population, and the uncertainties that accompany a switch in economic base. There are simply less people living in the Cleveland area, and therefore less people who will need hospital services at any given time.

Other causes are more closely associated with hospital practices and include the shift to outpatient services whenever possible and the new control mechanisms being mandated by the Federal government and many third-party payors. A growing percentage of patients are no longer admitted to the hospital, and those who are usually don't stay as long as they used to.

These trends have produced rapid escalation in estimates of excess inpatient bed capacity in the Cleveland area. It wasn't very long ago that various authorities were arguing as to whether 2,000 excess beds was an accurate estimate. Now some project the figure to be closer to 6,000, or nearly half of all hospital beds in Greater Cleveland (Crain's Cleveland Business 1985).

A GROWING SEGMENT

As in many other parts of the country, one segment of Greater Cleveland's population has continued to grow both in numbers and in proportion to the total population. That segment is the elderly, and this trend, of course, is particularly noteworthy to hospitals because older persons tend to use health services at a much higher rate than other segments of the population.

In fact, Western Greater Cleveland has a disproportionally high number of elderly residents. A hospital-funded study completed in January, 1984 relating to the age 65 and over population in a major portion of Fairview General's primary service area identified a senior population of 35,000 persons or 13.7 percent of the 255,000 people residing in the area which was the focus of the study. This percentage exceeds the national average of 11.3 percent; the Ohio average of 10.6 percent, and the total local county average of 12.8 percent.

Undoubtedly, these demographics contributed to a shift that had been observed at the hospital for some time. The number of Medicare-sponsored patients using Fairview General has been steadily increasing and has reached a point where approximately 50 percent of all inpatients on any given day are Medicare beneficiaries.

COMPETITIVE STRATEGIES

Given the increasing size and hospital usage patterns of the elderly population, various hospitals throughout the Greater Cleveland area began to look at this target segment as a potential source of additional admissions and launched promotional campaigns specifically designed to attract the attention of seniors.

One hospital near Fairview General began advertising that

it would waive co-payments and deductibles for all patients. This campaign, which used both commercial television and newspapers, had heavy emphasis on the elderly in the advertisements and collateral materials detailing this offer.

A hospital on the opposite side of town introduced its version of the Golden Care Plus program and offered to accept as payment in full whatever Medicare (or Medicare plus supplemental insurance) pays for inpatient and outpatient services at the hospital. This program was launched with a high visibility, intensive schedule of spots on commercial television.

Another nearby hospital began a supper club in its cafeteria with reduced meal prices for persons over 60 years of age. This program, while not heavily advertised, met with a high degree of success very quickly.

The floodgates opened. Hospitals began to offer the elderly a wide range of discounts, including price breaks on television rentals and telephones when hospitalized, and on cafeteria meals and health education courses when up and around. Free transportation for seniors to hospitals was introduced by at least two West Side institutions. Several hospitals purchased in-home personal emergency response systems and advertised their availability to seniors and caregivers. And, hospital-sponsored health fairs and educational programs for seniors became commonplace.

MARKET RESEARCH

During the period when many hospitals were thinking out plans for promotional programs aimed at the elderly, Fairview General received a letter from a patient who lived in North Olmsted, one of the major suburbs in the hospital's primary service area.

The basic thrust of this letter was a request that the hospital give consideration to allowing senior citizens and their relatives to park at reduced rates in the public parking garage adjacent to the physicians' center at the hospital complex. Among other reasons, the author cited the fixed income of many seniors, as well as the therapeutic value to a hospitalized patient of a visit from a spouse or other relative.

The letter writer was very active at the local senior center and he assured careful readership of his letter and consideration of his request by attaching a petition with 300 signatures. This might be called informal market research at its best.

The first response proposed to the request was that a card be issued which would allow the holder to be given a discount when parking in the garage. Fairview General's Public Relations Department produces a rich variety of publications for the hospital's staff, friends and associates, and it was also suggested that holders of this new card be given subscriptions to two of these publications. The idea of reduced television rental charges was also advanced.

Subsequently, three senior management officers met to discuss the idea and from that session emerged a consensus that the card concept be aggressively pursued and that a variety of services and discounts would be offered to persons applying for the card. Some of these services and reduced rates were developed especially for this program; others had previously existed and were therefore already available for inclusion in the benefits package. These benefits are described in detail in the following section.

At the same time the hospital was moving on the parking request, it was involved in planning a much more formal market research study on a series of geriatric services that had been under development for some time.

The results of the 1984 study cited earlier had brought into sharper focus the multi-faceted problems of the elderly and the hospital had been creating an integrated health care system that would continue over time and between providers and settings to address the needs of the aged population in its service area. A major grant was being sought from a foundation for that system, and the foundation had suggested that the services planned should be subject to proof of appeal and need through a formal market research study.

What finally came together then was the testing of a series of specialized services of a more clinical type that the hospital was developing for geriatric patients when hospitalized or in need of medical care and related supports, and, concurrently, the concept of a card which would provide Medicare-eligible persons with certain hospital services and discounts, the majority of which were aimed at the well-elderly.

The market research study was designed and conducted by a professional consulting firm headquartered in Chicago. The first phase of the research was done in the Spring of 1985 and involved five focus groups made up of the following target groups--geriatric patients who had been hospitalized at Fairview General, and at competing hospitals; caregivers; physicians; and the well-elderly. Shortly thereafter telephone interviews were conducted among a random sampling of 211 persons over age 65 and 100 caregivers, all living in Fairview General's primary service area.

THE SENIOR CIRCLE

Using the results of this market research, the hospital proceeded with final developments on its specialized programs and services for seniors.

The Senior Circle was the name chosen for the card. This name ties in with the hospital's logo and theme: "Providing a Circle of Care". The Circle of Care was selected for the hospital's logo because of its strong graphic potential and because of the fact that like a circle the hospital's services are continuous, always available, all encompassing, and provide care for all members of the family circle.

The card is very much akin to a common credit card in format. The patient's name and Medicare number are embossed on it using existing hospital equipment. The card is free, but an application must be submitted. The current age threshold is 65, but exceptions are made for disabled persons on Medicare.

These are the benefits of having a Senior Circle card, as presented in advertising and promotional materials:

* NO OUT-OF POCKET EXPENSES for covered inpatient and outpatient services for seniors who have Medicare and supplemental insurance.

* FREE help in filling out all Medicare and insurance forms.

* FREE personal financial counseling on health care.

* RISE -- a free information and referral service on social and health-related services in the community.

* PHYSICIAN REFERRAL SERVICE -- We'll help you find the right physician for any type of medical treatment you need.

* FREE parking when the card owner uses services at Fairview General.

* A 50% DISCOUNT on meals when visiting relatives or friends at Fairview.

* A 30% DISCOUNT on parking when visiting relatives or friends at Fairview.

* FREE subscriptions to the Fairviewer, Your Health and Fitness, and other health-related publications.

* NEVER ALONE -- Fairview's emergency response system that dispatches help to your home when needed. There is a monthly charge for the in-home unit, but installation of the unit, an instructional session, and an in-home system test are all provided without charge.

* SPECIAL speedy registration for all hospital services.

Subsequently, a community discount program was developed as an additional benefit. Local merchants in the Western Cleveland area were contacted about offering a discount to Senior Circle card holders, and more than 200 agreed to participate. A wide variety of businesses are involved, including a chain of drug stores, medical equipment suppliers, safety and security equipment dealers, restaurants, hardware, clothing shops, home repairs and housecleaning services.

The Senior Circle card is presented as "your key to service, whether you are using the hospital as a patient; visiting a relative or friend in the hospital; or looking to us for help on other matters involving your health and well-being".

Backing up that claim is a range of services that were developed consequent to the second main focus of the marketing research study. Those services include:

* The Senior Care Unit--this inpatient division has a specialized treatment program to help the elderly achieve maximum benefit during hospital stays. A team of professionals from many health disciplines are involved in the care of each patient.

* Geriatric Assessment Clinic--this service provides a special one-time evaluation for seniors with complex health needs and mental changes such as Alzheimer's disease. Again, a team of professionals makes a comprehensive health evaluation and plan of care.

* Senior Support Services--this program assures that older persons who need comprehensive care receive it in a coordinated way in their home. Registered nurses assess needs, help persons involved set goals, develop a plan to meet those goals, coordinate services, and follow-up to ensure needs are met.

* Senior Wellness--this is an outreach effort designed to help healthy seniors stay well. Nurses visit many locations in the community on a regular basis. Services include health screenings, such as blood pressure checks, and special monitoring, such as glaucoma testing.

* CARE (Community Assistance Resources for Elders) is a program in which trained volunteers assist seniors through telephone reassurance, light housekeeping, and errand running.

PROMOTIONAL CAMPAIGN

The advertising campaign for promotion of the Senior Circle card was developed by a professional advertising agency. All materials feature strong graphics of the card itself.

A large newspaper advertisement was developed and was used in both the west zone of Cleveland's daily newspaper, The Plain Dealer, as well as in a chain of weeklies--The Sun Newspapers--and other community newspapers.

The newspaper ads were also converted to direct mailers. These were distributed via purchased lists of over-65 residents in the hospital's primary service area.

A limited use of radio commercials was also employed at the start of the campaign.

News releases from the Public Relations Department succeeded in generating a good deal of favorable publicity for the program. And, of course, the Senior Circle was heavily promoted in publications produced by the hospital, two of which are mailed into all 110,000 homes in Fairview General's primary service area on a quarterly basis.

These steps were repeated a year later when the community discount program was introduced as an added benefit of the Senior Circle card.

A smaller ad has been developed for regular use in the community weekly newspapers. Experience has shown that these papers have been the most effective for promotion of the program.

Other promotional activities have included a contest in which employees were awarded prizes for signing up new members; giving out information on the Senior Circle at health fairs and other events; contacting senior housing complexes; working through churches; and promoting the card at senior centers and clubs. The seniors who sent in the petition which led to this program were true to their word--they signed up in large numbers.

RESULTS

Data obtained from the market research study questions involving the Senior Circle card was used by the consulting firm to project that 5,741 persons were likely to ever use the program. By the end of 1986--approximately a year and a half after the Senior Circle was first advertised--the total number of cards issued is approaching 15,000. This represents 43 percent of the estimated 35,000 persons over age 65 living in the hospital's primary service area. The program has a goal of reaching at least 50 percent.

But for the hospital's marketing purposes, the Senior Circle card really serves as a mechanism for distinguishing Fairview General's program from competing ones and for communicating with seniors about the services Fairview General maintains for them. The hope, of course, is that when Senior Circle members need hospital services they will choose Fairview General as the provider.

Studies show that this desired result is being achieved. Two mail surveys have been conducted in connection with offering Senior Circle members subscriptions to hospital publications. The sign-up card for the publications contained three questions relative to hospital usage.

Of the approximate 2,000 member responses received in these surveys:

* 33 percent of the respondents had used the Senior Circle card in connection with services at Fairview General, both of a medical and non-medical nature;

* 5 percent were persons converted to using Fairview General for hospital services--they indicated they had been a patient here for the first time as a result of being a Senior Circle member;

* 18 percent were patients with whom a stronger bond was forged--they had used Fairview General's medical services both before and after becoming Senior Circle members.

SUMMARY

The Senior Circle has been a successful marketing effort for
Fairview General Hospital. This outcome is particularly
gratifying because the project is the first full-scale marketing effort carried out by the hospital in response to the
rapid changes taking place in its competitive environment.
The project involved market research, product line development, promotion, and evaluation, more of which is yet to
come.

The Senior Circle has brought new patients to Fairview General, and has helped bond previous users to the institution
more closely. As such, it has been a first line of defense
against competing programs.

The Senior Circle has opened new communications channels
for Fairview General with both individuals and agencies. It
serves as a highly visible addition to the hospital's reputation for leadership and innovation.

Fairview General served more patients in 1986 than ever before in its history. Inpatient admissions were up by nearly
10 percent and total outpatient visits climbed by approximately 18 percent. Certainly, the Senior Circle was one of
the more notable initiatives contributing to that success.

REFERENCES

Crain's Cleveland Business (1985), "1989 forecast: Report
  halves hospital bed need," (September 16), 1.

MANAGED HEALTH CARE

As corporate benefits managers become more actively
involved in containing the costs of health services, the
trend points towards and increase in the managed approach
to the purchase of health services. This paper by Fine
addresses the issues by examining the perspectives of the
key players in this managed health care approach as well
as suggests how effective marketing strategies can
enhance greater acceptance of this concept.

MARKETING MANAGED CARE:
BRINGING PHYSICIANS INTO THE FOLD

Allan Fine, MBA
Account Executive
Rush Contract Care, Chicago, IL

J. Christopher Newman, MBA
Assistant Vice President, Corporate
Planning and Market Research
Rush-Presbyterian-St. Luke's Medical
Center, Chicago, IL

I.   Overview of Managed Care Today

Managed care has emerged in the last few
years as a significant health care
financing and delivery mode.

- - - - - - - - - - - - - - - - - --
Exhibit 1: Growth of Managed Care
Programs
- - - - - - - - - - - - - - - - - --

Reasons for managed care growth depend
upon the perspective: those who pay for
the care want reduced health care costs
with quality; those who provide care or
who channel the payment for care want an
increase in business volume.

- - - - - - - - - - - - - - - - - --
Exhibit 2: Perspectives of Managed Care
- - - - - - - - - - - - - - - - - --

Managed care influences the purchasing
decisions of health care

    o   by forcing the seller-
         hospital and physician - to
         exchange a discount for the
         prospect of increased (or even
         maintenance of the same)
         volume.

    o   by providing financial
         inducements for the buyer-
         employer and employee/consumer
         - to select lower cost
         providers.

- - - - - - - - - - - - - - - - - --
Exhibit 3: Contractual Arrangements of
the Players in the Managed Care Market
- - - - - - - - - - - - - - - - - --

Hospital perspective: managed care
presents a wide variety of contractors-
all with discounts paramount in mind.
Hospitals are motivated by the need to
maintain the loyalty of physicians who
might follow the contractual arrangements
of their PPO/IPA patients to other
hospitals.

- - - - - - - - - - - - - - - - - --
Exhibit 4: Hospital Perspective of
Managed Care
- - - - - - - - - - - - - - - - - --

How much of a discount to give?
Discounts and arrangements vary according
to the local market, the individual
hospital's costs of providing care, and
its willingness to price on the margin.
The pricing arrangements are based upon
the following:

    o   Hospital rates
         -    per diem
         -    per discharge
         -    per DRG
         -    flat scheduled rate
         -    charges less discount
         -    per cent of costs

The physician perspective is essentially
the same as the hospital's.   The basis
for the rates are:

    o   Physician rates
         -    relative value units
         -    HIAA fee schedule
         -    per cent of UCR
         -    scheduled rate (including
              DRG)
         -    capitation rate
         -    charges less discount

- - - - - - - - - - - - - - - - - --
Exhibit 5: Physician Perspective of
Managed Care
- - - - - - - - - - - - - - - - - --

To complete the puzzle of managed care,
it is important to look at the perspectie
of the payor.

- - - - - - - - - - - - - - - - - --
Exhibit 6: Payor Perspective of Managed
Care
- - - - - - - - - - - - - - - - - --

The payor, commerical carrier, Blue
Cross/Blue Shield, and independent plans,
contract with PPOs in order to offer
their cost containment advantages. Blue
Cross/Blue Shield has their own PPO.
Commercial carriers are contracting with
national networks of PPOs, such as the
Volunteer Hospitals of America (VHA) and
Adventists.

II.   Marketing Managed Care

Managed care offers the purchasers of
care the prospect of obtaining an equal
or better product at reduced cost.   On
that basis alone it is an attractive
product to offer.

Exhibit 7: <u>Spectrum of the Benefit Plan</u>
- - - - - - - - - - - - - - - - - - - --

The managed care market manager's objective is to make these basic characteristics known to the prospective purchaser. Unfor-tunately, managed care does not always save money for the employer and the employee/patient's experience or perception of the various aspects of the care package is not always favorable.

In a recent study (February, 1986) in Chicago performed by the Chicago Tribune, of the corporate benefits administrators who offered managed care products to their employees

o   18 percent felt the plans had <u>increased</u> costs, while
o   one-fourth felt that these plans had resulted in a <u>decrease</u> in company helath care costs.

The perception that managed care can reduce costs, though, is borne out in the fact that in addition to the 28 percent of the companies surveyed who offer managed care products to their employees, another 10 percent had plans to offer an HMO or PPO in the next twelve months. Managed care or not, 58 percent of the companies acknowledged that they had already or planned to negotiate lower rates with providers, and 47 percent had plans or had already implemented utilization review programs. Two percent overall planned or were already making HMO enrollment mandatory for new employees.

The hospital market manager's objective is to make available to his patient population, especially the corporations, an attractive, high quality, accessible, and low cost inpatient and outpatient services package. His competitive stance in this regard might well be: "I'll offer whatever managed care product is out there, as long as I don't run too large a risk of losing money on it, to make sure that my hospital not only doesn't lose any patients but also gains a few it wouldn't otherwise attract."

- - - - - - - - - - - - - - - - - - --
Exhibit 8: <u>Hospital Pricing Strategies for Managed Care</u>

- - - - - - - - - - - - - - - - - - --

- - - - - - - - - - - - - - - - - --
Exhibit 9: <u>Bringing Physicians into the Fold</u>

- - - - - - - - - - - - - - - - - - --

By virtue of sharing the same viewpoints of the competitive market, physicians and hospitals can help each other by collaboratively engaging in marketing and promotional programs.

- - - - - - - - - - - - - - - - - - --
Exhibit 10: <u>Marketing vehicles should:</u>

- - - - - - - - - - - - - - - - - - --

In addition, the hospital's management information systems should begin tracking the identity of patients' employers to assist managed care marketing managers in defining for their client prospects the pattern of current utilization.

III. THE FUTURE

Looking at one major market in the U.S.- the Metropolitan Chicago area - as an admitedly small sample, the managed care products now available are increasing rapidly in number and in market penetration.

- - - - - - - - - - - - - - - - - --
Exhibit 11: <u>Managed Care in the Metropolitan Chicago Area</u>

- - - - - - - - - - - - - - - - - - --

Two of the major medical centers in Chicago have offered HMO staff model plans: Rush-Presbyterian-St. Luke's Medical Center and Michael Reese Hospital. Many other independent HMOs have been formed, though the larger ones are the IPA model. The growth in the market share of managed care recently has been largely due to the conversion to IPA model HMOs from indemnity plans, not to staff model plans, nor to PPOs.

RPSLMC has recently formed both a PPO, Rush Contract Care, and an IPA model HMO, Access Health. These three products will be marketed together, since the future of managed care in the market place is to provide multiple options to the purchasers from one seller.

- - - - - - - - - - - - - - - - - --
Exhibit 12: <u>The Future of Managed Care</u>

- - - - - - - - - - - - - - - - - - --

Exhibit 1: Growth of Managed Care Programs

	June 1981	June 1982	June 1983	June 1984	June 1985	December 1985
Number of Plans						
Groups	153	168	181	180	212	235
(% of plans)	63%	63%	65%	59%	54%	49%
IPA's	90	97	99	126	181	245
(% of plans)	37%	37%	35%	41%	46%	51%
Total	243	265	280	306	393	480
Enrollment (000's)						
Groups	8,684	9,361	10,602	12,196	14,247	14,655
(% of members)	85%	86%	85%	81%	75%	70%
IPA's	1,582	1,471	1,889	2,945	4,646	6,397
(% of members)	15%	14%	15%	19%	25%	30%
Total	10,266	10,831	12,491	15,141	18,894	21,052

Source: "National HMO Census 1985," InterStudy, 1986.

Exhibit 2: Perspectives of Managed Care

Player	Motivating Factors Cost Containment	Maintain/Increase Volume
Employer	X	
Physician		X
Hospital		X
Employee	X	
Payor		X

Exhibit 3: Contractual Arrangements of the Players in the Managed Care Market

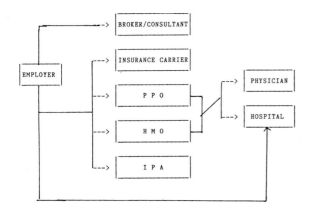

Exhibit 4: Hospital Perspective of Managed Care

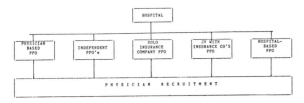

Exhibit 5: Physician Perspective of Managed Care

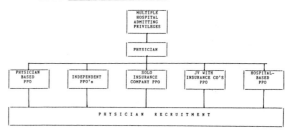

Exhibit 6: Payor Perspective of Managed Care

	PAYOR		
	COMMERCIAL CARRIER	BLUE CROSS/ BLUE SHIELD	INDEPENDENT PLANS
INDEPENDENT PPO	X	Have Own PPO	X
SOLO INSURANCE CARRIER PPO	X	N/A	X
JOINT VENTURE PPO	X	N/A	X

Exhibit 7: Spectrum of the Benefit Plan

SPECTRUM OF THE BENEFIT PLAN

FULLY MANAGED<-->SELF INSURED

HMO	PPO/IPA	FULLY INSURED		
Incentives Disincentives Utilization Review	Co-pays Deductibles	Carrier	Re-insurance Stop Loss	Administrative Services

Exhibit 8: Hospital Pricing Strategies for Managed Care

- o On margin: meet direct unit of service's expenses plus an increment for profit
    - effective as long as the volume is low enough not to increase the indirect expenses and the services offered at the margin are not replacement of current volume
    - yields most competitive prices

- o On average: meet the average unit of service's direct and indirect expenses plus an increment for profit
    - ensures profitability
    - may not yield competitive prices, with loss of volume

Exhibit 9: Bringing Physicians into the Fold

Physicians are brought together with hospitals through

- o sharing the same view of the competitive world of managed care
- o being forced to undergo pre-admission certification, case management procedures, and scrutiny of practice and care giving procedures.

Exhibit 10: <u>Marketing vehicles should</u>:

- o Stress the "hot buttons" of both employees and employers
- o Promote the cooperative relationship of the physicians with the hospital
- o Include mention of the managed care programs and the larger employers whose employees are members

Exhibit II: Managed Care in the Metropolitan Chicago Area

Product	July 1, 1985	July 1, 1986
HMO Staff Model		
Plans	3	3
Enrollment	241,880	277,500
HMO IPA Model		
Plans	8	10+
Enrollment	178,600	303,200
PPO		
Plans	N/A	14
Hospitals	N/A	119
HMO Group		
Plans	2	2
Enrollment	63,415	7,300
HMO Network		
Plans	5	5+
Enrollment	195,380	246,600

Exhibit 12: <u>The Future of Managed Care</u>

- o Triple and multiple option plans offered by one vendor
- o Formal links or joint ventures between managed care entities and between them and hospitals
- o Marketing will stress the factors of quality, convenience, and cost in that order

SERVICE MANAGEMENT

The importance of service management in the health care
industry has grown in recognition. The papers included
here present thorough coverage of establishing service
management programs in a health care setting. Examples
are drawn from outside industries as well as from health
care environments.

ACCOUNTABILITY THROUGH SERVICE MANAGEMENT

Kristine E. Peterson, K. E. Peterson & Associates, Chicago

ABSTRACT

Service management is the watchword for the future. Service management is the systematic approach for defining the hospital's services in a manner that is differentiating. Service management calls for targeting market segments and needs; conceptualizing how the service will be perceived by customers; defining operating strategies; and designing an efficient and effective service delivery system. It calls for a service strategy built on the organizational values. Finally, it requires measures of accountability to ensure superior service performance from every employee <u>and</u> every department.

INTRODUCTION

Over the past four years, American businesses have been learning lessons from excellent companies. As we voraciously read to stay in the mainstream of modern management thought, we have sustained ourselves on steady diets of admonitions from the authors who created the culture phenomenon and the second generation culture vultures who have made preaching and teaching "excellence" a big business.

As competition in the healthcare industry becomes more rampant; patients more discerning; payors more cost-conscious and physicians more entrepreneurial, hospitals are reaching deeper into their pocketbooks to fund their educations. They are paying big bucks to recruit marketing specialists from other industries; hiring a host of consultants from market research to guest relations; and flying off to numerous seminars and conferences that advertise the promise of the latest innovations in consumer-oriented marketing warfare.

Of all of the lessons that have been taught, one major lesson is yet to be learned: If we are to ride the crest of emerging trends, it is important not to get battered against the rocks.

It has happened over and over again. One business fad is replaced with another. We move from Theory X to Theory Y to Theory Z. With no more letters in the alphabet, we move to searches and then to passions. When the lust subsides, we use our marketing imaginations to re-invent our corporations.

To manage change amidst the turbulence, answers are sought. Those seeking the solutions are not unlike those who twist and turn the Rubic's cube a thousand different ways trying to solve the puzzle. After thousands of different configurations and as many failed attempts, most give up. The cube is abandoned on the shelf.

Which is where guest relations programs are being found in increasing numbers.

Guest relations was embraced from the beginning. It held great promise. It has not taken long, however, for high hopes to be dashed in disillusionment. The bugles which sounded so clearly when the guest relations program was launched have turned flat, if not sour. The banners have been taken down. As everyone ponders the question, "Where did we go wrong?" a few stubborn die-hards courageously ask, "Where do we go from here?"

WHERE DO WE GO FROM HERE

The first step is to go beyond, if you have not already, thinking of guest relations as a program, specifically a training program. Think of a multi-dimensional approach for delivering quality care that is directed to meet the needs and to exceed the expectations of the customers.

Guest relations was, is and forever shall be one of the most vital and essential strategies for distinctively positioning a hospital in a competitive marketplace; for differentiating services; for managing risk; for creating excellence; and for providing a workplace in which employees can be challenged, productive and fulfilled. The challenge now is to reach beyond and to create new strategies and systems to achieve superior service and performance. A transformation of the way service is conceptualized, managed and delivered is required for the future.

FUTURE TRENDS

As the concept of service management evolves, future trends that will be especially meaningful to marketing managers and executives are predicted.

Market Research

As marketing warfare has taught us, the battleground of competition takes place in the minds of the customers. That terrain is tricky and difficult to understand. Market research will continue to become increasingly important because of what it reveals about customers' attitudes, perceptions, needs and expectations.

Product/Service Design

As healthcare organizations become more knowledgeable about the demographic, geo-demographic and psychographic characteristics of their targeted markets, they will package their services in unique ways. Product and market segmentation will result in greater innovation to deliver those services in ways that are differentiating.

Delivery System Design

Systems for service delivery will be designed and redesigned for flexibility. Employees will be given the autonomy to break rules and make decisions that will be in the best interest of their customers.

Decentralization

Departments within the hospital will view their services as product lines. Decentralization will force managers to think of themselves as chief executives of their own "in search of excellence" companies. They will work harder to create their own service cultures within the context of the overall corporate culture; to solicit the cooperation of the "vendors" on whom they rely to produce their final product(s); to motivate those who deliver it to be more responsive; and to gain customer acceptance and satisfaction.

Individual Accountability

Employees will learn that taking part is not a matter of personal preference; it will be a part of the job. The department managers will make it clear to employees through job descriptions, performance reviews and pay policies. Recruitment, orientation, education and training will become powerful tools in promoting the desired behavioral traits. The superordinate value of customer service will trigger promotions, rewards and recognition.

Departmental Accountability

And finally, as hospitals become more attentive to research -- and more willing to pay for it -- they will scrutinize their services to determine whether customer expectations have been met. The feedback will provide new ways to measure service delivery effectiveness which will create greater accountability. Because every department in the hospital delivers a service to customer(s), customer satisfaction will become a key component of departmental goals and objectives. Feedback from the customer -- whether that customer is a patient, physician or another department -- will determine whether those goals have been met.

THE INFRASTRUCTURE

A service management program that will stand the test of time must have, at its foundation, an infrastructure. An infrastructure can be the difference between having to initiate redundant programs in a feeble attempt to achieve excellence -- and moving forward to obliterate the obstacles that prevent customers from experiencing less than 100% satisfaction. The infrastructure is comprised of two components: Measures of Accountability and Satisfaction Feedback Systems.

Measures of Accountability

The goal of service management is to create accountability for service excellence at three levels: organizational; departmental and individual.

Satisfaction feedback systems continually provide feedback on customer satisfaction and identify areas in which service improvements should be contemplated and made. The organization, itself, is accountable to act on this information and to initiate service improvements that will increase the levels of satisfaction experienced by patients, visitors, physicians and other service departments.

To do so, committees should be structured to review and assess barriers to customer satisfaction and to create programs, services and innovations that will result in greater levels of satisfaction for consumers and providers of service.

Each department is accountable for service delivery and must develop standards of excellence that will enable managers to define expectations and to measure the degree to which the delivery of their service(s) meets the needs and exceeds the expectations of their primary and secondary customers.

Every employee contributes to meeting the needs and exceeding the expectations of customers. Standards must be drafted and incorporated into job descriptions and performance criteria. Managers are responsible for communicating expectations; monitoring performance against the standards; providing regular and frequent performance feedback; counseling and coaching; rewarding and recognizing those who contribute; and ultimately dismissing those who do not.

Patient Satisfaction Feedback System

There are a variety of mechanisms that will provide ongoing feedback. These include:

Surveys - Surveys are the easiest and least expensive way to solicit feedback from the patient. The instrument must be designed to measure patients' overall satisfaction, to obtain diagnostic data that explains their satisfaction ratings, and to track the levels of patient satisfaction over time.

Complaint Management - Repetitive complaints signal recurring dissatisfaction with particular services. A system to log, classify, analyze and track complaints is necessary.

Telephone surveys - If conducted by qualified personnel, telephone surveys can provide revealing information about patient satisfaction.

Focus groups - The use of focus groups can satisfy a variety of needs: to identify sources of satisfaction and dissatisfaction; to stimulate ideas from the users that will increase satisfaction in the future; to define expectations that will assist the hospital in designing quantitative measurement instruments.

Personal interviews - Conducted by managers while the patient is still hospitalized, the personal interviews provide satisfaction feedback relative to specific services delivered by patient-contact departments.

Referral information - Others who have frequent contact with patients such as patient representatives, chaplains, administrators, physicians and physicians' employees can collect and refer patient satisfaction information.

Physician Satisfaction Feedback System

Gathering feedback from physicians is more challenging, but nonetheless important. Both quantitative and qualitative methods should be used to:

1) Track physician satisfaction with critical components of service;

2) Gather feedback relative to support provided to enhance practice development;

3) Identify service improvements that will create greater levels of satisfaction from physicians, physicians' patients, physicians' office staffs.

Departmental Satisfaction Feedback System

Satisfaction levels with the interdepartmental exchange of service should be measured on a bi-annual basis with each department offering performance assessments of those departments on whom they rely to deliver their services.

Employee Satisfaction Feedback System

An employee's willingness to contribute is influenced by the degree to which he feels good about who he is (self-esteem), where he works (pride) and what he does (purpose).

Monitoring employee satisfaction and opening channels of communication to actively encourage <-employee-> <-management-><-administration-> communication should be initiated through:

Internal surveys - Designed specifically to track employee perceptions on critical issues affecting service performance, surveys should be randomly administered at least every six months.

Opinion surveys - Comprehensive employee opinion surveys should be conducted annually.

Employee focus groups - Useful in isolating and solving problems, employee discussion or focus groups should also be structured to generate ideas and innovations for service delivery.

Communication forums - Feedback solicited through regular meetings between administrators and employees should be initiated on a regular basis.

THE SERVICE STRATEGY

A service strategy includes a statement of the business mission that defines the business. It is built on defined organizational values. This strategy for achieving superior service and performance should be keyed to the needs and expectations of the customers.

A service strategy for each department should also be developed. Every manager should be responsible for identifying the department's primary and secondary customers; the standards of expected performance and the driving values which will influence the delivery of the service(s) to achieve the stated mission/goals.

THE SERVICE DELIVERY SYSTEM

Each department should analyze its delivery system(s) and isolate breakdowns and barriers that inhibit efficient and effective service delivery. To do this, the manager should diagram the service cycle from the first to the last points of customer contact; analyze repetitive questions and complaints; review all procedures and policies. In essence, the purpose of this audit is to identify the degree to which the service system is structured for the convenience of the customer. Most systems are structured for the convenience of the providers.

THE SERVICE-ORIENTED STAFF

Employees must be educated first. What industry factors and changes have created the need for superior service? What organizational, departmental and personal benefits result from customer satisfaction? What is the individual's role and responsibility?

Expectations are communicated verbally, in writing and behaviorally. Every manager must be aware of all three channels because all three influence employee attitudes and behaviors.

Communicate expectations. Begin with candidates who interview for positions within the hospital/department; provide new employees with a comprehensive orientation to help them understand the high standards of expected performance; to indoctrinate them; to expose them to the history, traditions, values, 'rites and rituals' and every other cultural nuance.

Provide ongoing reinforcement to all employees. Offer training to enhance skills; feedback to reinforce positive behaviors; coaching to develop. Quality and productivity can be improved by generating commitment to value-driven performance.

SUMMARY

Service management requires a strong commitment to service excellence in strategy, systems and performance management. To competitively position the provider organization, service must become the standard. When it is designed strategically, delivered effectively and measured against the customer's wants and needs, superiority can be achieved and sustained.

USING HIGH TOUCH FOR MARKET SHARE ADVANTAGE AND PROVING MEASURABLE RETURN ON INVESTMENT

Paul H. Keckley, Ph.D.
The Keckley Group, Nashville, Tennessee

INTRODUCTION

Does "high touch" really matter? Does having a reputation for "warm, caring and helpful" attention by hospital personnel make a difference where it counts...on the bottom line, or is a warm fuzzy atmosphere only a last ditch effort by competitively disadvantaged hospitals to try to differentiate themselves? When push comes to shove, should administration invest in a new piece of equipment or a guest relations program?

At the heart of most hospital positioning strategies is the notion of "high touch," that is, the assumption that the consumer will choose one hospital over another because one is known for having an atmosphere more conducive to personalized attention or individual concern for the patient or the patient family. Often, this positioning notion is contrasted by means of expensive advertising campaigns against "high tech" or the hospital which is usually bigger and presumed to be more specialized and less "personal."

This presentation will answer two important questions about "high touch" positioning...

(1) Does "high touch" affect market share? Or, what is the relationship between a "high touch" image and actual use of the hospital?

(2) What can be done to improve "high touch" performance which will ultimately move market share?

To answer these questions, The Keckley Group has conducted an extensive analysis of thirty-six hospitals representative of hospitals of all sizes in varying market conditions and regions. The results of this landmark analysis, and the implications for marketing strategy, are significant for hospitals of all sizes and in every condition.

DOES HIGH TOUCH MATTER?

In their monumental treatise on organizational effectiveness In Search of Excellence: Lessons from America's Best Run Companies, Tom Peters and Bob Waterman noted that "excellent companies" tended to demonstrate a "service obsession" in responding to customer needs and wants. They offer a litany of illustrations ranging from car dealer Joe Girard who said he sent out thirteen thousand customer cards per month to giant IBM which answers every complaint within twenty-four hours. From Walt Disney Productions to Frito Lay, the writers forward a strong argument for companies which put customer service at the head of the line of operational concerns. In summarizing, they draw two important conclusions about service driven companies: "customer service is at the heart of every activity of the organization," and "almost every one of our service oriented institutions does overspend on service, quality and reliability."

In a similar vein, the work of Citibank's Dinah Nemeroff is noteworthy. In 1980, she analyzed eighteen high profile corporations attempting to isloate the "people" factors. Her hit list included giants like American Airlines, Disney, McDonald's, Westin, Hertz, IBM and others. Her conclusions were that three characteristics separated the "high touch" corporations:

(1) Effective high touch involves the active, intensive involvement of senior management.

(2) It involves a remarkable people orientation in product development, pricing, quality assurnace and promotion.

(3) It involves a high intensity of measurement and feedback.

In the healthcare industry, the notion of "high touch" has been popularized in an era where each hospital is attempting to find a means of differentiating itself. Some have chosen to position along product specific lines, using well-produced advertising to present their service lines in a manner which infers a higher level of quality or more convenient approach. Others have elected to build a reputation based on an institutional image rather than service line specific volleys. One popular tactic has been the use of "high touch" messages...how many of you know of a hospital which says WE CARE. In fact, several hospitals have spent their entire marketing appropriation on this central theme of "high touch." A recent campaign for a religious-affiliated hospital in the Sunbelt advised its market that "every one of our employees has been trained in guest relations...you can see the difference in their eyes." Was this investment of $80,000 for TV time prudent? Did the market come dashing because it had finally been advised of the availability of at least one hospital among the many which had "real" people delivering "real service?" Hardly.

Probably each hospital in this room has invested in a "guest relations" program in the past two or three years. Let's see the hands of anyone whose institution has not...

Current guest relations programs offer a smorgasbord for the choosing. Some are do it yourself, fill in the blank manuals for all employees. Some are "high tech" combinations of video cassettes and on-site supervised discussion...and ther's everything in between. In fact, probably the most popular consultant domain, and among the most lucartive along withwomen's healthcare and PPO development, is the area of "guest relations."

The key question I want you to consider is this: how many of you have bona fide data to support the claim that "high touch" investments within your organization improved the bottom line in your hospital in terms of market share improvements? Isn't that what everything boils down to? As a marketer, my task is to advise and facilitate the hospital's response to opportunities before the guy across the street realizes what has happened. All too often, investments in programs like guest relations are made without regard for projected results. In fact, very few hospital marketing professionals view guest relations as more than a necessary part of internal climate control. It's an expense. It's just one of those things which you have to do but you don't expect much to come out of it.

I wonder if Ralston Purina's Keystone Village operation on the ski slopes of Colorado has the same attitude. In January, we took our staff to Keystone for planning and playing. To our amazement, each lift operator, clerk, and ski patrol person and first aid attendant demonstrated exceptional people skills. Amazing for an employee core composed almost exclusively of college ski bums engaged at almost minimum wage for the allurement of free lift tickets and nightly carousing. Yet each was skilled in maximizing the value of Keystone for its customers. Each had mastered the art of "high touch." Is this investment just an expense to RP? Not at all. It's an investment. It is built on a complex system they have developed to screen applicants using a psychological profile which gauges people skills. It is monitored using roving mystery customers and formal measures of people skills. Complaints are correlated to annual sales and even more important, revenues from new and repeat customers. Dollars invested in their guest relations programs are investments in market share which would otherwise be spent in more risky return tactics such as direct mail solicitation or travel agent promotions.

We recently studied the correlation between market share and perceptions of "high touch" in thirty-six hospitals across the U.S. Using in-depth statistical analysis to isolate factors which related to "high touch" or "high tech" we found to our surprise some very startling things ...

(1) In the markets considered, the biggest hospitals were perceived to be highest on both the "high tech" and "high touch" measures. In fact, "high tech" positioning correlates strongly with "high touch" positioning.

(2) High touch correlations to market share of admissions is less strong than high tech.

(3) High touch matters most to women, especially women having a baby.

(4) There is only a small correlation between high touch factors and emergency room visits, and a relatively low correlation between high touch and consumer preferences for general medical care.

Does high touch matter? es, but it alone will not move market share. The data from this analysis clearly reveals that high tech is more important in today's healthcare environment than high touch. It syas that high touch factors such as the level of concern shown patients and the information given patients and patient families are important only if the products and services already in place are perceived to be of adequate quality.

TO POSITION AS THE HIGH TOUCH HOSPITAL IS NOT A WINNING STRATEGY TO GAIN MARKET SHARE. TO POSITION AS THE HIGH TECH HOSPITAL FIRST IS THE WINNING STRATEGY. HIGH TOUCH IS MORE EFFECTIVE IN REINFORCING MARKET SHARE THAN IN ATTRACTING MARKET SHARE.

WHAT CAN BE DONE TO MAXIMIZE THE IMPACT OF HIGH TOUCH ON MARKET SHARE?

The foregoing discussion focuses attention on the secondary role of high touch in attracting market share. Our data clearly indicates that having the right product, the right equipment, the right facility and the right practitioner are ultimately more effective in attracting market share.

This does not in any way obviate the usefulness of "high touch" in defen i g market share or in maximizing patient or patient family satisfaction, especially in markets where consumers perceive the supply of "high tech" is adequate and available through ore than one hospital.

How should hospital marketers approach "high touch" as a component of its strategy? Once again, the best lessons are those from other service industries.

In the airline industry, "high touch" is isolated to certain customer "sensitivities" and all investments are made specifically addressing these few. At the top of the list is delays in departure times. Piedmont is adamant about this, preferring to close the door of the gate precisely on the departure time rather than chalk up another DD.

In the hospitatlity industry, the Marriott Corporation has a similar strategy. A precise list of pressure points are isolated. Training is geared to reduce these pressure points, and evaluation and ompensation of employees is strongly related to eas rus of change on these pressure points. One key pressure point at Marriott is waiting times at check in, another is waiting time at check out. Do you wonder why Marriott was first to provide advance check out as a convenience? Or why Bill Marriott still answers complaints personally?

The examples are too many to recall here. The common ingredients are evident: hospitals wishing to maximize high touch performance should pay attention:

(1) Identify and isolate customer pressure points.

> For most hospital customers, our research indicates the following are the most sensitive of all issues:
> .....waiting times for admission, especially in ER
> .....failure to provide patient information by doctor or nurse
> .....failure of the nursing staff to answer call buttons
> .....lack of family amenities for extended inpatient stays
> .....lack of information about charges for care
> .....lack of respect for patient privacy

> Certainly there are others but these are the most important.

(2) Define staff behaviors which affect these pressure points.

> Take, for instance, waiting times in ER. That's a problem for most hospitals. Minor emergencies take a back seat to major e ergencies and that's as it should be. But does the customer understand that his/hers is a "minor" emergency? Usually not.

> The behaviors which staff can control in this regard involve (1) informing the customer of the nature of his/ her classification as a "minor" emergency, (2) telling him/her how long the wait will be, (3) providing amenities which will reduce the pressure such as a waiting area with TV, (4) reinforcing the customer's need with regular contact at least every ten minutes, and (5) providing information about the diagnosis and treatment procedures before dismissing the person to home care or an inpatient room.

(3) Measure, train and reward personnel based on these behaviors.

> The banking industry long ago learned an important principle: you can't expect your front line people to perform if they are not evaluated and rewarded on the basis of the desired behaviors. How many of you have specific performance evaluation procedures which define expected outcomes for "high touch" performance and then reward on the same basis? Very few, I would assume.

> This is the MTR model: MEASURE, TRAIN AND REWARD.

> Bank tellers are trained to remember cusomer names. They are routinely "shopped" to determine how methodically they employ their training, and they are compensated for performing in this important area.

The importance of MTR in hospital operations cannot be overstated. We expect orderlies to introduce themselves, yet compensation and reward for outstanding performance is missing in most hospitals. We expect our nurses to function as tour guides, baby sitters, and patient information specialists, yet we respond to their performance evaluations based on input from supervisors rather than input from patients and patient families. We choose doctors based on clinical skills, then express surprise that a doctor who refuses to take time to explain treatments is usually the target of litigation in which the hospital is joint defendant.

The Keckley Group has documented the importance of high touch as a secondary but important positioning strategy for its clients. We have correlated high touch by product line with sensitive pressure points and developed MTR models which respond to each one. Time does not permit presentation of each product line MTR model. One brief example may suffice:

In obstetrics, which is by far the most "high touch" of all service lines, these are the pressure points for customers:

.....the availability of adequate procedures and policy conducive for the involvement of the husband in the delivery
.....the willingness of the hospital nursing staff to provide a room which allows plenty of rest post delivery
.....the willingness of the physician to answer questions about the condition of the baby post-delivery
.....the willingness of the hospital to provide family members amenities during the pre-delivery waiting period
.....the willingness of the attending staff of doctors and nurses to preserve the dignity of the mother during labor and delivery, including the securing of privacy
.....the willingness of the admitting physician to provide the patient options for procedures such as anesthesia and discharge plans

Each of these pressure points involves performance by staff in specific ways. Each can be measured by contacting each discharged mother and the spouse/significant other to evaluate performance. Each staff member can be rewarded for performance in each performance area.

This is oversimplified. I realize it's easy to say we should evaluate and reward performance when, in the real world, many healthcare professionals afield the basics of human kindness. But the challenge is nonetheless real.

Before closing, there's one other lesson from industry which should be forwarded in this conclusion. Rewards have the most impact when they are more frequent, that is, it's better to provide incentives monthly or even weekly with less value than to have only one big winner every six months or a year. The lesson is to have everyone in the organization always striving to reach a higher performance level in sight of an attainable reward.

So, MTR, MEASURE, TRAIN AND REWARD, is a concept which will maximize your use of "high touch" in defending or attracting market share. Mothing will take the front seat ahead of the products you deliver in this era of high tech healthcare. But as certainly as IBM has discovered the importance of customer service in the sale of its computers hospital marketers may deliver high touch as the difference which makes the difference.

APPENDIX

Correlation coefficients based on data from 36 hospitals spanning five states: Florida, Texas, Utah, Tennessee and Virginia. (N=1400 interviews)

- How high touch correlates with...

	Correlation Coefficient	Significance Level
Hospital bed size	0.5665	99.9%
Hospital admissions	0.4320	95-99%
County market share	0.0451	< 80%
High tech factors	0.7300	99.9%
Consumer preference - serious medical care	0.3889	95-99%
Consumer preference - emergency room care	0.0791	< 80%
Consumer preference - general medical care	0.2416	80-90%
Consumer preference - having a baby	0.3335	90-95%

- TGK Database, January 1987

NOTE: "High Touch" is defined as showing concern for patients and giving personal attention to patients. "High Tech" is defined as having up to date equipment and technology and the ability to treat the most serious medical conditions.

WOMEN'S HEALTH CARE

Novak presents a case study of the successful attempt by
the Women's Hospital of Texas in developing a number of
geographically dispersed satellite clinics to service its
growing constituents. This distribution channel strategy
has effectively resulted in a network of linkages which
has generated increased referrals and other benefits to
the multi-institutional system.

THE WOMAN'S HOSPITAL OF TEXAS
HOSPITAL DIVERSIFICATION IN WOMEN'S HEALTH

Judith G. Novak, Chief Executive Officer

Woman's Hospital of Texas opened its first satellite office in May of 1985. It was named "The Woman's Place" and was located in Angleton, Texas. During the following year Woman's opened five additional satellites. Existing members of the physician staff were relocated to these facilities with the intent of accomplishing the following objectives:

1. To enhance the hospital's market share in selected attractive communities.

2. To assist participating physicians in expanding their patient base.

3. To enhance the hospital's image by expanding into other communities.

SERVICES

All satellites cater to the needs of women. They are staffed by a core group of physicians who specialize in women's health. Each core physician group covers the following speciality office services:

. Obstetrics/Gynecology
. Pediatrics
. Internal Medicine
. Plastic Surgery

Urology and oncology services are also offered at several of the satellite facilities.

In order to attract and retain customers, each satellite offers a wide variety of educational, wellness, and screening services. These services include:

. Exercise classes for pregnant women
. Exercise classes for older women
. Free hearing, vision, and breast screening (which are offered periodically)
. Free plastic surgery consults
. Educational programs covering numerous topics of interest to women (i.e.: new baby care, sibling rivalry, PMS, older adult care, weight management, preschooler communication, stop smoking, how to establish credit, singles only classes)
. Divorce and Menopausal support groups

PHYSICIAN PARTICIPATION

Medical staff members who relocate their practices to satellite facilities are offered free office space in return for their agreement to:

1. Allow all laboratory revenue to accrue to the hospital.

2. Provide free health screening and plastic surgery consults as needed.

When patient services are necessary, satellite physicians refer all of their patients to Woman's Hospital.

REVENUE AND EXPENSES

Each satellite's laboratory services provides the only direct source of revenue to Woman's Hospital. during the first half of 1986, the three satellites in operation generated a total of $43,523 in revenue. Each facility generates approximately $2,900 of laboratory revenue per month.

Woman's staffs each clinic with one registered nurse for office and market support. All other professional and/or non-professional staffing requirements and their associated costs are the responsibility of participating physicians.

As stated previously, Woman's assumes the leasing costs of all facilities. We pay an average of $3,200 per month in leasing expenses for each facility. In total, Woman's pays an average of $4,500 per month for each satellite's operating costs, which include clerical, office supply, and leasing costs.

FINANCIAL IMPACT

While the satellites are operated at a slight loss to Woman's, the true benefit of the satellite program lies in the number of patient referrals generated. During the first half of 1986 the satellites generated a total of 147 inpatient and 34 day surgery referrals. These referrals brought an estimated $547,000 dollars of gross patient revenue to Woman's. The total income, which can be traced directly or indirectly to the satellite program, is estimated at $167,000 for the first half of 1986. This is equal to a contribution of 28.8%.

SUMMARY

In conclusion, Woman's satellite program has resulted in the following benefits:

. Improved community recognition
. Positive physician relations
. Increased market share and revenue for both the hospital and its physicians

FINDINGS

. Total satellite associated gross revenue
for the first half of 1986 was $582,000.
Sources of revenue included:

1. Inpatient referrals ($513,100).

2. Day surgery referrals ($34,000)

3. Satellite laboratory services ($34,900)

. During the first half of 1986, Woman's
satellite program provided an estimated
$167,600 in total direct and indirect
income. This equals an estimated
contribution margin of 28.8%.

. The variable contribution (before fixed
costs) is estimated at $323,700 or 55.6%
of total satellite associated revenues.

. Woman's received a total of 147 inpatient
and 34 day surgery referrals from its
Kingwood and Angleton facilities during
the first half of 1986.

. Woman's physician satellite office program
has resulted in the following key benefits:

1. Improved community recognition.

2. Positive physician relations.

3. Increased market share and revenue
for both the hospital and its
physicians.

QUALIFICATIONS

. All inpatient and day surgery financial
figures are estimated assuming pricing,
resource utilization, and revenue
deductions are reflective of hospital
wide averages.

KINGWOOD, ANGLETON SATELLITES

FINANCIAL IMPACT ESTIMATE

First-Half, 1986

Revenue	
Inpatient	$513,100
Outpatient Surgery	34,000
Clinic Laboratory	34,900
Total	$582,000

Expenses	
Clinic Operating	$ 54,000
Hospital IP/OP	
Variable	174,600
Fixed	156,100
Total	$384,700

Gross Profit	$197,300

Revenue Deductions	
Inpatient	$ 20,520
Outpatient Surgery	9,180
Total	$ 29,700

Contribution Margin	$167,600
Percent	28.8%

Variable Contribution Margin (excluding fixed costs)	$323,700
Percent	55.6%

PHYSICIAN MARKETING

The papers in this section reflects the diversity of the
responses among physicians in their acceptance of marketing as applied to the private practice. At one end of
the spectrum, Kingsley's report of the project at the
Durham County Hospital Corporation where physicians are
being educated on what marketing really is depicts the
indifference and reluctance on the part of physicians to
embrace what they perhaps perceive to be the commerciali-
zation of medicine. On the other hand, Moore reports the
phenomenal growth - tripling of a 9 physician multispecialty group practice into a 27 physician group with nine
locations within a year. The goal is to become a 100
physician group within a few years. It appears that the
dichotomy of physician attitudes towards marketing and
the accompanying results has not changed in the past
decade.

Felt and King present a case study to illustrate how
hospitals can play an active role in enhancing its
medical staff's private practices.

TEACHING PHYSICIANS TO MARKET THEMSELVES

Bernard R. Kingsley, Durham County Hospital Corporation, Durham

ABSTRACT

Although it is often vitally important for physicians to engage in marketing themselves and their own practice, health care marketers have met with mixed success in "selling" marketing to the medical staff.

Planning to teach physicians how to market should be seen as a slow, deliberate process which requires demonstrations, cooperation and teaching by example. Once these steps are done more formal education can be provided in a seminar setting. Such a seminar should be geared to the medical staffs own perceived needs. A variety of methods used to increase the physicians interest in marketing are discussed here and the promotion and components of a meaningful seminar are provided.

INTRODUCTION

There has been considerable discussion between physicians and hospital administrators regarding the use and value of "marketing" which is often defined by the physician as no more than "selling" and "advertising".

Although hospitals often attempt to present themselves as independent entities in the market, the reality is that physician support is critical in any competitive hospital marketing area in order to maintain or increase admission rates.

Revenue generating efforts which focus on out-patient programs, such as wellness services, have difficulty offsetting losses, or potential losses in in-patient admissions since each outpatient service generates no more than 20% the revenue realized through a typical in-patient admission. Although new outpatient services and wellness programs can often be viewed as "loss-leaders", it is doubtful that any hospital can afford many of such "leaders" in days of declining admissions.

Any physician who regularly admits to a facility becomes increasingly more valuable as his or her practice increases. It is clearly to the advantage of any hospital to have physicians actively practicing marketing efforts and techniques.

During the past year the Durham County Hospital Corporation has taken an increasing interest in developing positive relationships with physicians and encouraging them to actively pursue marketing. This effort requires three distinctive activities:

I. Reinforcing the physicians' perception that it is in the hospital's interest to support them.

II. Educating the physician on what marketing really is.

III. Motivating and assisting the physicians to implement and monitor a comprehensive marketing effort.

These three activities were viewed as distinct phases in a deliberate effort to increase marketing on part of physicians. It can be easily recognized that many of the activities described occur in any hospital setting. More often than not, these activities are not seen as opportunities to educate however, and no deliberate plan is made to use them for such purpose.

Working Together

In order to arrest and diminish a growing "us vs them" attitude, the hospital marketing department developed a number of efforts to share information and the benefits of a low-level marketing effort.

The Marketing Department developed a PHYSICIAN LOCATOR service which consisted of a listing of the hospital's affiliated physicians by specialty and zip code. This was initially targeted at newcomers to the growing community of the Raleigh-Durham, NC Triangle area.

Sending this Locator to businesses which customarily distribute newcomer packets (real estate offices, banks and large industries which often transfer or hire employees) was perceived as a public service. Indeed, the local paper wrote a supportive editorial, missing the point that this brochure was essentially an advertising method.

Physicians who were initially neutral to the LOCATOR soon complained that they were not included. When a memo was sent to physicians requesting them to indicate if they wished to be in the second edition, 35% of all affiliated physicians responded within 24 hours, an unheard-of response to any administrative memorandum.

The LOCATOR is not only a tool to create a favorable image of the hospital and direct newcomers to certain physicians, it can also be used to teach something about marketing. Each edition expands the marketing orientation. For the second edition physicians were asked to list characteristics of their practice which makes them unique or of interest to newcomers, such as special office hours. The third edition will increase this effort to have physicians perceive their practice from a consumer viewpoint.

The LOCATOR is also used extensively in outpatient services which may require referrals to physicians. A bulletin sent to physicians (The Marketing Alert) advises them of these programs and to expect such referrals as a result of the LOCATOR. This has lowered some resistance to out-patient services.

Hospital advertising in print and electronic media prominently mentions the LOCATOR, again reinforcing that the physicians are tied to the hospital's advertising efforts.

Educating by Example

Although many hospital marketers lament the fact that physicians view marketing as no more than advertising, it is noteworthy that advertising is often the only marketing activity which is visible to the medical staff. If we are to teach all four traditional "P's" of marketing it is beneficial to involve the medical staff in all of them.

In addition to the P's of Place, Product, Promotion and Price, emphasis was placed on a fifth "P", the Patient.

The patient relations service of Durham County General Hospital was established and in operation for more than a year before physicians were formally advised of the service and the reasons for it. The service includes a PATIENT ACTION LINE which receives telephone calls from patients requesting information or make complaints. It also includes a patient satisfaction survey which is mailed out periodically.

Physicians responded well to information about this service, which essentially serves their (and our) patients. Reviews of the data generated through this service often generate suggestions from physicians for modifying services at the hospital. In many cases the results of this service also contained important information about consumer attitudes about physicians and local medical services.

It has not been lost on physicians that feedback about their own services (or, more often, about their practice staff) would be helpful. Physicians may be reluctant to have themselves viewed as a "product", but often recognize that they get little feedback regarding their patients' perception of the office environment and staff.

The hospital is currently offering to send out patient satisfaction questionnaires to patients of local medical practices. Since it would not be economical for physicians to do this on their own, this service has not been done before and will generate specific information to the physician, making him or her more conscious of consumer needs and desires. Assisting in the design of a questionnaire will also heighten sensitivity about marketing.

Physicians also become educated about marketing research and its applications by being involved in the development of new services and marketing plans.

Impressive academic credentials are not maximized if the consumer is unaware of them. Physicians respond well when told that patients are interested in their credentials and begin to recognize the need for education/information giving when they are advised that fewer than 5% of their patients are actually aware of their credentials.

Most all physicians have some characteristic in themselves or in their practice which lends itself to promotion. The problem most often is that they don't know how to promote or are reluctant to do so. Identifying these characteristics, and recognizing areas of consumer dissatisfaction is more easily dealt with and should be done first.

In an effort to provide a more formal method of teaching marketing ideas, a physician marketing seminar was developed. The seminar was designed to meet the needs of the consumer. Physicians were surveyed as to the need and possible inclusion of topics for such a project.

It is of no surprise to find that interest in a seminar was expressed primarily by those who rely on new patients from the community, rather than through the referral process. Internal medicine, family medicine, OB/GYN and Pediatrics were the fields in which physicians expressed the most interest.

Surveys showed considerable interest in areas such as local demographics and population growth, data related to show the competitiveness of health-care and consumer attitudes regarding hospitals and healthcare in general. There was considerably less interest in techniques which utilize such data, such as advertising and modification of services based on consumer perception. It was decided that this reflected a reluctance to participate more than a lack of interest since physicians were quite interested in how they might benefit from hospital advertising.

The survey, and discussion with physicians, also indicated some common misconceptions about marketing. All too often, for example, it is assumed that the consumers' concern about pricing would result in recommendations to lower fees. Many physicians were surprised to find that the data suggests that the concern for prices does not often translate into price sensitivity.

In some cases discussion revealed that the marketing department would actually recommend that fees be raised if the consumer's perception of the service justifies this. Pricing strategies which segment pricing and relate more accurately to what is being paid for were of interest when it became clear that this might permit raising fees.

The seminar is structured to be of practical use to the physicians. Local instructors are used and promotional literature indicates that the seminar will be of immediate benefit.

Another effort made to educate physicians to marketing techniques has been to ask them to approve hospital advertising for accuracy. This often provides the opportunity to advise them of the rationale for the advertising.

It has been noticed that physicians are much more likely to give credence to data generated at the local level and interpreted by an unbiased researcher. For this reason, much of the research available on the national level is ignored and emphasis is placed on local surveys (which often duplicate national data). Arrangements were made to have many of the corporation's survey data analysed and interpreted through an academic source (North Carolina Central University's Marketing Department).

Another method of education by example is to treat the physician as a consumer. Medical staff are often enthusiastic in providing input. Conducting surveys of physicians has been successful in obtaining their opinion, eliciting good will and educating them to marketing practices.

Surveys should be brief and to the point in order to minimize time required for them. They should be sensitive to definitions and they should be structured so that some educational benefit is gained.

In a survey of the DCHC staff it was found that many physicians insert "announcements" regarding their practice in the local paper, but few of the medical staff viewed these to be advertisements. Indeed, even physicians who used announcements which have some advertising flavor (mentioning specifics such as convenient office hours or location) claimed that they were not advertising.

By defining terms and structuring surveys asking for information about their practices, it is often possible to lead the respondent to a recognition that what he or she is doing is part of marketing.

Motivating and Assisting Marketing Efforts

It is fortunate that most medical services are in the very early stages of the product life cycle. This requires that consumers be educated about the product, rather than be sold on the basis of a particular branded service or price. Physicians understand and appreciate education.

The identification of physicians' efforts to be responsive to the patient and the identification of knowledge which physicians would like for their patients to have is a good starting point for marketing.

Physicians have become somewhat cautious of attending seminars which are either "another pep talk" or efforts designed to sell them on future services. Promotional literature is designed to overcome this.

Emphasis is placed on the fact that physicians will learn about local consumer trends and attitudes, techniques which will not only permit them to adapt their practice to the consumer's needs but also their own, and strategies which do not make more patients incompatible with present or higher fees.

Three documents are of particular interest to the market oriented physician. A patient questionnaire which can be utilized to obtain feedback and monitor staff, an evaluation of the practice which can be conducted by using a checklist, and a summary of demographic data which contains suggestions on what the meaning and potential uses of the data are.

Conducting surveys and comparing them with peers permit the physician to find his or her "niche" or market segment. These tools also indicate what positive elements of a practice the consumer will need to become aware of.

Evaluating a practice is most meaningful when numberical scores can be obtained and compared. The instrument used provides subtotals for different aspects of a practice and total scores which are useful for comparison.

It is helpful to share relevant scores which the hospital has obtained in its own self-surveys and patient surveys, though only if the hospital itself is committed to modifying its services based on the surveys. Most surveys, for example, will point out that waiting time is a strong source of patient dissatisfaction. It is useless to encourage physicians to make changes in response to that if the hospital itself is not doing so.

When utilized appropriately, self-surveys and patient surveys can be strong arguments for educating the public and modifying services.

The design and promotion of a seminar for physicians is difficult and time consuming, but may be one of the most meaningful tasks of a marketing department.

If a number of physicians have already become aware that marketing is more than advertising, and if they have seen that marketing may benefit the patient, reluctance to attend is often overcome.

Efforts promoting a physician marketing seminar should place emphasis on the following:

1. Information given is local and will be provided by local professionals.
2. Many of the tools provided are adapted from hospital use which has been proven to be successful.
3. Much of marketing involves consumer education.
4. Although pricing strategies are discussed, it is not assumed that fees need necessarily go down.
5. Many marketing task involve monitoring staff and having staff perform functions.
6. Hospital promotion can often be utilized by physicians for their own benefit.
7. The seminar is not used to sell physician services, but is complete in itself.
8. The seminar provides for interactions among presenters and attenders.

CONCLUSION

Encouraging physicians to market is a highly rewarding activity, but needs to be done in a slow process. Above all, physicians must be exposed to the various functions of marketing in order to overcome the thinking that this is "just selling and advertising".

Hospitals need to plan educational efforts and activities which are directed towards the physician and must demonstrate the use and success of marketing techniques. Steps leading to a successful marketing seminar for physicians are more important than the seminar itself. By recognizing the physicians' need to market and by considering the physicians as consumers we can "sell" marketing to those who are perhaps our most important customers.

Note: Patient Questionnaires for use in Physician Practices and evaluation forms for practices will be distributed during the Symposium and can be obtained from:
Marketing Department
Durham County Hospital Corporation
3643 N. Roxboro Street
Durham, NC 27704
(919) 470-7275

MARKETING A MULTI-SPECIALTY GROUP

Julie Rawls Moore

Atlanta, Georgia

ABSTRACT

This article uses a case study to outline the processes one marketing group used to market a large multispecialty physician practice. Included are the steps and timetable, data gathered, purpose and objectives of eight studies, reasoning behind some key decisions, an outline of parts of the final plan and the steps to monitor results.

INTRODUCTION

Marketing a physicians practice has become an exceptable part of the hospital marketing process. Physicians now realize that they are no longer exempt from the rigors of the market place and can be positively or negatively affected by how they respond to that marketplace. These progressive physicians are increasingly turning to their hospitals to assist them with this "foreign task".

The Healthcare profession has yet to gain the marketing sophistication of many industries and now there is a new set of challenges to add to our long list of objectives and projects. But this one may be a key to bring patients into the hospital. It is in the hospitals best interest to keep their admitting physicians viable as "business entities" through quality marketing. Because in most cases the more patients a physician sees, the more patients a hospital sees.

In early 1986, a hospital company affiliated with a well established nine man multispecialty Group. With this affliation, the Group opened a location in the hospital's new MOB and part of the Group moved to that location. The Group plans to grow rapidly to 100 physicians and become the premier group in the state by adding new and established physicians at new and established locations. Naturally the affiliate hospital is counting on this group to help fill its beds. In some months this groups census proportionately mirrors the hospitals census.

In about a year the Group had become a 27 physician Group with nine locations and is possibly about to add 13 more physicians in yet another location. Although the Group's patient base is strong it needs to be stronger to support past and future growth. Appropriate marketing as a part of the overall business planning process is very important not only for the hospital census, but for the viability and growth of the Group.

Fortunately, the physicians and administrative staff are very supportive of this marketing effort.

The purpose of this article is to show the process used to develop a marketing plan. It does not attempt to include all the research results or the entire marketing plan.

THE ENVIRONMENT

This Group is located in a MSA of just over 1.3 million, with a potential primary service area of 679,127. Little growth is predicted for the area except for two small areas, north and west of the city. The secondary service area has a population of 255,000 with growth in this area projected from a minus 17% to as high as 28%. The area is very young, with the majority of the population being under 34 years of age. There are over 4,000 physicians in the area and about 30 hospitals.

The competition comes from two separate arenas. The first has 2 large multispecialty groups. Group A has 120 full-time physicians and surgeons and 47 specialities and sub-specialties in seven locations. Group B has about 35 physicians in 5 locations. The second area has small, single specialty groups located in various parts of the city. Although hospital competition is very heavy, there is little physician marketing except for Group A. This marketing centers around the clinic rather than individual physicians. What physician marketing there is, is usually product line advertising plastic surgery or infertility services.

THE PROCESS

Initially a marketing committee was formed. The committee consisted of six physicians representing various locations, specialties and tenure. The Clinic Director and the Director of Nursing Specialties were also part of the committee. The purpose of the committee was to plan, introduce new ideas and approve all activities related to the Groups marketing. The committee met on an as needed basis throughout the original planning process, usually every other week.

At the outset of the study five broad goals were set. Following completion of the research, these goals were refined, prioritized and specific objectives were added. These goals were to:

1. Increase new patients from existing service areas (market penetration)

2. Increase retention of patients within the system (service development)

3. Initiate usage by new patients in a new market area (market development)

4. Identify new services to offer to new and existing patients-(diversification).

5. Establish this Group as a premier multispecialty group within the state.

To achieve these goals answers to several questions had to be found. Hopefully, the following questions would be answered by research:

-   What was the level of this Groups name recognition?

-   Would patients follow the physicians who were moving?

-   Would potential new patients in the new locations service area alter their habits of "going into town" to see a physician and stay close to home? How could the Group encourage this?

-   Did the community want a multispecialty, single specialty group or solo practitioner?

- What was important to the community when choosing or changing physicians?

- What type of attributes should be included in advertising?

- How satisfied were present patients and could the statisfaction be improved?

- How should the Group position itself against it's competitors?

To answer these and other questions several qualitative and quantitative studys were designed:

A. Facility audit - to assess how the patient saw the office, comfort of waiting and exam rooms, appropriateness and functionality of decor and image the office presented.

B. Customer Service audit - to identify problems, obstacles with service, measure intraoffice teamwork, communication, office morale and other components that effect how the patient is cared for and the patients perception of the office.

C. Physician and Office Staff interviews - to assess this groups expectations of marketing and the marketing process. Also gain the "insiders" opinion of the groups strengths and weaknesses, groups "position", main competition, and competitive edge. Also investigated was their opinion on their patients perceptions and any special questions they wanted included in the patient or community survey. Half of the physician and most of the staff were interviewed.

D. Competitive analysis - to identify the market leaders, challengers and followers and assess their strengths and weaknesses. Information was gathered as to services offered, hour, prices waiting time to get an appointment, image, etc. This helped identify areas of opportunity such as new services and underserved areas.

E. Focus groups - to aid in the development of questionnaires for the follow-up telephone surveys, ensure that all important issues were covered and that questionnaire language was clear and unambiguous. Another important purpose of this research was to provide a better understanding of the Groups image compared to competition, explore patient experiences at our Group versus competitors and learn what it would take to attract area residents to this physician group. Two focus group interviews were conducted. One group included present patients and the other was community residents at large, none of whom had any experience with our Group.

F. Patient satisfaction telephone survey - to assess patient satisfaction and areas for improvement. One hundred patients were questioned in 20 minute interviews. They were questioned on factors such as:

1. Name recognition
2. How they learned about the Group
3. Accessibility
4. Scheduling and billing procedures
5. Treatment by staff and physicians
6. Waiting time
7. Adequacy of facility
8. Quality of care
9. Hospital preference

This was helpful refining the target market.

G. Community telephone survey - to assess the Groups current position, opportunities for growth, community perceptions of the Group, what it would take to attract residents to the Group, competitors strengths and weaknesses and most desirable attributes for advertising purposes. Two hundred and eight interviews were conducted among a random sample of residents in one of the key primary service areas. Demographic requirements were set to allow generalization.

RESEARCH RESULTS

When the research was completed all questions were well answered with volumes of information. In summary here are a few key highlights:

- Only 1% of the community residents had top of mind awareness. Even some patients were unaware of the name of the Group.

- Many felt more information about the Group would increase the chance of usage.

- Those with less than 2 years with their present physician were most willing to switch. 28% said they were unaffiliated.

- 72% said they normally used a primary care physician.

- Attributes used in selecting a physician were "highly competent" and "took his time" with the patient. Other features were "update", ease of appointments and reasonable rates.

- There was no significant negative stigma to physician practicing in the hospital's area.

- The competitor weakness centered around rates and service amenities.

- There was a strong acceptance of the multispecialty concept for accessibility and convenience of having a variety of specialists available.

- Many equated small groups with warmth and caring and large groups with competency and accessibility.

- Nearly 9 out of 10 patients indicated their experience with the Group was outstanding or very good.

- Most patients knew of the clinic through friends or another physician.

- The few negatives centered around billing and the waiting room.

- Time spent in the waiting room directly correlated with satisfaction. The shorter the wait the more satisfied.

Research results were provided to the physicians in both written and presentation form.

Following the research results, an umbrella marketing plan was designed. Because of the geographic spread of the nine locations it was decided that plans would be established for the various locations in 3 separate stages divided by locations. The office next to the hospital was chosen to be first because the opportunity for growth was greatest. This office is one of the largest, the newest and the population of this area fit the target of 18-45 year olds with incomes of about $20,000, who had lived in the area less than two years and would be willing to switch physicians or were unattached. This area also had a high growth projection.

POSITIONING DECISION

The physicians wanted to be known as a highly accessible group that provides comprehensive personalized care. The large size and multispecialty aspect of the Group was seen as a benefit, because patients could stay within the system when referrals were needed and physicians could consult with each other. The disadvantages of a large group, such as concerns about "assembly-line medicine", patients being "lost in the system" or becoming "just a number" need to be minimized.

Since most of the physicians had recently joined the Group and brought their own patients with them interest was strong in retaining individual identities.

Lack of name recognition by the public enabled the positioning decision to be made as if the Group was brand new, but the physician did not want to lose the advantage of name recognition of individual prominent physicians, some of whom were new to the Group.

Competitive issues around positioning were identified through the research. The weakness of the largest competitor centered around lack of warmth, accessibility and rates, all attributes on which the Group is highly rated, but it was strong on competence.

This decision had two steps. First what the Groups composition was to be and second what their positioning attributes and image were to be. As to composition, this Group could be marketed as:

    A. 37 individual physicians
    B. individual single specialty groups
    C. 9 individual locations
    D. large multispecialty group.

Since the community's preference for multispecialty groups was significantly higher than their preference for single specialty groups and about the same as the preference for solo physicians, there was benefit in using a multispecialty position.

As to the attributes, did the Group stress it's large size and sophistication weakening the accessibility a warmth attribute or stress it's warmth and human side and risk diluting it's competency side. One seemed to contradict the other.

The final decision was a compromise. The Group would be positioned as a large multispecialty group with a humanistic style. To the community it would be a single large group. Internally, the patients would see the name of the group and the individual physicians names would be used on information sheets, stationery and any other patient materials. The group would be marketed as a highly accessible, comprehensive group who gave personalized care. And where physicians know and respect each other and feel comfortable making any referrals needed within groups - "like a family of physicians".

This positioning translated to soft colors, (off-white and soft blues) textured paper stock, a script lettered logo, cosier, inviting rearrangement of the waiting area with drinks, telephone, a writing desk and soft childrens toys. Bulleting boards and blankets were placed in the patient waiting rooms. Scrapbooks with physicians and family pictures were placed in the waiting rooms.

The advertising and public relations plan supported this positioning. A picture of a family (with dog) was shown in a 3/4 page ad that ran in all locations service areas. The attributes stressed were warm, personalized care, accessibility, reasonable rates and comprehensive services. A similar location specific ad was run for the new location next to the hospital. Since the majority of the residents surveyed used primary care physicians, the primary side of the group was presented. The header read "Exactly what is a family physician". The proposed tag line beneath the logo read "Just like your doctor used to be, only better".

MARKETING SYSTEM ESTABLISHED

Marketing needs to become as routine an operation as the monthly financial review. To that end several new systems were established within the Group to continue the marketing process.

1. The Physicians Marketing Committee will continue to meet at least every other month to review progress and assess needs for change.

2. A Referring Physician survey was designed and will be sent out on an annual basis to continue to monitor satisfaction.

3. Two questions were added to the patient registration form to help assess the effectiveness of the marketing activities:

    A. How did you learn about our Group? (If the patient was recommended by another patient they were asked if the group could send a thank you)

    B. What made you decide to use our group?

    Answers to these two questions are tabulated weekly, trended, examined by the group's director and used to guide future marketing decisions.

4. A patient survey was designed to be given to each patient at every visit. This will help monitor satisfaction and identify any problems as they arise.

5. A nurse call-back system was designed to assess patient satisfaction and check on patients health. A sample of patients are called each month.

6. Number of patient visits, demographics and geographic penetration will be compiled and monitored by the group's director.

7. A follow-up community survey will be done in a year to assess the sucess of the marketing effort.

RECOMMENDATIONS

Here are some recommendations to help manage a physician Marketing campaign. Most seem "common sense", but can be difficult to maintain or achieve.

1. Sound marketing process must be followed no matter how little support is received for it.

2. Find a physician who understands marketing to work with. If there is not one - teach one.

3. Show the physicians examples of other marketing studies or promotional pieces to help them understand your recommendations and make decisions.

4. Establish channels of communication and processes for approval prior to the start of any work. This can get muddled throughout the process, make sure everyone's authority is well defined.

5. Know it is going to take longer than the physician expects or finds acceptable.

6. Make sure all committee decisions are communicated to the entire Group.

7. Assign formal responsibility to one of the staff members for assistance in implementation. Hands inside the practice are needed as well as buy-in from the staff.

8. Give the Ad agency a copy of the American Medical Association Guidelines to Advertising. Have them meet with the physicians in their office to get a flavor of the Group.

PROMOTION AND PUBLIC RELATIONS PLAN

OBJECTIVES/ACTIVITIES

The following is a list of activities designed to achieve some of the refined goals and objectives.

1. To Increase Awareness of the Group in the Community thus improving name recognition

    A. Send direct mail Healthcare newsletters each quarter to target areas
    B. Place newspaper announcements of each physician group joining
    C. Give community speeches
    D. Participation in Health screenings in major malls in the Spring
    E. Physicians/staff joining community organizations
    F. Print staff business cards to be given to friends and aquaintances
    G. Sponsorship of a 10K run in the Spring
    H. Place physicians on radio and TV talk shows

    I. Work with local newcomers organizations

2. To Portray Sense of Openess/Friendliness/ Caring to Patients

    A. Place scrapbook in waiting room with pictures of physician, staff and families
    B. Send birthday and Christmas cards to all patients and referring physicians
    C. Develop letters to all new patients to send prior to and following the first visit
    D. Design thank you referral cards for physicians and friends
    E. Establish patient call back system
    F. Redesign stationary for softer image
    G. Send reminder cards for patient
    H. Order sympathy donation cards from Heart Association for families when patient expires
    I. Place physicians bio's in patient information packet

3. To become Key Source of Health Care Information for the Patient

    A. Give patient question sheets to help them remember their questions for the physician
    B. Provide information brochures on common illnesses
    C. Provide treatment information sheets
    D. Design monthly educational seminar
    E. Send new patient packet of information on the Group
    F. Send quarterly newsletter
    G. Place bulletin boards with Healthcare information in patient rooms
    H. Give health information book to all patients at Christmas

4. To Develop Sense of Presence in Office to Enhance name recognition with patients and make them feel like they belong

    A. Place Group name sign in waiting room
    B. Give patients pencils with Group name on it at each visit
    C. Rearrnage seating into small clusters
    D. Add writing desk, coffee and childrens toys to waiting area
    E. Add large sign to outside door
    F. Sew Group name patches on all physician/staff labcoats

REFERENCES

Moore, Julie R. "Hospitals and Physician: The Exchange Approach." Chapter 2, Persuading Physicians - A Guide for Hospital Executives, Editor: Robert Rubright (Aspen, 1984).

Moore, Julie R. "Marketing Your Practice: Patient Satisfaction Surveys: Ohio Family Physician News, September, 1984 and October, 1984.

My thanks to the following people and companies:

The physicians and staff of "the Group"
Keating MaGee and Associates, New Orleans, LA
Moosbrugger Research, LaGrange, Illinois
Wishard and Associates, New Orleans, LA
Dr. David Silvers, Tom Dolan, Rick Miller and Michael Ghani

	Pers. Resp.	SEP 2	9	16	23	30	OCT 7	14	21	28	NOV 4	11	18	25	DEC 2	9	16	23	30	JAN 6	13	20	27
PROCESS – TIMETABLE																							
Planning meetings		X	–	X																			
Market Committee Formation				X																			
Market Commitee Meetings					X		X				X		X		X							X	
Staff Liason Appointeu																							
Set Original Goals						X																	
Situation Analysis																							
Ficiality Audit							x																
Interview Physicians					X	X	X																
Interview Staff					X	X	X																
Customer Service Audit							X																
Competitive Analysis		X	–	–	–	X																	
Operational Audit		–	–	–	–	–	–	–	–	–	–	–	–	–	–	X							
Quantitative Research																							
Focus Groups							X	–	X														
Patient Survey							X	–	–	–	–	–	–	X'									
Community Survey							X	–	–	–	–	–	–	X									
Introduction of Ad Agency											X												
Strategy Formation																							
Goals Refined																X							
Positioning decision																X							
Patient Relations Plan																X							
Promotional Plan																X							
Public Relations Plan																X							
Advertising Plan																				X			
Expansion Plan																					X		

DEVELOPING A PHYSICIAN BUSINESS
AND HOW TO MAKE IT WORK

James R. Toth, Edge Healthcare Marketing, Inc., Nashville, TN.

ABSTRACT

Physicians are increasing their participation in the ownership of various components of the healthcare delivery
system. In some cases this physician ownership may take
the form of a joint venture with a traditional owner such
as a hospital. In other instances physicians are joining
together in sole ownership of a healthcare provider business, sometimes with the assistance of a management company. Of importance to hospitals and other providers is that
this phenomenon does not appear short-lived. An understanding of the motivation of physicians to participate in
these ventures can aid the marketer in better responding to
the physician as customer. Further, opportunities to
impact physicians exist at each stage of the development
cycle of a new physician business - from the planning
process through development to actual operations. Marketing opportunities exist for those who understand physician
needs and the process of developing a venture that meets
these needs.

PHYSICIAN NEEDS

Several primary marketing research studies were undertaken
recently by a healthcare development company. The firm,
which develops and manages outpatient businesses for
physicians and joint ventures between hospitals and physicians, was interested in defining physician needs with
respect to the non-clinical aspects of their practice. The
ultimate goal was to identify potential opportunities to
develop an "unbundled", physician-owned business.

Three stages of research were initiated: 1) Focus Group
discussions among targeted physicians; 2) Personal Interview Studies among physicians in selected market areas; 3)
Roundtable Discussions among opinion leader physicians.
The third research phase was undertaken to crystallize the
information gathered previously and to develop actionable
strategies to meet physician needs. These studies indicated that beyond obvious quality of care and related clinical requirements, physicians possess other, more personal
needs that rank high in priority.

Results of the "needs" research were grouped into five
categories that allowed the users to analyze needs and
classify potential need-satisfying services for physicians
(See Table 1).

Based on the findings of the research, it was felt that an
innovative approach to an "unbundled" traditional hospital
service would have high appeal, if it could respond to the
aforementioned needs. The research results actually became
a marketing tool in presentations to targeted physician and
hospital customers.

CONCEPT DEVELOPMENT

Physicians indicated that one hospital service that physicians were dissatisfied with and which they felt could be
greatly improved was outpatient diagnostic radiology. It's
important to note that the "problems" were generally
non-clinical.

The company envisioned that a service which corrected
existing perceived or real problems and which offered
satisfaction of physician needs (Table 1) would be attractive to physicians and other providers. Outpatient and
other radiological procedure incidence rates coupled with
physician response measurements showed that a free-standing
imaging center could be successful. Further, if the center
were owned at least in part by physicians then it would
have access to a built-in referral system. And if it
provided a superior service then it should attract a
significant share of the outpatient imaging market (notably
non-partner physicians). A description of the project is
provided in Table 2.

TABLE 2
PROJECT DESCRIPTION

Comprehensive Diagnostic Imaging Center
 	
- Limited partnership among area physicians
- Improved operational efficiency
- Customized services
- Unique Positioning
- Services
    CT
    Radiography/Flouroscopy
    Ultrasound
    Mammography
    Nuclear Medicine
    Cardiology
    Neurology
    Laboratory

GETTING OFF THE GROUND

Hospitals in the target city were approached by the company
and by interested physicians to ascertain hospital interest

TABLE 1 FIVE DERIVED CATEGORIES OF PHYSICIAN NON-CLINICAL NEEDS	NEED EXAMPLES
1) Assistance with Practice-Building and Development 2) Participation in Cost-Reduction Opportunites 3) Satisfaction of Ego Needs 4) Introduction to Time-Savings Innovations 5) Opportunities For Financial Investments/Income	patient generation overhead reduction need for control practice efficiency joint venture

TABLE 3
ORGANIZATION

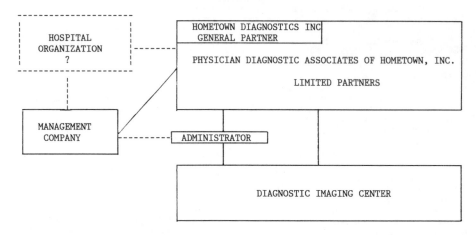

in a joint venture. No hospital would participate in the project for a variety of reasons, among them perceived loss of hospital-based revenues, loss of control to the physician group and/or the management company, off-campus location, etc. Physician interest in financial participation in the project was sufficient to warrant a company owned solely by area physicians. Six key physician "opinion leaders" were identified and agreed to become General Partners in the partnership. It was determined that 50 to 100 physicians would be allowed to participate as limited partners in the project. Table 3 shows the legal structure developed to implement the project. The management company was contracted with to 1) develop and organize the partnership; 2) syndicate the partnership offering; 3) arrange financing; 4) develop the facility; 5) manage the center; and 6) market its services.

Financial projections showed that an initial investment of $10,000 could produce essentially a break-even return after the first full operating year, with annual pre-tax returns of approximately $2500 in year two, increasing to $10,000 in year five.

THE ISSUE OF CONTROL

Hospital administrators often comment that they are concerned about loss of control if they were to become involved in a joint venture with physicians. Physicians have frequently complained about the loss of control they're feeling brought on by various changes in their practice due to reimbursement, alternative delivery and hospital operations.

It is suggested that physicians and hospitals already have at least an informal partnerhsip. Control issues arise and are addressed every week by a typical hospital. A joint venture could provide the opportunity for the hospital and its physician staff (and physicians on other staffs) to join in a project of shared control. What is to be avoided is the situation in which any party (hospital, physician group, other) attempts to take full control of healthcare delivery in an area. The following are two situations with clear messages about control.

In 1984, 50% of the surgeons in a medium-sized city in the Southeast decided to establish a physician-owned outpatient surgery center, without hospital involvement. It reached break even in its second month of

operation - perhaps the most successful such center in the U.S. On the strength of this, in late 1985 the same group and others decided to establish a freestanding diagnostic imaging center - again without hospital input or involvement. Approximately 100 of 170 physicians in the market became limited partners.   It opened in October, 1986, and is operating ahead of budget. It is now rumored that a new "physician company" may be next - incorporating outpatient surgery, outpatient radiology, laboratory, group purchasing, home fluids delivery, and perhaps its own alternative delivery system.

HCA has recently developed its "cluster market" concept in which numerous hospitals within a manageable area are clustered to function as a delivery system. It appears that this model would incorporate the HCA health plans that would be sold to industry and other groups. HCA's Physician Services Company, formed in 1985, would logically follow with its "physician company" model which is a venture between HCA and area physicians in a given market area. The model begins with an anchor concept to attract many physicians, such as a diagnostic imaging center partnership, and other physician-oriented services and programs are added. The end result for physicians looks like a response to the needs described in Table 1. Incidentally, a participating physician might add $15,000 annually to his bottom line through practice enhancement, income and cost-savings.

Which of the above is the more palatable situation? Would you like to be a hospital administrator in the medium-sized Southeastern city? What if yours is not one of the HCA hospitals in thier cluster market?

MARKETING OPPORTUNITIES ALONG THE WAY

One premise of this presentation is the observed growth in local physician organizations that, in part, protect and enhance the interests of member physicians. Hospitals and other providers certainly have an opportunity in their market to work with physicians if such an organization were to appear. Let's review the stages of developing a business with physicians and examine opportunities.

Initial feasibility study. When a new business concept is being evaluated, it makes sense for a hospital to become involved if the hospital's operations will be impacted. It's better to be in on the ground floor than merely part of phase three. The feasibility study is the single most important step in the project. Too many physician joint ventures are not properly evaluated and therefore can be set up to fail. The hospital can assist by helping provide appropriate feasibility assistance.

Project discussions. My observation is that there is no greater opportunity to align oneself with physicians than when discussing a new business project that will impact their personal needs. This "outside of the hospital" relationship provides a new perspective for hospital personnel. A much closer interaction with physicians is available.

Concept formulation. If 50 to 100 or more physicians in my market wanted to establish a new business I would want to be involved. The idea is to attempt to formulate the venture in the best interests of the hospital and others involved.

Syndication. The act of offering and selling a partnership in a market area has important strategic implications for a hospital. The syndication itself can be a vehicle to link the hospital with physicians on other staffs that don't normally admit to the hospital. An important springboard to satisfying clinical practice needs could be considered to be satisfying physicians' other needs.

Operations. Operating a business with physicians provides the setting to respond to physicians' desire for a voice in policy decisions. Physicians could be the board of directors that approves certain items. Their operations suggestions and medical policy decisions can be quickly implemented in the type of organization described. Control, income and ego needs can be satisfied through the new venture and a hospital can be a part of it. The hospital could offer marketing expertise to the new company. Then, marketing strategies undertaken for the new business could be linked to the hospital's strategies.

MARKETING NOTES

Not all such ventures have been successful. Typical marketing problems of awareness, comprehension and trial use are experienced. The greatest stumbling block may well be inadequate feasibility analyses before a project is undertaken. Our experience with less-than-successful centers reveals one or more of the following problems: 1) It was developed for the wrong reason(s); 2) Poor feasibility analyses; 3) Lack of a strategic plan; 4) Weak or misdirected marketing actions; and, 5) Poor tactical implementation.

Marketing a new outpatient business requires the same process that would be applied to a traditional provider business. Partnership and non-partner strategies, together with technology, sales, pricing and product line strategies have been successfully implemented in these types of centers to build revenues.

ENHANCING PRIVATE PRACTICE OPERATIONS/FINANCIAL PERFORMANCE

Cathy A. Felt, Manager, Peat, Marwick, Mitchell & Co., Kansas City, Missouri
Holly A. King, Consultant, Peat, Marwick, Mitchell & Co., Kansas City, Missouri

ABSTRACT

Hospitals, recognizing that physicians are their primary market, have developed a variety of marketing and support services to enhance the medical staff's private practices. An overlooked physician need, and major opportunity for hospitals, is the area of private practice operations/business planning assistance. We will discuss how hospitals can develop an innovative service to capitalize on this opportunity to enhance physician practices and therefore, increase physician retention/loyalty.

INTRODUCTION

Unfortunately, for today's physician, practicing good medicine no longer guarantees patient volume. Physicians and hospitals are realizing that, while the practice of medicine is a profession, the delivery of health care is big business. In order to compete effectively in an overcrowded marketplace, physician practices must utilize established business principles.

Hospitals are rethinking their marketing priorities after several years of committing large sums of money to consumer advertising campaigns with few tangible results. The physician is returning as the marketing focus as hospitals recognize the physician's key role, even in supposedly consumer-directed services such as obstetrics.

Practice enhancement services is a simple but effective physician marketing strategy based on the premise that benefitting the physician's practice will benefit the hospital. In order to be successful, the services must of course, respond to the needs of the particular physician's practice. Computer support, financial assistance, and promotional activities are important services that hospitals have been providing to their medical staffs. However, a major opportunity, which hospitals have largely overlooked, is the need for operations/business planning assistance.

Interviews and focus groups with physicians in all stages of practice, whether new, growing, mature or nearing retirement, revealed that physicians are very concerned about rising practice costs at a time when they are being forced to maintain current prices or offer discounts. Even among established, busy practices, the physicians complained that earnings are flat at best and cash flow is a problem at times. Many of the physicians indicated that they need to address practice issues/alternatives such as expansion, relocation, and changing patient mix. In addition, many physicians indicated they either did not know how to improve the operations and performance of the practice; or they had no interest in the management of the practice, but only wanted to "practice medicine". Thus, there is a large need for operational/business planning assistance, and hospitals, with their management and other resources and understanding of the physician private practice, are in a unique position to provide this service.

PRACTICE ASSESSMENT

The first step in providing operational/business planning services is a practice assessment. This will ensure that the physician's real needs are being addressed and the hospital's marketing resources are effectively used. To illustrate, expensive promotional efforts to direct new patients to a physician's practice will be unproductive if the physician is experiencing patient retention problems due to ineffective patient scheduling, inadequately trained office personnel, or poor office location.

The practice assessment begins with an examination of all aspects of the physician's practice, such as:

- Financial - billing, collections, cash flow and expenses.

- Operations - system analysis, patient flow, scheduling and patient records.

- Personnel - evaluation, job descriptions, training.

- Office facilities - location, access, atmosphere.

- Patient profile - mix, demographics and satisfaction level.

The next task is an analysis of the market factors likely to be impacting the practice. Such factors include:

- Competitors - location, pricing, office hours.

- Consumers - demographics, case mix, perceptions of providers.

- Other - alternative delivery systems, referral sources.

CASE STUDY

In order to demonstrate the benefits of private practice operations and business planning assistance, a case study of a practice assessment is presented.

Situation

The physician is a solo practicing obstetrician-gynecologist in an urban area. She has been in practice for three years. She was recruited by the hospital upon completion of her residency program and provided financial assistance to establish a private practice.

She spends three days per week at the main office adjacent to the hospital, a tertiary care facility located downtown, and two days per week at a satellite office located in a growing, affluent suburb. The hospital leases the physician space in both office buildings on a monthly basis.

The physician's patient volume has increased steadily each year, particularly in the newer satellite office. However, because of cash flow problems, the physician is considering closing the smaller satellite office.

Findings

The practice review revealed the following problems:

- Patient scheduling procedures were not documented or enforced. Over a 21 week period, a total of 160 appointments were either cancelled or missed by patients.

- An ineffective staffing schedule resulted in high hourly salary expense.

- The physical layout of the office impeded patient flow. Poor organization and scheduling resulted in patients waiting up to ninety minutes to see the physician.

- Operating expenses as a percentage of gross billings was 68 percent.

- Days revenue in accounts receivable was 189 days.

- The physician lacked OB/GYN coverage which limited office hours and patient volumes at both office locations.

Recommendations and Results

The satellite office was found to be in an excellent location and its success was critical to the physician's practice. However, in order to maintain the two offices, the physician needed to obtain additional coverage, increase productivity and lower practice costs. Specific recommendations included the following:

- Office personnel were trained in business office procedures and customer relations.

- New billing/collections procedures were adopted which resulted in higher gross billings, a reduction in accounts receivable, and fewer write-offs.

- Financial performance targets were developed and monitored on a regular basis to alert the physician to any negative trends.

- A "modified wave" scheduling system and patient recall system were implemented, resulting in a significant reduction in waiting time and an increase in the number of patients seen each week, with no reduction in the amount of time the physician spent with each patient.

- Additional coverage was obtained immediately and plans were made to recruit an associate as soon as it was feasible.

Six months following implementation of the preceding recommendations, the practice's cash flow and profitability had improved to the point that the physician was able to add an associate. This enabled the physician to keep both offices open all week, which further improved productivity and financial performance.

CONCLUSIONS

At a minimum, operations/business planning services should be provided to the physicians receiving financial support from the hospital, if only to protect and enhance the hospital's investment in these practices. Less expensive and more effective than extensive promotional campaigns, these services should become a key component of a program consisting of an array of physician support services designed to improve physician retention/loyalty.

SALES MANAGEMENT

In this article, Ken Mack explores an area of marketing
in the health care field that has often been overlooked -
personal sales. Here he presents a ten-point plan on how
this can be implemented.

GETTING INTO THE SALES GAME:
A CAPSULE TEN-POINT FORMULA

Ken E. Mack, Discover Marketing Innovations, Macedonia, Ohio

Nothing happens until somebody sells something--

There have been many shocks to the healthcare industry during the past two turbulent years, none more upsetting than the onslaught of the marketing phenomenon. And if marketing has come to healthcare with a vengeance, can sales be far behind?

No, say industry experts. In fact, the development of a healthcare sales force follows marketing and new product development as naturally as horses were once followed by carriages and love by marriage.

So, distasteful as sales may still be to some "old school" administrators, the fact is that once a hospital has entered a strategic planning mode, developing new products and a marketing plan, the products will have to be sold. Since advertising and public relations can't carry the entire sales load, a hospital-based healthcare sales force is the logical route to go.

THE TEN-POINT SALES DEVELOPMENT FORMULA

There are ten critical points to consider in developing a hospital-based sales force. All must be in place. All have equal weight. There are no shortcuts. The plan begins with ...

1. Executive Commitment

The CEO must play the role of initiator in the development of a sales force. This means that the CEO must believe in the need for a sales force, must be comfortable with the ethics of "selling the hospital's services," and must be prepared to invest the necessary capital and time--$50,000 to $100,000 per salesperson for up to 12 months--into a sales development program.

The CEO must be prepared to "sell" the concept to an often conservative board and must integrate the sales function with any marketing and planning functions that are already in place, always reassuring both that the sales force will enhance, not detract from, the entire marketing effort.

2. Marketing Plan with Sales Force Component

Today, most hospitals have at least the basics of a marketing plan. But how many of these plans include a sales force? Does yours?

If the existing marketing plan doesn't have a sales force in place, adding one is relatively easy. Here's how:

Or, looking at it another way, the sales force works in tandem with the public relations, advertising, support services, and direct mail marketing programs:

3. Identification of Products to Be Sold

Existing Hospital Products

To sell existing hospital products, the products must be clearly identified and "packaged."

List what your facility has to offer in these categories:

High Tech
- Diagnostic/MRI/CT scan/imaging
- Treatment--lithotripter
- Surgical--laser

Special Markets
- Women's center
- Sports medicine
- Geriatric center

General
- Wellness programs
  -Smoking cessation
  -Weight-loss programs
  -Cardiac fitness
- Unique use of space
  -Hotel/hospital
  -Osteoporosis clinic
  -Bakery

Each of the preceding represents a separate and unique product together with a separate and unique customer-- and must be treated as such. An analogy might be the old Heinz '57 Varieties--all different, all special, and all a potential profit center.

Hospital Products under Development

Hospital products under development, often stimulated by market research and customer demand, also require a sales force to market them successfully, especially when they are initially presented to potential customers.

4. Identification of Customers

The health care facility has three major groups of customers for its products and services (in addition to its sales to other hospitals). There are:

- Consumers
- Physicians
- Business and industry organizations

Each of these groups has its own unique characteristics that must be addressed by the sales force in attempting to market products to them.

Consumer Market Characteristics
- Caring
- Service oriented
- Knowledge of patients

Sales Force Response
- One-time calls only

Physician Market Characteristics
- Scientific
- Technical
- Medical terminology

Sales Force Response
- Repeat calls
- Cannot place current business in jeopardy

Business and Industry Market Characteristics
- Familiarity with corporate personnel policy
- Bottom-line approach
- Knowledge of insurance

Sales Force Response
- Call until sale is made
- Update periodically

5. Sales Manager

A sales manager is one of the first key players to bring on board to build an energetic, enterprising sales force. The right sales manager can bring needed knowledge and experience to be applied to the development of job descriptions, supplemental sales materials, benefit and compensation policies, motivational incentives, and realistic sales quotas. This type of outside expertise is particularly important to the health care industry, which hasn't had time to develop expert sales managers.

6. Setting Sales Targets

"Don't expect any miracles" is a safe and realistic thought to hold in mind during the first twelve months of an infant hosptial sales force's life.

High-volume sales depend on the product mix, the degree of support provided the sales force, the sophistication of the sales training and recruitment effort, and the local competitive market. A real sense of how well the fledgling sales team is doing won't be evident for at least four operating quarters.

7. Support Services

It is important to remember that the sales force does not sell in a vacuum. There must be strong support for the sales team by the following functions or you will cripple the efforts of the sales personnel.

- Public relations
- Advertising
- Planning
- Market research
- Marketing
- Operations/technical support

8. Sales Training and Motivation

Salespersons need a lot of TLC. A tragic and costly error is to give them the products and send them out into the field without adequate training, co-training, or ongoing motivational support.

Most hospitals are not equipped to offer the necessary training in sales and must look to outside training resources to ensure the success of the sales force effort.

9. Compensation

A sales force is not cheap. Decisions have to be made as to what compensation structure to adopt out of the many to choose from, including

- Salary only
- Commission only
- Salary and commission
- Salary and individual bonus
- Salary and group bonus
- Salary, commission, and bonus

The annual cost of a sales force (one full-time person) includes all of the following:

● Experienced salesperson	$25,000 to 35,000
● Office space (amortized)	8,000 to 10,000
● Office equipment	1,000 to 2,000
● Secretarial support	6,000 to 7,000
● Transportation (auto)	4,000 to 5,000
● Sales materials	1,000 to 3,000
● Insurance and miscellaneous	2,000 to 3,000
TOTAL	$47,000 to 65,000

10. Evaluation of Success

Before success can be realistically measured, the following elements must be in place:

- A timely reporting structure must be built and enforced.
- Measurable goals must be set and clearly defined.
- An ongoing analysis of market information must be maintained.

WRAP-UP

These are exciting times for the health care industry. Building a sales force is just one component out of many designed to move the health care industry into a position of leadership in the marketplace.

RURAL HEALTH CARE

The market dynamics that rural hospitals experience differs
in many respects from that encountered by urban hospitals.
Galanti and Prout's article specifically addresses the
plight of rural hospitals and provides a marketing model
that requires relatively lower financial resources
compared to the non-rural counterparts.

ECONOMICALLY MARKETING A RURAL HOSPITAL

Susan Galanti, Cunningham Associates, Sacramento
Linda Prout, Tahoe Forest Hospital, Truckee

ABSTRACT

Many rural hospitals are having their
markets compromised by outmigration of
appropriate patients. The marketing process
used to develop communications and
operations to attract consumers is common to
many hospitals. However, most rural
hospitals must market on a significantly
lower percentage of financial resources
compared to their non-rural counterparts.
This case study describes the marketing
process and two resulting programs used by
Tahoe Forest Hospital to economically
promote the hospital to their rural service
area.

INTRODUCTION

Tahoe Forest Hospital is a 42-bed, acute
care hospital located in Truckee,
California. This district hospital has a
primary service area population of 15,000
year-round residents. However, since the
hospital is close to popular Sierra Nevada
mountains and is only about two miles off
the main thoroughfare between Sacramento and
Reno, this population may peak at 100,000.
The area's economic mainstays are the
recreation industry and related services.

The hospital's cash flow cycle is unique due
to its dependence on the winter ski season
and summer tourist season. Hospital
occupancy flourishes when the winter
blizzards visit the Sierras, usually from
early November until April. This dependence
on nature requires a great deal of
flexibility in the timing of hospital
resource expenditures. These challenges are
met under the stewardship of management team
members who function in diverse roles
including patient care providers, community
spokespersons, service directors, and
marketers.

Tahoe Forest Hospital, like many other rural
hospitals, is faced with distinct threats
from "big city" providers in adjacent
communities. Reno, Nevada, is located about
45 minutes away and offers two large
hospitals. One hospital is a significant
competitor with Tahoe Forest for the area's
major surgery market. The other large Reno
hospital is a major competitor in the OB
services market. Additionally another small
hospital is located in nearby, affluent
Incline Village, Nevada. This hospital
competes with Tahoe Forest in the minor
hospital services market.

Above all, the research Cunningham
Associates has conducted for Tahoe Forest
Hospital indicates that the hospital, like
many other rural providers, fights a
negative phantom image as described in Lynne
Cunningham's article "Onion Rings,
Strawberries and Rural Hospitals" in
California Hospitals' premier issue,
October/November 1986. "It begins with the
public attitude that everything good is in
the big city and that everything in the
rural community is second rate. That
applies to doctors, nurses and hospitals.
If you were a good doctor you'd be
practicing in the big city. If you were a
well-trained nurse you'd be caring for
patients at the big hospital. Because you
are a small hospital you obviously can't
have good doctors and well trained nurses.
Of course that's not true - but you've
become a victim of a negative phantom
statistic."

The larger Reno hospitals have poured vast
resources into public education regarding
what to look for in a hospital service.
Since much of this advertising has been seen
in North Tahoe communities, Tahoe Forest
Hospital has capitalized on this increased
awareness by providing preferred service
features and some additional features
meeting perceived needs that are unique to
their service area. The hospital has been
marketed with minimal advertising for the
past five years using the PRIMOe marketing
model.

PRIMOe--A MARKETING MODEL

PRIMOe is a marketing model developed by
Lynne Cunningham of Cunningham Associates.
Cunningham Associates has worked with Tahoe
Forest Hospital for five years conducting
market research and developing market based
strategic plans. PRIMOe is an acronym for a
flexible model that has been successfully
used by dozens of health care clients. Its
simple, evolving steps are easy to use for
facility-wide marketing plans and can also
be used for product line, department, and
audience specific plans.

P--Purpose

Ideally, the marketing purpose is defined by
a marketing task force composed of the best
thinkers in the hospital. In Tahoe Forest
Hospital's case, management team members had
the most pervasive influence on all levels
of the hospital's operations. They were
chosen and continue to serve as a marketing
task force. Because the rural hospital's
management team members function in a
multitude of roles, their input into the
market segmentation rationale and
determination of further research needs is
invaluable.

FIGURE 1

Research Decision Matrix

Market Segment	Priority High/Med/Low	Method Quanti/Quali	Confidential High/Med/Low	Internal Objectivity	Resources--Yes/No Tech. Skill	Time
CONSUMERS-COMMUNITY -or- By age group By sex By residence area						
PAST PATIENTS i.e. By service Emergency Dept. Med/Surg Drug/Alcohol By age By sex						
EMPLOYERS-GENERAL -or- By industry By size						
EMPLOYEES i.e. Licensed Unlicensed Support Management						
BOARD						
VOLUNTEERS						
PHYSICIANS-GENERAL -or- By specialty						

R--Research and Analysis

Often, conducting market research entirely through outside providers is prohibitively expensive for smaller hospitals. So, Cunningham Associates helped Tahoe Forest Hospital develop a largely in-house market research function. Many market research activities can be completed internally depending upon the organization's resources, priorities, the necessity to maintain confidentiality and objectivity.

The marketing task force should begin by establishing priorities. What needs to be known about which audiences? The kind of information sought from each audience determines the importance of confiden- tiality. In-depth problem solving information is best developed from focus groups or interview research. Physicians and employees are not likely to be as frank and open with a hospital employee researcher as they would be with an external consultant. This is particularly true in a small hospital with no insulating layer of management between marketing staff and the employees. Finally, the task force assesses the internal capabilities of their staff. Does someone on the staff have the time, technical skills and objectivity to conduct the research? Figure 1 is a matrix that may be helpful in conceptualizing this decision process. The sample matrix indicates that the sample hospital should use an external consultant for physician research, patient satisfaction research with past patients from the drug and alcohol unit, employee research, and a quantitative consumer survey. Tahoe Forest Hospital has reduced its consulting expenses by having staff members trained to conduct appropriate qualitative research and low sample size quantitative research.

I--Internal Audiences.

Internal audiences are the medical staff, employees and volunteers at the hospital. These audiences are frequently the hospital's major marketing resource and vital to any marketing plan's success. Internal audiences should be involved in the research process from the first planning steps. Carefully consider internal audience needs for information, feedback opportunities, and direct contact with the hospital's decision makers.

M--Marketing Mix

The marketing mix is an action plan addressing researched needs and perceptions. The mix is designed to meet marketing goals within the organization's capabilities. Any organization's marketing mix typically includes product descriptions, positioning strategies, pricing strategies, distribution plans and promotional strategies.

changes in services to accommodate consumers' needs are often implemented slowly. The marketing director at Tahoe Forest Hospital attends all meetings that may result in changes in operations. The director and other members of the marketing task force keep consumers' needs visible during program development and implementation. The marketing director has increased responsibility for positioning and communications to internal and external audiences. A communication plan has been developed to parallel the service implementation schedule.

Communication plans are usually developed to address each significant audience. Internal audiences may be medical staff, employees or board members. External audiences are usually grouped by age, sex, income and education, but Tahoe Forest was an anomaly. The first community survey for Tahoe Forest Hospital indicated the different towns in the service area had very different needs and preferences for health services. Thus, the communication plans for external audiences were developed for groups of communities with common needs. For example, a recent quantitative community survey indicated that 10 of the 11 communities in the service area would be likely to use urgent care services if they were available in the residents' town. Qualitative research indicated that more affluent residents from several towns worked in Reno, one hour away, and were interested in urgent care for extended hours. Communities with less affluent residents (and more self-insured residents) were likely to be interested in urgent care because they thought this may be a less expensive alternative to the emergency room. Local physicians indicated they would not support an urgent care center, yet they were very willing to offer extended hours and lower prices than the hospital's emergency room to attract more patients. These features were positioned and promoted to the communities in accordance with the communities' perceived needs.

O--Objectives

Objectives are more specific than the marketing purpose. An objective usually states the expected outcome of a marketing effort addressing a specific issue. The outcome is usually quantitative, such as the number of callers asking for more information. Goals can be qualitative, such as improved employee perception of communications with administration.

e - Evaluation

The marketing process is not complete until the evaluation mechanisms are in place and evaluation data is collected, analyzed, and feedback is provided. Feedback of evaluation information to internal audiences is essential to sustain marketing efforts. Additionally, efficient ongoing evaluation is also an economical way to update the marketing data base.

APPLICATION OF MARKETING MODEL AT TAHOE FOREST HOSPITAL

A 1983 community survey revealed the strengths and weakensses of Tahoe Forest Hospital.

Strengths:

. Excellent reputation in the community.

. Good primary name recognition among permanent residents.

. The hospital of choice for emergency care, minor surgery, and obstetrics.

. Good availability of primary care physicians.

. Convenience.

. Excellent staff.

The weaknesses of the hospital that were perceived by the community are common among many smaller semi-rural hospitals. They included:

. The area residents are unfamiliar with the health care services in the community. Most particularly, (1) they perceived a lack of physician specialists, and (2) They were not aware of the home health and hospice programs.

. Lack of available skilled nursing beds.

Responses to this community research included:

. Promotion of the physician specialty services existing at the facility and the technical equipment available to help care for area residents.

. Establishment of a sports medicine clinic in Tahoe City.

. Aggressive promotion of the home health and hospice program.

. Construction of a 28-bed distinct part skilled nursing facility in 1986.

. Recruiting of more OB/GYN specialists to the area.

. Development and promotion of health education classes.

. Expansion of facility ancillary services.

. Development of a newsletter for the hospital's employees and physicians.

. A series of health and hospital articles placed in the local newspaper.

. Promotion of appropriate services to seasonal residents.

. Development and promotion of a Tahoe Forest Hospital speakers bureau.

. Institution of a biannual health fair.

Most of these responses had been implemented by 1986.

The following changes had occurred in the market since 1983.

. **Increased advertising from Tahoe Forest Hospital and competitor hospitals.**

. **Increased population growth in some towns equidistant to Truckee, Incline Village, and Reno.**

. **Additional provider specialists in the area.**

The issues at the close of 1985, as perceived by management, included:

. Affordable health care

. Outmigration of patients appropriate for Tahoe Forest Hospital.

. Consumer awareness of the area's hospitals, clinics and physicians.

. Community health care needs.

. Advertising effectiveness.

. Physician development.

The markets the management team felt must be addressed included the medical staff, patients, employers, senior citizens, young and middle-aged consumers, employees, and seasonal residents.

Research

The management team decided to conduct research using surveys mailed to the medical staff, employers, and hospital employees. The purpose of this research was to collect baseline data on communications and interest in cooperative ventures.

The hospital retained Cunningham Associates to conduct a large community survey and several focus groups with consumers and past patients.

Significant economies were realized in the qualitative research through innovative cooperation incentives, no-cost facilities, and recruiting by the marketing director. Additionally, the hospital's marketing director learned to conduct future focus groups with appropriate audiences, thus decreasing the hospital's dependence on outside consultants.

Analysis

The 1986 community survey provided interesting tracking data for the hospital.

The reputation of the hospital, medical staff, and quality of care had improved since 1983.

. The consumers perceived improved availability of health promotion and mental health services in the area.

. There was a sharp increase in awareness of Tahoe Forest Hospital among seasonal residents.

. The consumers perceived an increased availability of services for the elderly, such as home health, hospice, and extended care facilities.

. The perceived availability of physician specialists and state-of-the-art hospital care had improved since 1983.

All of these findings were confirmed by the increased utilization of the hospital. However, the study also indicated that a large influx of new residents to the area were not aware of medical services in the community and held the "phantom" impression that small hospitals are second rate. This finding was confirmed and further clarified in focus group research.

Internal Audiences

The initial research results were presented to the entire management team during a retreat. The team then brainstormed a list of responses to the opportunities presented and prioritized that list. The management team agreed that improved guest relations would be the most effective means of improving the community's awareness of Tahoe Forest Hospital. The hospital is the second largest employer in the area. Good word-of-mouth recommendations from the employees and patients would result in increased utilization of the hospital. Guest relations encompassed:

. Establishment of a central mission.

. Increased communications with employees.

. Guest relations training.

. Increased feedback to employees.

The second priority identified by the management team was to increase communications with the medical staff and promote their specialty capabilities. Industry experts find that 80 percent of hospital admissions are based on physician recommendation. But, if consumers don't access area physicians, appropriate admissions may be lost.

Marketing/Communications Plan

Implementing the management team's recommendations was going to be a challenge. The hospital's cash flow in the winter is dependent on a ski season starting Thanksgiving weekend. This season, Tahoe had only partially opened ski areas by New Year's Day. Implementing a typically priced guest relations program was prohibitively expensive.

Guest Relations

The marketing director scheduled three focus groups of past patients to determine service factors causing patient satisfaction. It became very evident during these groups that some segments of the staff, such as nursing personnel, were doing an excellent job on guest relations. These nursing personnel could serve as role models for other employees—if they could be caught doing something right this could be related to the entire staff.

The service factors causing patient satisfaction were shared with employees in another three focus groups. The objectives of the employee focus groups were to:

. Share research information.

. Obtain input into patient satisfaction standards from the hospital's experts, the front-line personnel.

. Find the most meaningful way to identify and describe great performance to the entire staff.

. Have the employees "buy in" to the guest relations program by including them in the planning stage.

The marketing director established a patient representative program at the same time. Tahoe Forest Hospital may have three to ten discharges per day. The patient representative would see each patient once for a short time during his or her hospital stay. If up to talking, the patient was asked a few short questions on his or her satisfaction with services at the hospital. Patients were also given a patient satisfaction survey and a service information sheet. The patient representative also could "catch employees" doing something right. The patient representative program also provides patients immediate access to a non-threatening problem solver.

The patient representative shares compliments with the entire staff through the hospital newsletter and postings on the bulletin board. Complaints are typically addressed with the management supervisor. These are usually resolved before the patient is discharged from the hospital.

Physician Promotion

Focus group research with area consumers indicated that more recent residents from one community were not usually aware of physicians in other nearby communities. If they weren't pleased with a provider in their community, they would go to Reno for services and be lost to the entire Tahoe medical network. The management team decided to implement a "physician finder" service. A small newspaper ad was developed and placed in the local newspaper, distribution 18,500. The ad appears once every five to six weeks. Prior to the newspaper ad, with the service ad in the telephone book, calls averaged four to five each week. After the newspaper ad began, the number of calls increased to 10 to 12 each week, and admissions increased by 10 to 14 each week. The same ad was developed

into a direct mail piece. These media distribution channels were selected because the community survey indicated that recent residents were most likely to respond them.

On the hospital side, the switchboard personnel were asked to route physician finder calls to the administrative secretary and medical staff coordinator. The physician finder "system" is a filebox of information on physicians in the area organized according to specialty service. The physicians receive a monthly report during their medical staff committee meetings on the number of calls received by the physician finder service. The physicians are also given the percentage of callers referred to physicians in the North Tahoe area and the number of callers referred to physicians out of the area because the caller needed an unavailable specialist.

OBJECTIVES AND EVALUATION

Guest Relations

The hospital conducted a patient satisfaction survey for baseline data prior to implementing the patient representative program. The results of this survey were shared with department managers. The same survey will be distributed to past patients in July. The percentage of change in patient satisfaction will indicate the impact of the guest relations program.

Physician Promotion

The objectives of the physician finder program are multiple.

. Increase utilization of local physicians with a secondary increase in utilization of Tahoe Forest Hospital.

. Stem the outmigration of patients to Reno.

. Collect data to support the physician community in recruiting selected specialty providers.

The first objective is being met. The second and third objectives will take longer to evaluate. The second objective will be evaluated through physician interviews regarding changes in their practice volume. The third objective will obviously be accomplished when the medical staff elects to recruit needed specialists to the area.

HEALTH CARE MARKETING ON TRIAL

A feature common to a dynamic and evolving discipline is
the frequent examination and scrutiny it receives. Some
of its most severe critics are often from within. In
this article, Allen and Eich review the arguments for and
against health care marketing. Questions about its
future are also discussed.

MARKETING ON TRIAL

Bruce H. Allen, San Francisco State University, San Francisco
David P. Eich, Akron Children's Hospital, Akron

ABSTRACT

The marketing function in health care has come under
serious scrutiny and criticism in 1986. Questions have
been raised as to whether there is an adequate
organizational payback from investments in marketing and
advertising. Doubt has also been cast upon the
capabilities of health care marketing managers and their
competence to achieve results in a complex and
increasingly competitive industry. Confidence in health
care marketing professionals and the importance of their
role seems to be on the decline. This article critically
examines the arguments for and against health care
marketing. A differentiation is drawn between marketing
and marketing management, and questions are raised about
the future of the profession.

WHY IS MARKETING ON TRIAL?

A recent study by SRI Gallup in Chicago indicated that
U.S. Hospitals planned to spend more than $1.1 billion on
marketing in 1986 (HOSPITALS, Nov. 20, 1986, p.64). The
average annual hospital marketing budget was over
$225,000 with larger facilities spending nearly $500,000
(excluding marketer's salaries). Advertising was the
biggest portion of the budget, representing almost half
of a typical hospital's marketing budget.

By private industry standards, $225,000 is not a large
marketing budget for diversified, multi-product
organizations which serve a wide scope of market segments
and constituencies. But compared to a few years ago,
when the healthcare industry was not in a competitive
marketplace, marketing expenditures have grown
substantially. For example, according to HOSPITALS (Nov.
20, 1986, p. 64), hospital advertising budgets have
nearly doubled since 1985. Another survey showed that
advertising expenditures had increased 147% between 1984
and 1986 (Modern HealthCare, Sept. 26, 1986, p. 25).

At the same time as marketing budgets were growing,
nearly three fifths (57%) of CEO's from a 1986 survey
were "dissatisfied with the performance of their
marketing staffs (MODERN HEALTHCARE, September 26, 1986,
p. 25)." Reasons given by CEO's were: staff lacks
marketing knowledge, marketing work force and funding are
insufficient, and failure to produce measurable results.
Even though they were dissatisfied, over two-thirds of
CEO's planned to spend more on marketing during the next
two years than they did in 1986.

Based on CEO's concern's for measurable results and an
adequate return on their marketing investments, there is
some evidence that hospitals have called a "marketing
time-out (HOSPITALS, June 5, 1986, p. 50)." According to
Philip Kotler and some other industry experts, hospitals
suddenly began to advertise and use other marketing
tactics when admissions began to fall and their markets
became increasingly competitive. Many hospitals were
looking for short-term census increases which never came.

The current controversy about the success or failure of
health care marketing provides substance upon which to
base the following CHARGES against the profession:

o Marketing has been FRAUDULENTLY misrepresented and
oversold as to its potential to attract additional
customers, revenues and market share in the health care
industry.

o Marketing funds have been EMBEZZLED from demonstrated
areas of need in the line organization, and wasted on
marketer's salaries, ad agencies, consulting fees and
other self-serving marketing expenses.

o Marketing executives have NEGLIGENTLY damaged their
organizations' competitive positions by being careless in
implementing tactical marketing when they should have
been developing longer-term strategies first.

The health care marketing profession stands accused of
some very serious crimes. But, the traditional view of
innocent until proven guilty does not stand up in a
highly competitive industry marketplace. Health care
marketing is a major investment for an organization in a
declining market. Investments that are not capable of
paying back a high return should be terminated. To
achieve long-term status as a key managerial function,
health care marketing must answer the serious charges
lodged against it. The profession of Health Care
Marketing Management is on trial for its life.

THE CASE AGAINST HEALTH CARE MARKETING

There are a number of criticisms that can be made against
health care marketing. In MARKETING FOR HEALTH CARE
ORGANIZATIONS, Kotler and Clarke (1987) cite many of
these negative claims:

o Marketing Wastes Money: Resources that should be
devoted to patient care for the poor and elderly are
squandered (with few measurable results) on advertising,
glossy publications, marketing personnel and
entertainment to woo doctors or other prospective buyers.

For non-profit hospitals, these wasted dollars could have
been devoted to charity care.

o Marketing Is Intrusive: Advertising, direct mail, and especially telemarketing violate the privacy of consumers. Also, advertising for health care services such as treatment for drug and alcohol problems, cancer, male potency, and other sensitive services can cause alarm among consumers. In addition, telephone or mall intercept market research may interrupt consumers and offend them.

o Marketing Is Manipulative: Due to messages about health services that consumers have not been exposed to before, they may make decisions without proper facts. For example, in a true emergency situation, they may choose an urgent care center which has misrepresented itself instead of going to an ER.

o Marketing Lowers Quality: the health care provider with the best advertising agency will be selected (at a higher price) over the provider with the greatest expertise and patient sensitivity.

o Marketing Causes Fruitless Competition: Health care organizations in a community should work together on behalf of the patient. This is how the system operated in the past. But, when organizations are pitted against each other in "Marketing Warfare", they cease to cooperate and the patient suffers.

o Marketing Creates Unnecessary HealthCare Utilization: With costs and insurance premiums already being too high, marketing seeks to create demand for health services that are not really necessary (ie. plastic surgery, upgraded maternity services, unnecessary visits to the ER, etc.).

Some additional criticisms are:

o Marketing Advocates Two-Tier Health Care: New products and services are being developed for the "private pay" patients which cannot be afforded by the poor and elderly (ie. plastic surgery, concierge services, upgraded maternity packages, chemical dependency treatment). The poor are exposed to the promotion for these services, but cannot access them via Medicaid and Medicare.

o Health Care Marketing Is Too Complex and Difficult: Because the industry environment changed so rapidly, health planners and PR managers were promoted into high-level marketing positions. These managers, untrained and inexperienced in marketing, are unprepared to plan and execute successful marketing programs in the U.S. economy's most complex industry. There are few marketers from private industry who are able to understand the health care industry and its complex structure. The lack of preparedness, experience and knowledge among marketing executives may be the reason for the apparent high turnover rate.

o Health Care Organizations Are Anti-Marketing By Nature: Hospitals are bureaucracies composed of mini-organizations of specialists (including physicians) who are independent and see themselves as unique. Effective marketing requires cooperation, coordination and interdependence in support of an organizational focus on the customer's needs. This is nearly impossible for the typical hospital structure.

o There Are Very Few Examples Of Marketing Success: With substantial budget increases for advertising, marketing research, staff and consultants, there are very few known situations where marketing has made a major shift in competitive position and market share for health care organizations.

Thus, taking into account only the shortcomings, one could conclude that while marketing had an exciting introduction to health care, it does not have a bright future. If the aforementioned premises are accepted, the verdict is that marketing departments (and executives) have no place in health care organizations.

THE CASE FOR HEALTH CARE MARKETING

Marketing can be defined as a social process through which a society achieves a standard of living via an integrated network of exchanges involving products, services, support, ideas, concepts or anything of value. In other words, the marketing process automatically occurs as exchanges take place.

Since exchanges are (and have been) constantly taking place involving health care organizations and their customers (consumers, employers, government, etc.), marketing as a social process cannot be on trial. Health care organizations are inherently engaged in marketing, they have no choice.

Do we have a mistrial, for lack of a defendant? No, because health care marketing management may be the culprit. The inherent exchange process called marketing cannot be placed on trial, but the way health care organizations are (and have been) managing marketing can certainly be scrutinized. Marketing management is the managerial process through which exchanges are created which should result in beneficial outcomes for both the organization and its customers. In a competitive marketplace, it would be nearly impossible to find a very successful company without excellent marketing management.

FORTUNE magazine recently published its list of the corporations most admired by over 8,200 senior executives, directors and analysts (FORTUNE, Jan. 19, 1987, pp.21-31). The most admired companies are well-respected organizations known for their marketing expertise and innovation. By industry categories, some of the winners were:

Aerospace - Boeing
Diversified Financial - American Express
Apparel - Liz Claiborne
Chemicals - DuPont
Electronics - General Electric
Office Equipment - IBM
Motor Vehicles - Ford
Instruments - 3M
Soaps,Cosmetics - Procter & Gamble
Retailing - Dayton Hudson

Some of the lowest rated companies were: TWA, Financial Corp. of America, Manville, Bethlehem Steel, American Motors and BankAmerica. These low rated companies are not known for marketing excellence and are definitely not industry leaders. It is clear that all of these companies are engaged in marketing. But the most admired ones are managing it in an outstanding fashion, while the least admired are simply not succeeding.

The case for marketing is based upon the fact that managed marketing works throughout private industry (health care is a hybrid of non-profit and for profit), when it is done well. It has been proven that marketing can be managed in competitive industries and that it is a precondition for sustained competitive advantage. Firms having successfully managed marketing demonstrate measurable, sustained results in support of their missions, when compared with the competition, and show high returns within the context of an industry's financial structure.

These successful companies have reaped the major advantage of marketing management, they have achieved higher customer satisfaction within their target markets. A focus on marketing analysis, planning, implementation and control has enabled them to achieve competitive advantage. All types of organizations, from large corporations to physician practices, can reap the benefits of marketing management.

Although not widely publicized, there are numerous health care marketing successes, where marketing management has apparently made a difference. Some examples are:

o The strong competitive position attained by Kaiser Permanente in West Coast markets. In the Bay area and Los Angeles, Kaiser has obtained market shares in the 25% to 35% range. But this has not been a sudden success, it has taken decades to accomplish. Kaiser is now managing their marketing more aggressivley due to competitive challenges.
o The dramatic growth of Maxicare health plans. In contrast to Kaiser, Maxicare is a for-profit company that has grown rapidly via innovation and acquisition. Strong marketing management focused toward employers and consumers is a major factor in Maxicare's achievements.

o The product-line marketing and sales management programs pioneered by Humana. Back in the late 1970's and early 1980's, Humana was gaining market share with products such as Cradle Club, Senior's Courtesy Club and InstaCare emergency services. Humana was also successfully applying sales concepts in their relations with physicians.

Regional/local competitive gains via marketing have also been accomplished by hospitals:

o NKC Inc. in Louisville, Ky., with its innovative product line development strategies, as exemplified by the Women's Pavillion, has enabled the organization to compete effectively in Humana's headquarters city, against four Humana hospitals.

o Erlanger Medical Center in Chatanooga, Tenn. used a multiple product-line marketing approach, and a new women's center, to achieve a 6% market share gain, an improved payer mix and an $11 million surplus (Health Care Competition Week, 9/29/86, p.3).

o Community Hospitals Of Central California in Fresno developed and implemented a comprehensive set of marketing strategies focused toward consumers, physicians, employers and employees to achieve a 5% increases in total admissions and patient days, a 27% increase in revenues and a 150% increase in profits during a two year period.

These are just a few examples where managed marketing proved successful. Obviously, there are case studies of marketing management successes and failures throughout the healthcare industry. Today's successes can become tomorrow's failures if the competition retailiates effectively, or market conditions change. Thus, successful marketing management is not just the launching of new products, it is managing throughout the product life cycle and across competitive environments.

Thus, health care marketing management is really no different from private industry. It requires long-term marketing management approaches. The pitfalls of short-term marketing are exemplified by many of the companies profiled as excellent in IN SEARCH OF EXCELLENCE that are now having serious marketing problems and competitive reversals.

One important additional factor is that health care CEO's and administrators are short-term results oriented. In contrast, good marketing management takes time to pay off and then should return long-term dividends. Hospital administrators have a tendency to want results daily (such as census statistics), rather than taking the time to allow marketing programs to work. Many fine marketing programs have received a premature burial just as they were beginning to work. Marketing management is not a quick fix, but instead a long-term investment.

To sum up, health care marketing is not on trial, but marketing management is. If health care marketing is in trouble, it is because of the inability of marketers to:

o Perform adequate analysis of marketing challenges and opportunities.

o Develop corporate and product line strategies, plans and programs that are innovative, focused, differentiated, and can be implemented.

o Build and staff marketing departments with well-trained and energetic marketers who will involve line managers in the marketing processs.

o Demonstrate leadership with peers from operations, finance, and other administrative areas in gaining support for marketing initiatives.

o Gain top-level support for strategies and budget allocations necessary to successfully implement marketing programs.

o Measure results using multiple indicators, and make programmatic adjustments when warranted.

o Give proper credit for successful results to the operations staff and employees on the front lines who have provided outstanding service to the customer.

If these critical aspects of marketing management are successfully executed by health care marketers, the accusations will cease and marketing will be elevated to its rightful stature as an essential managerial process within the health care industry. Based upon the performance of marketing management in private industry and its potential for application in health care, the verdict should be NOT GUILTY of the charges made against it.

THE JURY IS OUT

The cases for and against marketing have been presented.
Although marketing is experiencing both success and
disillusionment within the health care industry, it is
still relatively new as a key managerial function. It is
not too late for marketing to reach its potential, but it
definitely is not too early. The challenge is for
marketing management practitioners to achieve a high
level of performance and clearly demonstrate the
potential of well-managed marketing.

In a recent speech, Dan Beckham (Past President of the
Academy For Health Services Marketing) summed the
situation up quite well (Marketing News, Sept. 26, 1986,
p.4):

"If marketing professionals today don't demonstrate their
own competence and that of their profession, they'll be
job hunting, and marketing is going to get a black eye in
health care....a lot of folks in marketing positions
today won't be in marketing positions two years from
now."

Yes the jury is still out - but not for long.

REFERENCES

FORTUNE (1987), "America's Most Admired Corporations,"
Janaury 19, 18-22.

HEALTH CARE COMPETITION WEEK (1986), "Chattanooga
Hospital Attributes Dramatic Turnaround To Marketing,"
(September 29), 3-4.

HOSPITALS (1986), "$1.1 Million Spent On Hospital
Marketing in 1986," (Nov. 20), 64.

HOSPITALS (1986), "Hospitals Call A Marketing Time Out,"
(June 5), 50-55.

Kotler, Philip and Clarke, Roberta (1987), MARKETING FOR
HEALTH CARE ORGANIZATIONS, Englewood Cliffs, N.J.,
Prentice-Hall, Inc.

MARKETING NEWS (1986), "Skillful Marketers Will Survive
Health Care Shakeout," (Sept. 26), 4.

MODERN HEALTHCARE (1986), "57% Of CEO's, COO's Aren't
Happy With Marketing Staffs," (September 26), 25.

Bruce H. Allen, Ph.D. Executive Director of the National Center for Health Care Marketing Studies and a Professor of Marketing in the Business School at San Francisco State University. Dr. Allen was formerly Vice-President for Marketing Strategy at a California-based multi-hospital system.

Joseph A. Boscarino, Ph.D. Corporate Vice President for Marketing and Business Development for Jersey Shore Medical Center in Neptune, New Jersey. Prior to this, he had spent the past seven years as a senior healthcare consultant in commercial market research firms, which included Allied Research Associates of Chicago and Market Opinion Research of Detroit. Prior to entering the health care consulting field, Dr. Boscarino served a two-year post-doctoral internship in Health Services Research at the West Haven VA Medical Center and Yale University. He holds a Ph.D. in Social Psychology and has published numerous healthcare articles.

Sheryl H. Boyd, Ed.D., Assistant Chairman of Internal Medicine and Associate Professor in the Health Organization Management Program. Prior to joining Texas Tech University in 1985, Dr. Boyd was the Director of the Health Services MBA Program at the University of Dallas, Irving, Texas for seven years. Dr. Boyd's special areas of health services interest are improving and facilitating health promotion strategies for rural and senior citizens.

Murray Cantor, President of MRC Research, holds a Ph.D. in mathematics from the University of California in Berkeley. Author of numerous articles based upon his work in applied mathematics and data analysis, Cantor has received research grants from the National Science Foundation, the Smithsonian Institution, and the University of Texas at Austin.

Christine Cameron, Director of Sales for Mills-Peninsula Corporation. She has been in the hospital sales management field for seven years, concentrating primarily on providing products and services to the employer market. She also manages a home health care sales force covering eleven counties in northern California.

Nancy Clasen, Marketing Manager for Carondelet Community Hospitals, a 1,100 bed health care system located in Minneapolis, Minnesota. She has held previous marketing positions with Control Data Corporation and National Care Rental Systems, Inc. She holds a masters degree in history.

Kathy L. Divis, Associate Director for Marketing at the University of Alabama Hospital in Birmingham. She holds an MBA from the University of Alabama at Birmingham and a BSBA from the University of Nebraska at Omaha.

David Eich Vice President of Marketing at Akron Children's Hospital. Mr. Eich was Vice President of Marketing at Nebraska Methodist hospital and has had extensive marketing experience in private industry. Mr. Eich is a member of the Academy Board.

John A. Eudes, Associate Administrator for Marketing at the University of Alabama Hospital in Birmingham. He holds an MBA in Marketing and a BSBA from Northern Illinois University and is a Certified Public Accountant and Certified Management Accountant.

Cathy A. Felt, Manager in Peat Marwick's Kansas City office, has provided health care strategic planning/marketing services to hospitals and physicians for the last six years.

Trevor A. Fisk, Associate Executive Director, Marketing and Planning at Thomas Jefferson University Hospital in Philadelphia, which he joined in 1985. Previously, he headed marketing for seven years at Cooper Hospital/University Medical Center in New Jersey. Prior to entering health care, he worked in marketing for fourteen years in the education, travel, insurance and other industries. Trevor Fisk holds degrees from the London School of Economics and M.I.T. He has contributed to several books and various journals and recently published a full-length book on health care advertising methods.

James C. Folger, President, Northwest Healthcare Consulting. Substantial product management experience with H.J. Heinz and Monsanto. His healthcare expertise includes positions as Marketing Development Manager for Humana, Inc., and Director Marketing & Planning for a reginal referral hospital.

Daniel P. Franklin, President of Illinois Health Plans, Inc. (wholly-owned subsidary of VHA Illinois), a health care marketing consulting organization specializing in alternative delivery systems (HMO's, PPO's). Mr. Franklin's prior experience includes extensive non-health care related small business consulting and development. He has also served as director of planning and market development for one of Illinois fastest growing HMO's.

Susan Galanti, Senior Associate with Cunningham Associates, a market research and communications planning firm specializing in health care. Galanti has over 11 years of experience in the health care industry and holds degrees in occupational therapy and hospital administration.

E. Preston Gee, Director Marketing and Strategic Planning for Sacred Heart Hospital in Eugene, OR. Prior to his healthcare experience, Mr. Gee was an educational software product manager for Fisher-Price. Mr. Folger and Mr. Gee are scheduled to publish a definitive new text, Product Management for Hospitals: A Winning Strategy in 1987.

Eileen E. Gibbs, R.N., Past President of the Lubbock General Hospital Auxiliary. Mrs. Gibbs devotes 25-35 hours per week in volunteer service to Lubbock General Hospital.

Ellen F. Goldman, Principal with Lammers & Gershon Associates, Inc., a health care consulting firm specializing in planning and development services. Ms. Goldman directs the firm's Business Development Services, including strategic planning, marketing, market research and new venture studies. She has over ten years experience in health care services development, both as a consultant and as a corporate director of a health care system.

Arthur E. Gross, Director of Marketing at Johnson County Memorial Hospital, Franklin, Indiana. He has fifteen years of hospital management experience. He has a Master's Degree in Health Administration from Indiana University and a B.S. Degree in Business Administration from Butler University in Indianapolis. He has been responsible for the development of several innovative and successful advertising programs which have been recognized for their excellence by other organizations.

Tim M. Henderson, Senior Associate with McManis Associates, has consulted with hospitals and other health care organizations and has particular expertise in the development and execution of marketing strategies and programs.

Henry T. Jacques, Assistant Administrator at Fairview General Hospital in Cleveland, Ohio. His responsibilities include promotional campaigns, advertising, public relations and fund-raising. He has been a daily newspaper reporter, NASA public information officer, and college lecturer.

David A. Kantor, Vice President, Marketing and Sales, for Bethesda, Inc., a regional, integrated health-care system based in Cincinnati. Mr. Kantor's career has focused on the marketing of services in the transportation, computer services, and health-care industries. He received his MBA from the Wharton School.

Mike Kaufher, Senior Vice President, Corporate Communication, with the Geisinger health care system in Danville, Pennsylvania. He joined Geisinger in 1978. Prior to that he was a Vice President with the Maryland Hospital Association in Lutherville, Maryland and had previously directed Public Relations and Development for a community hospital in Maryland.

Paul H. Keckley, Widely known in health care as a leading proponent of marketing accountability in the new consumer era of healthcare. His firm provides market research and strategic planning expertise to more than seventy hospitals annually.

Ronn Kelsey, Responsible for Strategic Planning, Corporate Marketing and Business Planning for Saint Agnes Medical Center, brings twenty years of broad health experience in general management and marketing of health care related products and hospital services on a domestic and international scale. Mr. Kelsey, Corporate Marketing Department and Saint Agnes were recently awarded the 1986 Hospital Innovators Award from the Association of Western Hospitals/3M Company.

Holly A. King, Recently joined Peat Marwick as a consultant. Previously with the Miami Valley Hospital System, she developed their medical staff marketing-support program.

Bernard Kingsley, Marketing Director, Durham County Hospital. Previously employed with the Ohio Department of Mental Health as Educator, Clinical Psychologist and Administrator. Has also been involved in marketing with a major retail chain (Circuit City Stores, Inc.). Holds M.A. Ed. from University of Alabama in Birmingham and M.B.A. from Ohio University.

Catherine F. Kinney, Ph.D., Administrator for Community Health Services at Catherine McAuley Health Center in Ann Arbor, Michigan. She has planning and operational responsibilities for a broad range of non-inpatient services, including services to the disadvantaged.

Douglas Klegon, Ph.D., Associate Administrator for Planning and Marketing at Henry Ford Hospital and its related subsidiaries involved in a wide range of health care delivery and financing products.

Michael S. Leibman, Senior Associate with McManis Associates, has consulted in organizational and human resource management for over seven years. During the last several years, Mr. Leibman has directed several large healthcare strategic and organizational studies.

Karen Lyon, Research Associate with the Minneapolis based firm of Anderson, Niebuhr. Designs and conducts market research for clients in various segments of the health care industry.

Ken E. Mack, President of a healthcare marketing organization called Discover Marketing, Innovations. He has had marketing positions with General Electric, Stouffer's and Akron General Medical Center. He lectures nationally and has a marketing MBA.

Cindy Matthews, Marketing Manager of Rehabilitation Services at Baylor Institute for Rehabilitation, Dallas, Texas. She received an M.B.A. degree in 1983 from the University of Dallas. She also holds M.S. and B.S. degrees in speech pathology from Southern Methodist University.

Julie Rawls Moore, Director of Marketing for the Southern Region of AMI where she is responsible for the marketing of 18 hospitals, Occupational Health Centers and many Physician Practices. Prior, she was VP of Marketing for MedAmerica Health Systems and Miami Valley hospital in Dayton, Ohio.

Frederick H. Navarro (BA, MA), Research Operations Manager for Peabody Marketing Decisions, has extensive experience in healthcare marketing research and with advanced statistical analysis.

Judy Novak, R.N., Ed.D., CEO of Woman's Hospital of Texas in Houston. Prior to her current position, she was assistant administrator at the hospital. She is a noted speaker for the American College of Healthcare Executives and the American Hospital Association. Ms. Novak serves on the editorial board of The Wonder of Life program and is a member of the Interprofessional Network of Consultants. She developed the first sibling class in the country to assist children in coping with the pregnancy of their mothers. She was recently honored by being selected a distinguished alumni of San Jacinto College and as one of Houston's Top Ten Women on the Move.

Kristine E. Peterson, President of K.E. Peterson & Assoc., a Chicago-based firm specializing in strategy, systems and staff development to achieve customer-driven and service-oriented health care delivery, has worked with over 500 U.S. health care organizations and is widely recognized for her work in organizational development and service management. Ms. Peterson has been featured in Hospitals, Modern Healthcare, FAH Review, Hospital Forum, USA Today, and Working Woman magazines. In 1978, she worked with Marriott Corporation to develop the health care industry's first nationally-utilized program of guest relations. A graduate of the University of Texas with a B.S. in Advertising/Communication, she has done graduate work at the University of Oslo, Norway. Her professional experience includes sales, sales motivation training, health care market analysis and public relations.

Linda Prout, Director of Marketing for Tahoe Forest Hospital located in the Sierra town of Truckee, California. She is a newspaper columnist on health and health care issues for two local publications. She has been involved with promotion of health and fitness programs and activities in rural areas for over 5 years. She received a B.S. from the University of California at Davis.

Sharon K. Rexroad, Marketing Manager at The Methodist Medical Center of Illinois, in Peoria. In addition to her role in researching service needs of older adults, she has product line responsibilities in community education and awareness, psychiatry, and rehabilitative services. She received her MHA from the University of Minnesota in 1983.

Michael Richmond, President of Healthcare Consultants, Inc., has started four health maintenance organizations. His roles include senior marketing staff and consulting positions in charge of research, planning, product development, hiring, advertising, marketing and sales.

Marc D. Rubinger (BA,MA), Vice President for Marketing of the Peabody Group, is a healthcare software consultant who specializes in design and development of health care-decision support applications. He is a frequent speaker on the strategic use of computer software in support of management decisions.

Janet L. Scheuerman, Partner of the health care consulting firm Herman Smith Associates, directs all activities in the firm's division of Strategic Planning and Marketing. She has worked with health care providers across the country in marketing research, market segmentation analysis, and joint hospital/physician marketing endeavors as well as strategic planning.

Arthur S. Shorr, President/founder of Arthur S. Shorr and Associates, Inc., a health care management consulting firm in Tarzana, California. A twenty year veteran in the industry, Mr. Shorr specializes in physician/hospital business development and emerging entrepreneurial opportunities.

Jim Thalhuber, Associate Executive Director for Marketing at Courage Center, a regional rehabilitation facility in Golden Valley, MN for adults and children with physical disabilities. Prior to joining Courage Center in mid-1986, he served as Director of Marketing for Carondelet Community Hospitals in Minneapolis-St. Paul where he was responsible for market research, planning and communications. Thalhuber holds a masters degree in business from the College of St. Thomas.

John Thoens, Executive Vice President and Chief Financial Officer for Saint Agnes, brings fifteen years of broad health care experience in working with non-profit health care organizations, including seven years as assistant treasurer with the Robert Wood Johnson Foundation of Princeton, New Jersey. Mr. Thoens has extensive experience in joint ventures with physicians/hospitals and alternative health insurance programs.

Ellen Tobin, President of Health Surveys and Marketing, Inc., a Columbia, Maryland marketing research firm. A former health care administrator and therapist, she is the developer of the PERC System for the measurement of patient satisfaction. The firm trains staff in health care organizations to conduct focus groups and survey research.

Warren E. Todd, M.B.A., Manages the marketing, public relations, community education, physician liaison, and market research functions for a major regional teaching hospital in Central New Jersey. Prior to entering the hospital industry, Mr. Todd's health care background included ten years of marketing and general management experience in both medical products and health care services. This background in health care is complimented by Mr. Todd's earlier experience in consumer marketing.

James R. Toth, President, Edge Healthcare Marketing, Inc. a Nashville-based consulting company. Previously he was Vice President of MedInc, a national outpatient center company, and Director of Field Marketing for Humana, Inc.

David J. Vander Schaaf, M.H.A., Responsible for developing health care facilities, strategic market plans and coordination of market research projects for SRI Gallup, a national research and consulting organization. Prior to joining Allied Research Associates and SRI Gallup, Mr. Vander Schaaf worked in planning and marketing for a metropolitan teaching hospital. His earlier background includes administrative responsibilities for a 160 bed rural hospital.

Susan Welker, Manager, Administrative Services of Illinois Health Plans, Inc. with responsibility for policy development and implementation as well as ADS project management.

Eve W. Yeargain, Has worked as a marketing practitioner and consultant for health care providers since 1973. She holds an M.B.A. in Marketing from Southern Methodist University and is vice president of The Marketing Works, Austin, Texas.

Sandra L. Yost, Has worked in the psychiatric and chemical dependency field since 1970. Working throughout the system in many facets, she has a keen understanding of the field. She spent 13 years with Comprehensive Care Corporation in various capacities, including Director of their national 800 call center. She spent two years with Horizon Health Corporation as Regional Marketing Director and for the past two years with Recovery Centers of America which operates the New Beginnings Chemical Dependency Programs nationally. She is currently Vice President of Marketing.